The Free University
A Model for Lifelong Learning

The Free University

A Model for Lifelong Learning

Bill Draves

AP **Association Press**
Follett Publishing Company/Chicago

Designed by Karen A. Yops

Library of Congress Cataloging in Publication Data

Draves, Bill, 1949–
    The free university.

    Includes bibliographical references.
    1. Continuing education.   2. Continuing
education centers.   I. Title.
LC5219.D7   374   80–21040
ISBN 0–695–81443–5

First Printing

To my father
who taught me to write.

*That the natural state of man
is ecstatic wonder;
That we should not settle for less.*

—from the Midpeninsula Free
University Manifesto

Contents

Foreword

by Malcolm Knowles

The need to continue to grow and develop throughout life appears to be built into the human genes. Carl Rogers describes it as the one basic need or striving of human beings, with all other needs being subsidiary to it.

This need has expressed itself throughout human history in many forms. There is evidence that preliterate man engaged in a fairly systematic each-one-teach-one process. Informal study circles are described in the historical documents of ancient China, India, Israel, Greece, Rome, and Egypt—sometimes with master teachers such as Confucius and Lao Tse in China; the Hebrew prophets; Socrates, Plato, and Aristotle in Greece; and Cicero and Quintilian in Rome; but often with peers helping one another. The guilds and churches served as centers of learning in the Middle Ages. In the centuries since then, there have appeared in Europe such vehicles for continuing learning as folk high schools, temperance societies, study circles, and workers education associations. In Chapter 5 of this book Bill Draves describes some of the early forms the need for continuing learning has taken in this country—the Junto, lyceum, public library, YMCA, chautauqua, and others.

9

Until the approach of the twentieth century, these informal associations were the *only* instrumentalities for continuing learning by adults. Then, as formal educational institutions—public schools, colleges and universities, and later community colleges—became established, they played an increasingly dominant role in the education of adults. The spirit of the adult education movement began to change. The focus began to shift from learner-centered learning to teacher-centered instruction. The content of adult education started taking on the characteristics of the prescribed curriculum of the schools rather than being organized around the curiosities, life problems, and developmental tasks of the learners. The spirit of pedagogy began to prevail.

During the fifties, there began to be a growing dissatisfaction with the lock-step of the formal educational establishment, and alternative forms of adult learning gained new vitality. The Great Books movement, the Great Decisions program, Metroplex Assembly, human potential growth centers, the community education movement, educational brokering agencies, and community action projects (ACTION) were examples of this trend. Even the established educational institutions, particularly those in higher education, have responded to the new mood with experimentation with nontraditional programs, external degrees, and the granting of academic credit for prior learning.

Certainly one of the most promising of the new institutional forms for continuing lifelong learning is the free university. It expresses in purest form the philosophy of learner-controlled self-directed learning, and it is the freest from the constraints of traditional schooling. For this reason, this is an important book. I, personally, hope that every educational policy-maker in the country will read it and be stimulated to reexamine the philosophy, program, and methodology that govern the institution for which he or she is responsible.

It will be most useful, of course, for people who are interested in joining in with this pioneering effort to make lifelong learning available to adults at their convenience in terms of time, place, pace, interests, and resources. For them it provides a rationale as well as a blueprint for action.

A more timely book I cannot imagine.

Malcolm S. Knowles

Acknowledgments

This book is really the result of years of endeavor, not by the author, but by the learners, teachers, and staff who make free universities happen. To their effort, creativity, and commitment I am most indebted. My friends and colleagues in the free university movement who have had much to do with this work include Sue Maes, Dennis DuBé, Julie Govert, Jim Killacky, Greg Marsello, Ed Dobmeyer, Jim Schupp, Joe Rippetoe, Julie Coates, Lona Jean Turner and Bob Wagner.

My appreciation goes to those who have contributed to this book, including: William Johnson and Michael Rossman, for lending their archives; Aimee Horton; Robert Calvert, Jr., Beverly Wilhelm, and Marianne H. Roffman, for review and comment; copy editor Sue Bacon, for eliminating a thousand commas from the manuscript; Jean Lesher at Association Press, for her enthusiasm for the project; typists Donna Haynes, Gayla Brown, and Molly Magee; and Susan Warden, for her support and prompting of the few amusing anecdotes in the story.

Part I
Where We Are

*Courses organized in the freedom
of free universities often reflect a sense
of ecstatic wonder, this 'new' rediscovery of being alive, of having a 10-
million-year storage of life-wisdom in
our blood. We have lost the idea of
how rich and infinite our capacities
really are!*

Robert G. Greenway

Chapter 1

Anyone Can Teach—
Anyone Can Learn

In Pawnee Rock, Kansas, population 400, a seventy-year-old gentleman teaches a class on wood splitting. Eighteen people sign up, motivated by the craft of the axe, as well as a desire to use wood to supplement their heating during the winter.

In Cincinnati, record-store clerk Jim Hatch, a college dropout, teaches a class on the anthropology, history, and religion of "The Mysterious Maya."

In Boulder, Colorado, a class in 1973 on "How to Start a Radio Station" leads to the formation of a new public radio station, which began broadcasting in 1978.

In Olsburg, Kansas, population 170, twelve-year-old Sarah Nelson briefly stuns her mother by telling her that she has just signed up for a class in blacksmithing.

In Kansas City, Missouri, East German–born Georg Moncki teaches a class in "Conversational German" in a bar.

These are a few of the thousands of examples of an exciting trend in adult learning today—people sharing skills and knowledge with each other through a free university. From Washington, D.C., where you can learn how to crash a foreign embassy party, to rural Oklahoma, where you can learn how to make beef jerky, hundreds of thousands of Americans are participating in free universities, in what United Press International calls the "hottest current development in adult education."[1]

There are now approximately 200 free universities and learning networks[2] in the country, and they enroll more than 300,000 participants a year, according to the National Center for Educational Statistics. Both the Educational Testing Service and the College Board list free universities as one of the major providers of adult learning.

Richard Peterson, in his study of lifelong learning for the Educational Testing Service, writes that

> free universities appear to be genuine educational innovation—at least in the United States. They allow people to learn without the trappings or rigidities found in most conventional schools. . . . The free universities and learning exchanges are both extremely important models for serving the vast numbers of learners who are not motivated by the desire for credits and credentials.[3]

Rolf M. Wulfsberg, of the federal government's National Center for Educational Statistics, says that "their stability, their innovative approach to education, and their low cost of operation make them particularly popular today."[4] Free universities have gained enough respect, in fact, that the Kansas legislature in 1979 passed the first free university legislation in the country, providing state monies to help set up free universities in small rural towns.

A free university is defined as an organization that offers noncredit classes to the general public in which "anyone can teach and anyone can learn." Citizens offer to lead classes and may teach practically anything they want in any manner they wish. The free university acts as a link between those who want to teach and those who want to learn.

Free universities differ in structure. About half the free universities are sponsored by a traditional college or university, about one third are completely independent organizations, and another 12 percent are sponsored by a community agency like a library or YMCA. Half the free universities charge no fees to the learner. Some allow their teachers to charge fees; many do not. The Denver

Free University has both teachers who charge and volunteer teachers. The structure of the free university is usually determined by the character of the community it serves. The Brooklyn Skills Exchange in New York, for instance, charges fees of $20 to $30, and pays its teachers. The Center for Community Learning in Russellville, Arkansas, charges no fees and does not pay its teachers.

Even the free university's name reflects the nature of the community: The Animas Free School is in Durango, Colorado; the Center for Participant Education in Tallahassee, Florida; the Learning Connection in Columbus, Ohio; the Class Factory in Houston, Texas; and Sundry School, also in Houston.

Free universities were started on college campuses in the early 1960s and gained a reputation and visibility as alternative organizations offering political courses for an active student body. The first free university grew out of the Free Speech Movement in Berkeley, California, in 1964, and free universities spontaneously sprouted on hundreds of college campuses across the country. Although the student activism of the 1960s died down in the seventies, the development of free universities remained strong.

After a mild decline and a nosedive into anonymity in the media, free universities became a vehicle for a new trend in American society—lifelong learning. In the mid-1970s more free universities started again, existing free universities experienced enrollment jumps, and free universities moved off campus in orientation.

By 1976, free universities were found in large cities, in small rural towns, and in college communities where they meshed with the community.

With their new popularity came visibility once again, as free universities were viewed as a new way for adults to get together to learn. The Associated Press reported,

Free universities have made a full turn. Known variously as open education exchanges, communiversities and experimental colleges, they have moved from the activist and often underground university of the 1960s to the adult education wave of the 1970s.[5]

And *Newsweek* noted at the turn of the decade of the eighties,

Free universities, it turns out, are as accurate a barometer of American tastes as their radical founders always hoped. . . . Today they are hotter than ever—but with a difference. Fiery activism is out. Disco lessons, tai chi exercises and fix-it courses are in.[6]

What makes free universities different from other noncredit educational providers? One of the most distinguishing characteristics of free universities is the philosophy that anybody can teach and anybody can learn. Free universities are the only nationally coordinated organizations that allow an individual to teach anything he or she wants, provided it is legal. "We see this as an educational implication of the First Amendment, that anyone can share his or her ideas, whatever their perspective, in a group situation," says Seth Horwitz, former head of the Free University at University Park, Pennsylvania.

That openness to ideas attracts unorthodox ideas and unheard-of concepts. "When a man came in a few years back and wanted to teach 'Swimming and the Effortless Effort of Zen,' I thought he was a bit crazy," recalls one free university director. "The course was a philosophical approach to swimming. But we ran the course, a lot of people signed up, including an avid swimmer on our staff, who said the course was excellent. So who is to say what is a good or bad idea?"

Some of those unheard-of ideas have become quite popular. In the late seventies, people began to offer courses on preventive and holistic health in free universities. Then, such topics were regarded as offbeat. Today, the health topics are not only among the most popular in free university catalogs but also a national trend. Free universities also claim to have led the way in solar energy, appropriate technology, and nuclear power courses.

A second distinctive feature is that while free universities are not necessarily "free," they are the most cost-efficient adult learning. A study conducted for the National Center for Education Statistics showed that the average cost per class for a participant was less than $10. That cost included cost to the sponsoring institution, to the government, and to the participant.

This low cost makes it possible for any community, large or small, to have a free university. In Olsburg, Kansas, a volunteer committee runs the Olsburg Rural Educational Opportunities (OREO) program on a budget of $200 a year, which is raised at an annual summer flea market. That $200 goes into brochures. In Boulder, Colorado, the Community Free School has a budget of more than half a million dollars and charges fees. A local survey, however, showed that most Free School classes cost less than those of other local providers.

Another feature, self-directed learning, is not particularly new and follows in many of the traditions of adult education. "Learning should be a two-way process," says Dennis DuBé of Boulder. "Free universities do not guarantee learning; it is not a consumer product. We are not in the business of putting on intellectual Johnny Carson shows for nighttime diversion. Learning rests with the teacher and the participants." Thus free universities are helping to take learning away from its institutionalized "providing" mode back to a time when learning was a sharing process that both teachers and learners undertook together. Free universities act as a linking mechanism, as an educational clearinghouse, and shy away from taking responsibility for class content and process as much as possible, putting that responsibility instead on the participants.

The free universities have a broad appeal. They are more than just another way to get a course. They contain something special, something fascinating, for just about everyone who comes into contact with one. For the average person, free universities are an enjoyable and relaxed way to learn. At the same time, they hold out a tantalizing offer to teach something in return. It is a fresh approach to learning, unhindered by computer cards, deans, or complexity. For community and civic leaders, free universities contribute to community development, starting new projects beneficial to the town and supporting other community ventures.

Other adult educators look at the free university as an innovator, as an experimenter with process, content, and structure. Some of its operational aspects may be tested and fail, but many have caught on and made free universities—without a financial push from government or industry—highly successful educational organizations.

The free university, either in its component parts or as an entire model, is beginning to be adopted by other adult education organizations. Charles Bunting, deputy director of the Fund for the Improvement of Postsecondary Education in the Department of Education, told a free university conference, "In the future, other educational providers will look more like you, not less."[7] Professor Gordon C. Godbey of Pennsylvania State University writes,

The university, extended or resident, is not free. Nor is it free from the domination of faculty, administrators, and pressure groups who exercise influence on what is offered, as well as when and by what teaching methods. Although this may be well and good, it is decisive and it is limiting. However, there is such a thing as a "free university"! . . . Universities can move a long way toward one of their stated goals—an informed electorate sympathetic to learning—by supporting "free universities."[8]

The free university need not be another threatening, competitive, adversary institution but can provide a vision and an operating model. The number of institutions that have adapted the free university model to their own institutional structure is expanding. There are free universities sponsored by many different community groups and organizations from schools to churches. The potential for other existing social, community, and educational institutions to do the same is great.

But professional educators aren't the only people who can run free universities. Just as anyone can participate in a free university, anyone can start one as well. Five years ago, Sandy Bremer hired an answering service and started Open University in Washington, D.C., working at it during nights and weekends. One year later, she quit her job to take on Open University full time, and today she employs four other people and enrolls more than 10,000 participants a year.

In Dighton, Kansas, farmers Vance and Louise Ehmke wanted a little more stimulation over the long winter nights than just the television. They helped start People to People, a rural free university that offers more than fifty classes a year to the county's 2,800 residents.

The main ingredients for starting a free university are an office, a phone, and human energy. Free universities start with as little as $25 for the first brochure. Currently, there are three basic free university models. The first is the campus-community model, in which a free university is associated with a college and reaches out to the community as well. The second, the rural small-town free university, was developed in the last five years by Jim Killacky and Sue Maes at University for Man, in Manhattan, Kansas. They have set up twenty-five free universities in towns as small as 170 people, using volunteer teachers, half-time paid coordinators, and advisory boards. A third model, the independent fee-charging free university, thrives in larger cities. These free universities charge fees from $5 to $40, usually pay teachers, and are separately incorporated. Denver Free University, the largest, now enrolls 17,-000 participants. It has grown so large that the staff has helped set up another free university in Denver to "compete" with it. Other large independent free universities are in such towns as Indianapolis, Oakland, San Francisco, Tucson, Tulsa, and Houston.

Where will free universities be headed in the future? "We'd like to see a free university in any community that wants one," says Julie Govert of the Free University Network, the national association of free universities. "One area full of potential is cooperating with other agencies, such as public libraries, in setting up free universities. Free universities are not so much another institution as a new vision and a new model. Any person or organization can set up a free university, and we hope to utilize existing resources, agencies, and people in the community."

Perhaps so many people are intrigued by free universities because they are more than just education. Among other things, free universities attempt to provide a sense of community. That role, once held by churches, by family, by clubs, and sometimes even by government in times of national emergency, is never fulfilled by any one organization. But the free university partially meets that underlying need in all of us to feel part of something larger than ourselves. Free universities provide teachers and learners with a "community of scholars," a feeling of learning with others.

In pursuing learning for all, free universities have had to attack some mental blocks. They unhesitatingly propose that "anyone can teach and anyone can learn"—anything. That notion, of intruding upon sanctuaries of knowledge that have previously been unlocked only through a series of prescribed doors available only to a few, is heretical. We have been taught that knowledge is a commodity attained by going through prescribed steps, usually from elementary through intermediate to advanced. But a new concept of learning—as a process that anyone can tackle at any point—unleashes a deluge of possibilities for people to learn and act. In that sense, free universities are a new vision of what it means to learn. With resources available to all, people are free to learn any subject they wish and to teach any subject they want to. The consequences of learning anything inevitably lead to behavioral changes and to people's believing that they can do anything. When people believe that, they begin to act, to start things, to initiate democratic activity, to participate more in society.

The 1980s will see great changes in adult learning. Many of those changes are unforeseen now. No one knows much about what adult learning will be like at the end of this decade. We know something about the demographics of our society, but not a whole lot. We do not fully understand what self-directed learning is, or how one becomes a self-directed learner. We do not have an accurate gauge as to when it is appropriate to direct one's own learning and when it is appropriate to be taught. We do not know why people participate in different adult learning settings.

Free universities will continue to stand on the cutting edge of adult learning in this country, developing new concepts, and adapting with the changing learning needs of the general public. Juxtaposing a society of learners and teachers and our traditional education institutions, the free university remains one of the most vital organizations linking formal learning with the needs and interests of the general public.

Whether from the viewpoint of a learner, a teacher, or an educator, the eighties will be an exciting time in lifelong learning, and free universities will have a large role in contributing to the challenge of making us truly a nation of learners.

Chapter 2
A Visit to Three Free Universities

For a close-up view of free universities, we can examine three programs to see where they are, who runs them, and how they operate. Our tour will begin in the Rocky Mountains, where the Denver Free University is representative of large and independent free universities. We then will head to the East Coast and visit the Baltimore Free University at Johns Hopkins University, a medium-sized free university representative of the campus-based free universities in the country. Finally, we will go back to the heartland of the country to the wheat fields of Kansas and visit the Clay County Education Program in Clay Center. It is a successful small-town free university and representative of the rural free university model.

Denver Free University

With the serene and beautiful Rocky Mountains as a background, the city of Denver is a contemporary metropolitan boom town. The Denver life-style combines a little of the sophistication of eastern cities with the western spirit of adventure.

The Denver Free University (DFU) is part of the bustling city in which it is set. The second largest free university in the nation, DFU enrolls more than 17,000 participants a year. Formed in 1969, it is also one of the older free universities. Although DFU started on a college campus, it quickly separated from the university in 1970 and became an independent organization. It has a board of directors, a staff, volunteers, teachers, and, of course, learners.

DFU is located in the Capitol Hill area near the state capitol. As with most free universities, DFU's offices are fairly small, and only a handful of classes meet there. Most classes take place in the community—in homes, churches, community centers, businesses, and schools.

The offices are located on two floors of a modest old storefront office building. On the first floor are two large rooms for dance—the current most popular course—with wooden floors, big mirrors, and sparse furnishings. Upstairs are DFU's offices, a conference room, and a coffee room.

The offices reflect color, activity, and organization. Colorful past catalog covers made into posters line the walls of the main office. A large cloth banner with the DFU logo decorates one wall. A receptionist listens to a classical music station on the radio. Long rows of file boxes line tables around the edge of the room.

But there are also signs of technological efficiency—electric typewriters, push-button phones with four lines, adding machines, desk calculators, an answering machine, a mimeograph, and a copy machine. Recently, a Denver newspaper reporter covering the DFU tenth anniversary visited the offices, pointed to the copier, and remarked, "That alone shows you've come a long way in ten years."

Throughout the other four staff offices are books about management: Marlene Wilson's *Volunteer Management, The Modern Practice of Adult Education* by Malcolm Knowles, and the *Free U. Manual.* Among the orderliness of books, files, and machines are plants, movie posters, art, notices, and news clippings.

An in-out board for the nine regular workers is posted by the exit door.

One of the inner offices looks like the main strategy room: its walls are covered by large color wall maps of the city of Denver. One map shows the location of classes and teachers' residences. Yellow pins mark class locations, and red pins indicate the teachers' residences.

Another map has several hundred red pins marking catalog distribution points. "We've got to analyze this map," says staffer Tracy Dunning, pointing out the clumping of red pins in some neighborhoods and scattered pins in other areas of the city.

Another map shows the public schools and school districts. The school locations that are underlined are where DFU holds many of its classes. The staffers add that they hope to locate more classes in public schools around the city.

Through the offices is a hallway leading to a conference room flanked by a large kitchen and another meeting room. That is the extent of the Denver Free University facilities. The five offices, dance studio, kitchen, and conference rooms are considered spacious for most free universities confined to single offices.

The staff occupying the offices also reflects a mixture of orderliness, efficiency, exuberance, and friendliness. The staff ranges in age from eighteen-year-old receptionist Deborah Harris to fifty-nine-year-old Grace Johnson, who is assistant class coordinator.

Mary Ann Van Buskirk is the financial and business coordinator. Tracy Dunning is the class coordinator. Steve Estroff is volunteer and public relations coordinator. DFU has two receptionists, a maintenance manager, an assistant registrar, an assistant office coordinator, a board of thirteen directors, and numerous volunteers.

But who's in charge? "We're still working with shared responsibility among the three primary coordinators," explains Dunning. "We can always go back to traditional management schemes." After three years, the experimental management system seems to be working. Enrollments are still growing. The catalog is a slick sixty-page brochure produced four times a year. Until recently it was printed on glossy "*Time* magazine" paper, with rich color photos and art, the envy of every free university layout artist and catalog designer.

DFU's courses reflect the modern man and woman, exploring the latest trends. For Winter 1980 there are approximately 400 courses. Standard adult learning subjects are offered, such as fine arts, arts and crafts, dance, repair classes, and recreation. But DFU also has courses for children in social issues, spirit, holistic health, and personal growth.

Under Holistic Health are courses in "Psychosynthesis," "Fear," "Right Brain Exploring," "A New Baby at My House," and "Infant Massage."

Seven courses are offered in a section called Macrobiotic Cooking, including "Cooking with Seaweed."

The Body section includes yoga classes, martial arts, tai chi, and "Survival in the Streets: Self-Defense for Women."

The Spirit section can take you from "Past Life Regression and Time Travel" to "Studies in the Gospel of John." The Dance section is usually popular, although the types of dance rise and fall in popularity. At the turn of the decade, disco had plateaued, and country-western swing and clogging were gaining. Ballet, modern, jazz, and ballroom are all well attended.

Music classes are geared for everyone from the casual listener ("Classical Music for the Complete Idiot") to the professional ("Songwriting") with a good deal of hearty practice thrown in ("Singing and Understanding German Folksongs").

The Language section includes literature, such as that of Herman Hesse; writing, "To Be a Writer, Write;" foreign languages, including conversational Arabic and intermediate Mandarin Chinese; and speed reading. Classes are still offered in the Social Issues section, which used to be much more prominent in free university curricula. They include such current topics as Latin America, pornography, and nuclear energy.

Children are welcome at the free university and can take courses in ballet, poetry, and building and playing a dulcimer.

The Arts and Crafts section has a steady fare of photography, drawing, calligraphy, quilting, and many others.

Personal Growth is a big section; its fascinating course titles ask questions or offer answers—"The Creative Use of Aggression," "Stop Messing Yourself Up," "Creative Intimacy," "Men: It's OK to Be Single," and "What Do I Want Out of Life?"

The Tools for New Directions section is unique, with scores of classes and seminars on how to direct your own life, including "Life/Work Planning," "Self Realization," and "Overcoming Self-Defeating Behaviors." The reading for one course is the book *Frogs into Princes*.

Practical courses abound: repair, construction, finance and business, law and jobs, investment and selling, and gardening.

DFU plays around with its Playing section, teasing and tempting learners with "Ghosts and Ghoulies," "Sweet Loretta's Coffee House," and "Juggling." For the less adventuresome, there are "Trout Fishing," "Bridge," and "Volleyball."

Finally, a Potpourri section has what you couldn't find else-where—"Video Awareness," "Popcorn," and "Practical Taxidermy Appreciation."

If you haven't chosen at least five classes you'd like to take from those mentioned, there are 350 others. DFU's catalog reflects contemporary social life. A reader can discover the trends and the outer limits of what adults are interested in learning and doing today. Unlike traditional higher education, each DFU catalog is different, reflecting the shifts in American interests, concerns, and life-styles. Three years from now, one can look at the catalog and find the changes in American learning habits.

The Denver Free University, like a dozen other free universities, celebrated its tenth anniversary last year with justifiable enthusiasm. It has grown tremendously in numbers and staff and organization. It has retained most of its original philosophy and concept and still is a springboard for individual thought and action in the community.

DFU staff member Cheryl Moffitt outlined DFU's history in a recent catalog:

A close knit group of seven people started the Denver Free University in 1969. Neil Rosenthal, president of the University of Denver student body, had been to Berkeley. He came back to Denver with the idea of starting a free university similar to San Francisco's, which began as a result of the free speech movement of the early 60's. With a thousand dollar grant, he empowered Marc Lefkovics, one of the original organizers of DFU and still a member of the board of directors, and others to organize the first term.

"It was a different time, politically, than it is now," recalls Marc. "By starting DFU we were attempting to make a sociological statement about the changes needed in education. It was a ripe time for the idea of learning for learning's sake. In other words, learning and teaching without the direct rewards of grades and money. I had attended a progressive high school and had been totally disillusioned with my college experience. It seemed that the most important thing in college was learning to cheat very well, to do the least amount of work for the most amount of profit (grades)."

The base of operations for DFU was a coffeehouse on South

Pearl. Instructors and community members volunteered their time. That first term, 250 students signed up for forty-six courses. Eventually, DFU split from Denver University, moved several times, and grew to its present size.[1]

Now DFU has between 200 and 250 teachers a session, and four sessions a year.

Teachers must volunteer their time the first session; after that they can charge for their services. Surprisingly, a good many teachers choose to remain volunteers after the first session. DFU sets a limit on the amount teachers can charge, which averages $12 an hour, and adds its own registration fee.

The variable fee structure means that a course from DFU can be taken for as little as $4, with an upper limit around $30—still very reasonable for big-city education.

In adherence to the free university philosophy that "anyone can teach and anyone can learn," there are no restrictions on participants who come to DFU, and any person can offer a class. All teachers are interviewed by class coordinator Dunning. They must be honest in stating the course description and their qualifications.

During our visit to DFU, a potential teacher walks in with an appointment to see Dunning. He is Steve Hunter, a house analyst who examines homes for construction defects for buyers and sellers of local real estate in Denver.

Dunning examines Hunter's course outline, which seems to be in good order. She schedules his class for the junior high school space DFU uses. Then she asks, "Why are you interested in teaching a free university course?"

"Well, I've taken several courses but never taught one before," Hunter says. "But I am writing a book on how to become a landlord, and I thought I could get some good questions and concerns I haven't thought of from the students.

"I'd like to bring in some experts—a zoning specialist, a construction expert, a tenants' union organizer—just to shake things up a bit, and maybe even a psychologist on tenant psychology. I don't know if there is a tenant psychology, but there might be one. It's just one area I'd like to explore. I have questions to ask these experts, but I thought the students might also have them.

"Having the students to bounce my ideas off of, and their questions to the other experts, would really help me formulate the material for my book."

Hunter's class should do well, Dunning predicts. Over her shoulder on the wall is a short prayer, "Lord, Help Me To Know What's Cooking Before It Boils Over."

Nothing, however, seems to be boiling over right now, as Dunning is in a position to know what's cooking in adult learning. "I love it," she says. "Where else could I learn about so many intriguing subjects on a daily basis?"

The teachers at DFU come from all walks of life. Some have taught elsewhere; many haven't. Some are old, like seventy-year-old Jane Tanenbaum, a professional student and former member of the Martha Graham Dance Company. Some are businessmen, like Joe Sabah, who heard about DFU on the radio. He has taught his class "How to Get the Job You *Really* Want" ten times already, and he was so enthusiastic about DFU that he joined the board of directors.

Some are professional teachers, like Elaine Norona, who says without embarrassment, "I'm a really good teacher." Norona had been a professional belly dancer in the Far East for ten years when her sister, who lived in Denver, encouraged her to come home and enclosed a copy of the DFU catalog in one letter. When Norona, with a background as a teacher at Arthur Murray studios, did come back to Denver, she began teaching DFU classes out of her home. "It's a very gratifying experience," she says. "Students walk in, and waltz out.

"I tell my students I can teach anything—even the minuet. One time I was called on it—two people needed to dance a minuet for a play they were in. Fortunately I had seen it on late-night television once and could teach them the steps."

Some have had no experience teaching before. Don Marchese works for Xerox Corporation. He wants to be in employee training and development someday but was told he needed some teaching experience. So he started teaching astronomy at the free university.

"I hadn't taught before," he says. "So it was pretty much of a challenge. I didn't learn astronomy in school but by being observant. I learned celestial navigation from my father."

About thirty people sign up for Marchese's class every session. Many of them are campers who want to identify the stars they see so clearly at night.

"Sometimes we use a basic classroom," Marchese explains. "But we also get out of the city and view the sky. We also use the local planetarium. People talk to each other. The teacher is the hub, but we learn from each other."

Although he could charge, and his classes are popular, Marchese continues to be a volunteer for DFU. Why doesn't he charge for teaching? "I don't know. I may. I wasn't really thinking about that. I'm more interested in meeting new people."

The rewards for teaching at DFU seem almost greater than the money a teacher could make from it. That seems to be the attitude of another DFU volunteer teacher, David Margolis, whose business is making money. Margolis has run a successful financial planning agency in Denver for eleven years, and his course description exudes confidence. "I can show you how to be one of the select 5 percent who achieve financial independence," it reads. "I will destroy the myths about investing that keep people from winning the money game." Why does David Margolis teach at the free university? "I love to talk," he freely admits. "The little guy needs help, and I get a kick out of doing it. It's a catharsis. There is a small course fee, but I ought to be paying the students. A waiter who took my class wrote me this summer and said he had gotten into real estate sales and that I had been the impetus to change his profession."

Margolis also has his own nontraditional teaching techniques that seem to work. He asks the students to write a letter telling him why they are in the class. After each class, he writes a letter back to them summarizing the meeting. At the end of the session, he throws a pizza and beer party at Shakeys.

What do the participants think of DFU? As we sit in the office, a prospective student comes in to look over the catalog. It turns out Sky Wise has already taken courses at DFU. Like many other people we talk to around here, he knows what he likes in learning.

Wise's current class is in watercolors, and he likes his free university teacher because he provides a lot of information about technique. "I've had studio art classes before, but not as good as this one. It may seem odd that you can learn more in a free university unstructured way. You teach yourself, but a good teacher will have a whole lot of information."

Wise has seen some classes he didn't like at DFU as well, such as the aesthetics of music theory course, taught by a musician who was involved in atonal music.

So how can he tell which courses are good? "There are so many more DFU courses I'd like to take," he goes on. "It's pretty easy to tell. The folksy, general course descriptions—you know you are taking a chance. If the guy lays it out clearly, it's a good course. The fee means something too. And people's experience has a lot to do with it too."

If DFU's students and teachers are independent-minded, they are not a small minority in Denver. Despite (and many would maintain because of) its informal and friendly atmosphere, DFU has become a large and successful provider of adult learning.

Writing in a Denver weekly, Patricia Calhoun says,

> Over the last ten years DFU has grown from a small knot of alternative classes offered at the University of Denver into the educational pacesetter in Denver. It used to be that people taking adult education classes naturally turned to the local colleges and universities for a course roster. Now a person looking for a course will likely start at the Denver Free University.[2]

Baltimore Free University

For our second free university tour, we go to the East Coast to visit the Baltimore Free University on the campus of Johns Hopkins University. The Baltimore Free University (BFU) is typical of the campus-community model of free universities.

The Johns Hopkins campus is a big park in the middle of a working-class city. Two quads are set in the middle of the grounds. In one of the quads is the student union, which in earlier days was a YMCA. The free university is located in the student union, run from the suite of offices the chaplain has. BFU itself has part of only one office. The free university has a desk, two file cabinets, and a bookcase.

To understand the Baltimore Free University, one needs to look beyond that big park to the city surrounding the campus. From the beginning, BFU has been oriented to the community surrounding it. The community is probably several communities. To the east is a mixture of middle-class and retired people, seven churches, and a shopping strip. To the west are the lower middle- and working-class people. To the north are apartment buildings, and one mile to the south are some of the worst slums in Baltimore.

The participants in the free university reflect the diversity of neighborhoods around Johns Hopkins. Folks come from all over the city and the county. "The free university really has a good mixture of people," says free university director Judy Reilly. Eighty-five percent of the participants come from the community, and the other 15 percent are associated with Johns Hopkins. Most fall into the age range of nineteen to thirty-five, but many are over sixty.

BFU was started in 1960 by chaplain Chester Wickwire; Jim Regensberg, a student; and Mike Saffle, the assistant chaplain at Johns Hopkins then. Many saw the early free university as a platform for what was happening in the 1960s—a means to discuss war, racism, and women's issues. Although the beginning was a bit shaky, the free university eventually got on its feet.

Wrote one reporter in 1971,

> After approximately two years of halfhearted effort, with six course offerings—more or less—at the start, and with little acclaim or acknowledgement from anyone, the Baltimore Free University has finally come into its own. Last semester, offering a variety of 44 subjects from Appalachian Culture to Urban Problems, BFU enrolled about 500 students, ages 15–50, as diverse as the course offering themselves.
>
> BFU is aiming toward expansion. Next year they hope to offer twice as many courses as are in the present catalog. The emphasis is in two areas: vocational subjects directed towards residents of the inner city and more useless subjects to attract its traditional students.[3]

That expected "expansion" never came, and statistically the Baltimore Free University has grown little since 1971. It now offers approximately eighty courses a semester and still enrolls around 500 participants a semester. Unlike most free universities, the participants, even in the early years, came from the community, not the student population. That is still true today. Although some of the motivation for starting the free university may have come from a social consciousness, the course offerings of BFU have not changed much since the early 1970s either.

Some of the courses offered in 1971 were on wine making, fibers, wood sculpture, home repairs, drug addiction, social engineering, Afro-American music, black literature, alternative journalism, drawing, silk screening, Shura Aboda, yoga, mysticism of Teilhard, motorcycling, documentary film making, legal aid, Herman Hesse, and poetry.

What comes through to the casual observer of the Baltimore Free University is not a remarkable array of statistics, participants, budget, or staff, but a concern for the joy and enjoyment of learning and teaching in a free university. This is reflected in the diversity of participants—probably the most outstanding feature of BFU. BFU was probably one of the earliest free universities to begin reaching older citizens, and the elderly both learn and teach in the free university. Part of the reason that older citizens attend the free university here is its proximity to their homes. Another reason is that the free university's fee of $5 per course is affordable to the elderly. Surprisingly, the elderly do not seem interested in such "typically elderly" classes as macrame, arts and crafts, and talks on social security.

"The older people take every course," says Reilly. "One seventy-year-old woman takes the massage courses. Another wants swimming, or frisbee throwing, or cooking. The older people are a lot of fun."

The elderly also teach interesting courses. Bennet Gold, a retired schoolteacher, teaches English as a second language to foreign students. Howard Langford, eighty-five, teaches issues in human survival. Marjorie King, seventy, does a class in interior design. She even had a "recital" at the end of the course. The students refinished chairs, did house plans, and put together displays of their work and plans for interior design, complete with samples.

The Baltimore Free University also has many participants from the black community. They too are attracted to the free university's low cost, and despite its location in a rather conservative university, the free university has a good image in the community. This may be due to Chaplain Wickwire, who has a reputation for working with the black community.

BFU also has about a half dozen black teachers as well. They teach Spanish and German, women's courses, film making and cartooning, poetry, and others.

Although teachers do not get paid at BFU, Reilly maintains that there are a lot of other rewards. "They are very happy to be in the free university. They are teachers at heart." Many of the teachers are repeaters, and perhaps as many as half keep on teaching at the free university. "They really like the experience of meeting people. They are the best people I've known," she says. In keeping with the ideal of allowing anyone to teach, BFU does not screen any of its teachers. The open-minded system apparently works, for there have been major complaints about only two courses in the past two years.

BFU has its series of staple courses, like auto repair, ballet, sailing, massage, bicycling, and yoga. But it also has some unusual courses. Arnie Goldberg teaches a course on the assassination of Abraham Lincoln. George Phelps takes his German and Spanish language students to the German and Mexican embassies in Washington.

James Pipas, a postdoctoral fellow at Hopkins, teaches a course on "Modern Science for the Rest of Us." "Lay people need to know more about science," Pipas says. "We are living in a fast-moving technological world, and the people need to make political decisions. Often they do not know what is behind some of the decisions, or how they affect life on this planet."[4]

Pipas structured his two-hour classes with lectures first, then informal discussions. "They get pretty heated sometimes and sometimes spill over into the Rathskeller nearby over some beer drinking." More than 100 people registered for the course.

The operations of BFU are kept simple. The free university is run by Reilly, the coordinator, who is a paid staff member of the chaplain's office but has other duties in addition to the free university. About her job she says, "I just keep it running. I don't really direct it; I coordinate it. I match it all up. There is joy and pain in the work. I hate the administration—the juggling of space, the complaints, the students who want a million-dollar course for five dollars, the registration period. I like the concept, the teachers, the brainstorming, going to the classes." Reilly is supervised by the chaplain, and officially by a board overseeing the student union, but the free university is fairly autonomous in its everyday operations.

Former BFU director Jim Case sees two reasons for the endurance and success of the free university experiment in Baltimore. First, the concept of free learning has enabled the free university to consistently attract teachers and students interested in what it has to offer. Secondly, Case sees the sponsorship of the chaplain's office as providing a solid base and continuity (despite ups and downs in student interest) to develop a clientele of students and instructors.[5]

What does the rest of Johns Hopkins University think of the free university? "I think we're basically ignored and sometimes criticized," says Reilly. Part of the anonymity rests with the unusual funding situation in the chaplain's office. Originally a part of a private YMCA on campus, the chaplain's office raises much of its own programming budget each year, thus giving it some freedom and control over its own programs.

Although the university evening college helps by giving space for classes to the free university, there are periodic criticisms of the free university by some in the administration. According to Reilly, "They take us through the wringer each year. Some think we are taking money and parking places away from the university. They see us as competing. It's really silly." Reilly's greatest fear is losing some of the space on the campus that BFU gets for classes. With many people in the community living in apartments too small for classes and only two churches in the area able to provide space, BFU relies on the university to provide much of its classroom space.

Reilly maintains that the free university doesn't really compete with the university. The university pays its teachers and offers credits and standard academic courses. The free university uses volunteer teachers, offers no credits, and offers nontraditional subject matter.

The free university, like all organizations, has its problems. The problems most apparent to BFU now are space, recruitment of teachers, and lack of involvement from the university. Money does not seem to be a problem. Although the modest $4,000 yearly budget does not cover the coordinator's staff time, it does take care of the expenses of brochure printing, telephone service, and supplies. BFU has a great deal of support within the chaplain's office. The free university is seen as one of three most positive programs in the office, along with a tutoring program and a film series.

"The free university can be very effective," Reilly says. "It pulls together people who might not ever meet, ideas that might never be had in any other setting. It is a sharing process, and very meaningful."

Clay County Education Program

The third free university that we shall visit is representative of a relatively new type of free university that is blossoming in rural

America—the small-town free university. One of the more vibrant of the small-town free universities is the Clay County Education Program (CCEP) in Clay Center, Kansas.

Clay Center is located in north-central Kansas, forty miles from the nearest four-year college and community college. It is a farming community, and the free university sessions are geared to the wheat crop. Summer classes are sparsely attended because that is harvest time. Clay Center itself is a town of 5,000 people, and another 5,000 live in the county and the small communities surrounding it: Green, Idana, Morganville, Oak Hill, Longford, Fact, Clifton, and Wakefield.

To get to Clay Center, you drive through the gently rolling hills of Kansas, where the sky is big, the farms far apart, and the wheat golden. Clay Center is a typical small town. As you drive in, you come down the main street, past the grain elevators and grain cooperative that is the heart of almost every Kansas town, past the Pizza Hut and A&W Drive-In, to the town square. The courthouse, built in the 1800s and made of native Kansas limestone, graces the town square. Banks and stores surround the square. The town library, a renovated Carnegie library also built in the 1800s, is across the street.

The free university offices are now in the courthouse, symbolic of the central and accepted role that CCEP has gained in the community. But like other free universities across the country, the office is not much more than a phone, a desk, and a few files. The real activity takes place all over town—and in CCEP's case, all over the county.

The people who teach in CCEP are volunteers, and there are no fees for the classes except for materials. A board of advisers oversees the program and advises and supports the two part-time paid coordinators of CCEP, Coni Witters and Judy Bigler. The board members reflect a cross section of the community: a retiree, a minister, a school principal, a farmer, and a banker. Perhaps because it is education, perhaps because it is not yet an ingrown organization, CCEP often brings people from different social strata together. Thus, a low-income welfare mother may find herself seated, at first uncomfortably, across the table from a wealthy civic leader, and find for the first time that they have something in common and something of interest to each other.

Classes at CCEP meet in all sorts of buildings, a testament to

CCEP's complete integration into the community. Just take a look at the local newspaper, the *Clay County Dispatch*, and its frequent pictures of CCEP classes around town. During the last two years, the paper has run photos of six women and lots of food at a cooking class called "Lean Cuisine," at the local high school; a living room full of people for Coni Witters's class on making pictures with scrap cloth; a rhythmic aerobics class exercising at the Elks Club ballroom; a summer aqua exercise class for older people in the municipal pool; and a calligraphy class in the Episcopal church basement.

Other classes meet at the public library, the two banks, and many other public and private meeting places throughout the community.

The spirit of community education has infiltrated the community not just in its class locations but also in its involvement of a cross section of the population.

One summer evening in 1978, for example, the Associated Press visited a CCEP class in the village of Idana, a town of around 100 people, just thirteen miles west of Clay Center. Reporter Scott Kraft later wrote,

Three wooden pews were his classroom, a piano bench his lectern. The bare light bulbs flickered as a summer storm threatened. But to the thirteen inquisitive minds assembled in the tiny church basement in north central Kansas, there was no setting anywhere more fertile for learning. Because beekeeping was the subject, and John Schweitzer, a wiry seventy-three-year-old in green work clothes, the teacher.

And from the two young women in the front to the middle-aged men in the back, his audience listened, questioned, shared and learned. For his recent teaching debut, Schweitzer offered baby food jars of honey—"just enough for a flapjack"; gave advice to a farmer with an ornery swarm of bees on his land; and recommended that beekeepers keep their swarms away from the honeysuckle—"it'll make your honey smell like dirty socks." Then there was that down-home smile and an embarrassed gesture. "When a bee man gets to talking—why, he sometimes says too many things."

In church basements and living rooms and even on backyard patios across the country, a few people are talking and a lot of others are learning—without grades, homework or pressure. That growth has its roots in people like Schweitzer, a service station operator by trade, and in places like Idana, where it's a half-minute walk from the center of town to acres and acres of Kansas wheat.[6]

CCEP brings people together in an informal and relaxed atmosphere that stimulates learning, enjoyment, and community pride. People find out that their neighbor knows about Korean cooking. A fifteen-year-old boy teaches macrame to a group of older women and bridges a generation gap.

CCEP classes are popular. In the spring of 1979, CCEP offered fifty-nine classes and had 936 participants register, just for that one session. About half the people come from the county rather than the city of Clay Center, an achievement which took years.

The free university in Clay County radiates a folksy rural charm. Its brochure is filled with drawings that, according to former director Bev Wilhelm, are "quite tacky, but people love them."

CCEP, like other free universities, plays a big social role in bringing people together and providing entertaining evenings. One teacher admitted that a participant came to the class at her home just to see the inside of her house.

But CCEP also fills a major educational need in the community. With higher educational institutions far away, it is the only extensive adult education program in the county. And not all the courses are in tractor repair and macrame, by any means.

There is yoga for people over fifty, and biofeedback was a big course in the late seventies. There is a course on women in jazz, and others on foreign languages, philosophy, religion, and other intellectual topics.

CCEP's success with issue-oriented and serious topics has not been easy. Like other adult-learning programs, CCEP has had to buck the winds of popular sentiment for more leisure-time classes, as well as a mistaken impression that only leisure and recreation classes will gain large enrollments. Wilhelm notes that many people would approach her and say that they didn't want to have to think at a CCEP class. Yet CCEP has offered some of the most serious of all free university topics. A course in the Russian Revolution, taught by a local doctor, was so popular that it was repeated the next year, as was a course on comparing society in the sixteenth century with society in the twentieth century. Taught by a minister, the class had more than twenty enthusiastic people sign up. Adult education oddsmakers would probably have given that course a 100-to-1 chance of drawing twenty enrollments in a small rural town.

Both the issues courses and the arts get a fair hearing at CCEP. Dorothy Roebke has offered several drama presentations on artists through CCEP, including ones on painter Grandma Moses and musician Pablo Casals. Roebke researches the artist thoroughly and then presents a one-person dramatization of him or her. With Casals, the famous cellist, she attempted to familiarize people with the cello and something about it. She is now planning to do something on women's poetry, examining women's search for themselves in the modern world.

Roebke's goal is to increase the community's knowledge about the arts. She also had a hand in getting CCEP off the ground. "I had an eye on the arts and saw community education as a vehicle to bring the arts to the people," she says. "And when the program was having trouble in the early stages getting off the ground, I said 'stay in the buggy, we'll get it done.'"

As a free university teacher, Roebke subscribes to the philosophy about sharing knowledge. "People just bloom when they teach. They have so many hidden talents, and some feel like they are a dummy if they didn't come out of a college. But when they teach through community education, they feel their own worth."[7]

The program runs on just $4,500 a year. About $3,000 goes to pay the coordinators' salaries, and the other $1,500 pays for brochure printing, telephone service, stamps, and travel to a few free university workshops. The money comes from the county supervisors, who are annually amazed at how far $4,500 goes. Each year Gary Griffiths, the vice-president of Hutchinson-Royal, the town's biggest industry, and a former board member of CCEP, clearly and convincingly presents the CCEP case before the county board of supervisors.

Like most other rural free universities in Kansas, CCEP got its start with help from University for Man (UFM), a large free university in Manhattan, Kansas.

UFM outreach director Jim Killacky recalls the challenge of a university professor in 1974 that first sparked his interest in starting a free university in Clay Center. The Kansas State University professor in political science, specializing in rural areas, advised Killacky before the program was undertaken that the project would never fly in Clay Center. Killacky recalls, "He put his feet up on the desk and said, 'Killacky, if you ever pull off anything like that in Clay Center, it'll be a miracle.' "

Spurred on by the skeptics, Killacky organized a humanities program on rural life for several small towns in central Kansas, including Clay Center. The successful humanities program led to local interest in having a UFM program in Clay Center, and when UFM received a major federal grant to do free universities in rural Kansas, Clay Center was at the top of the priority list.

UFM not only provided Killacky's expertise but also placed two full-time VISTA volunteers in Clay Center. Barbara Swain and Jim Gehman were young, enthusiastic, and, ultimately, skilled in transferring the program to the local townspeople.

As in other Kansas towns, residents displayed caution about the program. Kansas is a conservative agricultural state where local people feel, not without a good deal of justification, that too much federal money is wasted on temporary, unproductive projects run by outsiders that stop when the federal funding faucet is turned off. So Swain and Gehman needed to convince the local people not only that this outside federal project was worthwhile but also that they, as VISTA workers, were not condescending to the rural residents. They were successful, and a year later, a local coordinator was hired to run the program.

The two VISTAs began their work in the local Episcopal church basement in 1975. They organized a town meeting there to explain the program, round up local leaders for the advisory board, and start the program. When they left a year later, the program sought local funding from the county supervisors and hired Witters as coordinator. The office was moved into the county courthouse, and the program began to expand to include rural residents outside Clay Center.

Between 1975, the first year, and 1979, enrollments jumped 350 percent. Registrations run at 1,500 a year, a whopping 15 percent of the county's population of 10,000. "It's passed the experimental stage," observes one civic leader.

Four years later, Killacky would note,

The Clay County program is a success largely because we've been able to stay out of it. It's run by local people; local people are doing the teaching. They're doing a fantastic job. The beautiful thing is Clay County has proved to a lot of skeptics here that a program like this will be accepted and perpetuated without outside pushing, outside money.[8]

In Clay County, Kansas, the free university has "made it." It is accepted and respected by the leadership in the community; it is both social and serious, and it has captured a warm sense of people doing something for themselves and enjoying it.

Chapter 3

A Look at the Data—
And the People

Having examined three different kinds of free universities, we are now ready to step back and look at free universities overall—their numbers, types, and budgets, and their people—learners, teachers and staffs. These data, together with a survey of the participants in free universities, give us a picture of free universities nationwide.

Until 1978, little data had been collected on free universities. There were rough guesses as to numbers of free universities and estimated total participants around the country but not much else. Free university organizer Blair Hamilton did the first free university directory in 1968, when most free universities were in their infancy. It contains valuable quotes from free university leaders, catalogs, and newsletters of the time but little overall analysis. Professors Paul Lauter and Florence Howe did some sound work on collecting information on the numbers of free universities and why they started for their 1970 book, *The Conspiracy of the Young*, and included a chapter on free universities. The most complete work was done by Jane Lichtman in her excellent book *Bring Your Own Bag*, in 1972.

While national directories of free universities were published in

1974, 1975, 1976, and 1978, they contained mainly names and addresses of local organizations.

In 1978 the Free University Network, the national association of free universities and learning networks, received a small grant from the National Center for Education Statistics for a comprehensive data collection on free universities and learning centers for the first time in their fifteen-year history. From that study came most of the statistical information that we have about free universities. Some of the data confirmed previous hunches; some of them were new.

The first free university person to realize the value of statistics locally and to make use of them was Dennis DuBé of the Community Free School in Boulder.

DuBé began collecting data on participants at the Free School in 1975, and his studies on catalogs and courses have also led to a more studied and analytical approach to the operation of free universities.

The lack of concern about (and in some instances, avoidance of) data collection is understandable in light of what free universities were trying to do in the early and mid-1970s. Like any other educational innovation, free universities wanted to be judged during those years on qualitative rather than quantitative grounds. This was so partly because free universities were creating a new model. Like all new model builders, they were concerned with the formation of the model and its ultimate worth, rather than its immediate success as portrayed by statistics.

Free university people were trying to establish a philosophy of learning and to create a learning environment. They were aware that those two qualitative aspects of education could not easily be measured.

Also, during the early 1970s, free university statistics, had they been compiled, might not have been very impressive. In the realm of higher education, universities had just enrolled the greatest number of college students the world had ever seen, numbering in the millions. With university staff and budgets in equally enormous proportions, the free university movement's statistics might have seemed paltry indeed.

Finally, data were not particularly useful to free universities in the early years when they were experimenting with methods, people, and philosophies. They were also mindful of the excess of data collection that higher education and the government were prone to do in the sixties, and of the relative uselessness of those data. Early free university people were mainly college students or college graduates, and keenly aware of the mounds of information that they as students were asked to give—to the university, to the government, and to the countless graduate students and professors doing research on them. The volume of data that these institutions collected, the perceived invasion of an individual's privacy, and the few relevant outcomes that the data produced left a negative impact on free university people.

Since 1975, more free university people have realized the benefits of data collection for their own organizations and have begun to collect limited data.

Free universities are still reluctant to ask too many questions of their participants and teachers, to invade privacy, or to pose embarrassing questions (such as income, marital status, and sometimes age).

By 1978, free universities not only recognized that proper and limited data collection could benefit them but also realized that their statistics in learning were now impressive enough to be touted in local and national circles. By that time some of the larger free universities—such as Seattle's Experimental College, Denver Free University, Communiversity in Kansas City, and the Indianapolis Free University—were the largest providers of noncredit classes in their metropolitan areas. In 1978, the respectable College Board, through its Future Directions for a Learning Society project, listed free universities for the first time as one of the major providers of adult learning in the country, along with fifteen other types of providers, such as the military, Cooperative Extension, and religious agencies.

Seeing that free university enrollments nationwide were a respectable 200,000, but still far below most of the other adult education providers, one free university staff person told Rexford Moon, then head of the Future Directions project for the College Board, "We're last." "Yes," replied Dr. Moon, "but you made the list."

That listing was the first recognition statistically that free universities had joined others in being a major provider of adult learning in the country. That same list, including free universities, would soon appear in an Educational Testing Service report on lifelong learning and in a Federal Task Force's Lifelong Learning report that stemmed from the passage of the Lifelong Learning Act by Congress.

From then on, free universities would often appear alongside other adult education institutions in media stories on adult learning. They received a good deal of attention in Ron Gross's book *The Lifelong Learner,* and they were included in stories on adult learning by the Associated Press, *Glamour* magazine, and others.

To some extent, the free universities' greater acceptance of and interest in data collection coincided with greater attention given to data collection in adult education overall.

When adult educators John W. C. Johnston and Ramon Rivera did their pioneering study entitled *Volunteers for Learning* in 1965, it was the first analysis of data in adult education in recent years. In 1969, the National Center for Education Statistics (NCES) did a series of reports on participation in adult learning. In 1972, NCES also published a study on adult education in community organizations and one on noncredit activities in colleges. But the state of the art was not advanced in other adult learning institutions either.

For instance, while higher education can measure enrollments in terms of actual people, adult learning providers can count only registrations. That is, if one person takes two classes, it is counted as two registrations. If a person takes one class in the spring and one in the fall, that is counted as two registrations as well, even though it is the same person. So almost all adult learning enrollments are based on registrations, rather than unduplicated people counts.

For free universities, it is estimated that participants take one to two classes per session, so that if a free university has 2,000 registrations, probably around 1,500 people have registered.

The emergence of statistics and data in other adult learning situations helped put into perspective some of the statistics that free universities were encountering, particularly the seemingly awful ones.

The dropout rate—the percentage of people who drop a class before it is finished—and the number of classes cancelled because not enough people signed up for them were embarrassing "closet" figures for many free universities. They were admittedly high— at least high by prevailing college and university standards, the only other figures free universities had to compare them with.

So free universities in the early seventies justified those high dropout and cancellation figures by virtue of the free university philosophy.

"We're the only educational set-up in Berkeley with community feedback," said Larry Miller, a coordinator at the Free University of Berkeley, the nation's first nationally recognized free university, in a 1969 interview. "We pride ourselves on our failure rate—we may start a year with 150 course-groups, but many fail, and we let them, just because the community doesn't want them, while Cal (University of California–Berkeley) is full of obsolete courses."[1]

With respect to the dropout and cancellation rates of courses, higher education operates in an educational environment whose constraints are of a different variety. In the university, few courses are listed that may have to be cancelled. Required courses are ensured enrollments. And, of course, college students, searching for credits and a degree and having paid substantial tuition, are not likely to drop many classes.

But free universities still regarded their dropout and cancellation rates as problems until recently, when rates at other adult learning institutions became public. It is now known that the free university dropout rate for a given class, which may range from 25 to 50 percent in some cases, is not unusual and that other institutions have similar dropout rates. The percentage of cancelled courses at other educational institutions is also the same as, or sometimes even higher than, at free universities.

Although free universities may have seen some of their statistics in a negative light and thus did not wish to pursue or illuminate those statistics too highly, we now know that the data for adult learning in this country are completely different from data for higher education.

As free universities move into the 1980s, they are encouraged by their overall statistics—age, participation, and courses—and more aware of the value of data for developing their organizations. Thus, the 1980s should produce even more statistical data for free universities.

Here, then, is a look at the data for free universities. Most of the information was collected in 1978 and 1979.

NUMBERS AND KINDS
OF FREE UNIVERSITIES

There are now approximately 200 free universities and learning networks in the United States. Learning networks are organizations similar to free universities. They act as referral services and link individuals in the teaching-learning situation rather than set up classes or groups. Philosophically, learning networks are identical to free universities, and they often are included in free university activities.

The National Center for Education Statistics (NCES) survey lists 146 free universities and 42 learning networks in its 1978 study. Since 1976, new free universities have been starting at a rate of more than twenty per year, so that there are probably about 160 free universities now.

Of the 146 free universities in 1978, about a third (47) were started before 1971. The oldest free universities are Experimental College at Davis, California, and Experimental College at UCLA. Both are fourteen years old. Nine other free universities were started before 1969.[2]

Another thirteen free universities turned ten years old in 1979, and nine are celebrating ten years of existence in 1980. Several others were started before 1971 and then revived in the 1970s after a period of dormancy.

Most free universities are associated with another organization, although a recent increase in independent fee-charging free universities is making this less the case. However, 55 percent of the free universities in the country are sponsored by a college or university. Most of the parent colleges are large universities, although some small private colleges have recently taken a greater interest in free universities. Only one community college in the country— Monterey's Peninsula College—sponsors a free university, University for Man, Monterey.

Roughly a third of all free universities are independent organizations. Many of these are large fee-charging organizations in metropolitan areas, such as Class Factory in Houston, the Skills Exchange in Toronto, and Open University in Washington, D.C. But small rural free universities comprise another segment of the independent free universities. The Rooks County Community Education in Rooks County, Kansas (population 7,628), and People to People in Dighton, Kansas (population 1,540), receive funding directly from their municipalities. The Forum in Winter Park, Colorado, charges fees.

The other 12 percent of free universities around the country are sponsored by a community agency or institution. The New

Orleans Free University is sponsored by the New Orleans Public Library; Communiversity in Champaign, Illinois, is sponsored by the YMCA; and the TREE (Trego Recreation Education Environment) program in Wakeeney, Kansas, is hosted by the local recreation department.

Free universities are found in many different kinds of communities—in large metropolitan areas, small rural communities, and college towns. These locations range in size from the nation's largest city, New York, which has several free universities, down to Olsburg, Kansas, where the world's smallest free university thrives in a town of just 170 people. There are free universities in forty states, with a greater concentration of free universities in the Midwest, stretching from Ohio to Colorado, than on the coasts where they first appeared in the sixties. States with quite active free universities include Kansas, Colorado, California, New York, and Illinois. Several cities have more than one free university. Boston has four, Houston has four, and Baltimore has three.

PARTICIPANTS

Soon after the College Board estimated total free university enrollments at 200,000, the NCES survey produced new figures putting that total at more than 300,000 participants a year, with 298,255 in free universities and another 26,849 in learning networks.

The average free university enrolls around 1,500 participants a year. This is small compared with schools and colleges but large compared with other community organizations such as YMCAs, churches, and civic organizations. The largest annual enrollments for the local community organizations were fewer than 1,000 participants a year for the Red Cross, which had the highest average enrollments per community organization.

In actuality, most free universities have fewer than 1,500 participants a year. There are a few medium-sized free universities, with enrollments from 1,500 to 3,500, and about twenty-five large free universities with enrollments of more than 3,500 participants a year. These larger free universities, on the whole older and more developed organizationally, account for more than half the registrations nationally. They are usually located in metropolitan areas where the population base for education is quite large.

Of 146 free universities surveyed in the NCES study, 80 free universities had enrollments of fewer than 1,000 participants a year, 43 had between 2,000 and 5,000 participants, and 17 had more than 5,000 participants a year.

The sixteen largest free universities and their 1978 enrollments were

1. Experimental College, Seattle, Wash.	28,000
2. Denver Free University, Denver, Colo.	17,000
3. Open Education Exchange, Oakland, Calif.	15,500
4. Indianapolis Free University, Indianapolis, Ind.	15,000
5. Community Free School, Boulder, Colo.	13,000
6. Open University, Washington, D.C.	13,000
7. University for Man, Manhattan, Kans.	12,000
8. Sundry School, Houston, Tex.	10,500
9. Wisconsin Union Mini-Courses, Madison, Wis.	8,500
10. The Skills Exchange, Toronto, Ont.	8,500
11. Center for Participant Education, Tallahassee, Fla.	8,000
12. Experimental College, Corvallis, Oreg.	8,000
13. Free University, University Park, Penn.	8,000
14. Communiversity, Kansas City, Mo.	7,000
15. Orpheus, San Francisco, Calif.	6,500
16. Wichita Free University, Wichita, Kan.	6,000

The enrollments are a significant increase over previous reporting periods. In 1968, Blair Hamilton estimated enrollments at around 100,000, and in 1972, Jane Lichtman put the total between 120,000 and 200,000 participants.

The profile of learners in free universities is similar to that of learners in other adult learning organizations. There is a predominance of learners in the age bracket from twenty to forty, more women than men, few minorities; and the average formal level of education tends to be higher than that of the rest of society.

But free universities have made progress in breaking out of these restrictive participant categories to reach the elderly, the young, rural residents, and those making less than middle incomes.

Participants range in age from preschool children to senior citizens in their seventies and eighties. In tracking the age of participants at the Free School in Boulder over a five-year period, DuBé found that the range of the 50th percentile age grouping was expanding, thus showing greater diversity in ages, and also that the average (mean) age of participants was getting one year older each year.

Joseph K. Rippetoe, director of research and development for University for Man, Manhattan, has led the way in constructing a participant profile for both the campus-based free university and the rural free university.

In an exploratory study, he gathered data not only on age, sex, and identity of UFM participants but also on participants' reasons for taking a UFM course. He found that

sixty percent identified themselves with Kansas State University, either as a student, student spouse, or faculty/staff member. Sixty-five percent were women. The mean age was 28 with a range of 9–71. Thirty-seven percent were participating in UFM for the first time. . . . The most common reason for participation was to "gain general knowledge or skill which satisfies personal curiosity or interests," a reason noted by 91 percent. Seventy-four percent of the respondents noted that the course actually met this need. Vocational skills and interests was the second most common reason for participation, though noted by only 32 percent.[3]

Rippetoe also surveyed the Neosho River Free School (NRFS) participants in Emporia, Kansas (population 23,100), in the spring of 1977. NRFS is an interesting case. Although it began in 1971 as a campus free university, since 1976 it has been oriented toward the community. Its participant data reflect that shift, indicating that campus-based free universities can reach the general public at large.

Rippetoe found the age distribution to be from seventeen to ninety-two, with a mean age of twenty-nine. Women constituted 79 percent of the population, men 21 percent. City of Emporia residents accounted for 57 percent of the participants, while college students at Emporia State were 28 percent of free university participants, and rural Lyon County residents 9 percent; out-of-county people, 5 percent; college faculty, 1 percent; and high school students, 1 percent.[4]

Rural free universities, which serve small-town communities with few college students and a disproportionate number of older persons, tend to reflect community demographics. Thus, the average age of the small-town free university participant is greater, and the percentage of women participants is even higher than for campus or independent free universities, but participant reasons for taking the free university course remain roughly the same.[5]

TEACHERS

On the whole, the people who teach in free universities share the same characteristics as the learners, largely because of the free university's belief that "each one of us has some knowledge or skill that someone else would like to know." This promotion of "peer teaching," as it might be called, or "neighbors sharing their skills with one another," as free university people would probably state it, helps make the teacher profile in a free university much like the learner profile.

In small rural communities, for instance, free university organizers have made concerted efforts to tap local talent in the community, rather than bring in outside experts even where it is possible. Many, if not most, teachers in free universities took free university classes before they taught. Many teachers in free universities have not taught before.

The free university teacher is not exactly identical to the free university learner, however. The Denver Free University in its 1978 annual report shows that approximately 65 percent of its students were women and 35 percent men. The sex ratios are reversed for teachers, with men constituting approximately 60 percent of the teachers and women, 40 percent. The residence of DFU teachers and students also differs somewhat. For DFU, 85 percent of its students come from the city of Denver, and 15 percent come from the suburbs. Of its teachers, however, a slightly greater percentage (20 percent) live in the suburbs.

Beyond these rough statistics on teachers, our information comes mainly from example and case studies of teachers. We know that the age range for teachers and students is equally wide. In Clay Center, Kansas, fifteen-year-old Slade Griffiths taught macrame, primarily to women old enough to be his grandmother. Many children's classes are taught by other children. At the other end of the life cycle, senior citizens often teach at the free university, and most free universities eagerly welcome older people as teachers because senior citizens have a lifetime of experience and skills, and society offers few avenues for older folks to share what they know with others.

A panel on the history of Olsburg, Kansas, sponsored by the Olsburg Rural Educational Opportunities (OREO) program there, had five members, all over the age of eighty.

"We could see their eyes light up three weeks before the day the class started," recalls free university organizer Barb Nelson. "They were very excited about doing the program."

Sue Maes, director of University for Man in Manhattan, Kansas, recently received this letter from a family of free university teachers:

> Last night over dinner my family had a remarkable conversation. It reflects and almost underlines the diversity of educational sharing which UFM facilitates, and I wanted to share it with you. It began when we asked my father, who is 82 years of age, about the creative writing class he will be co-leading this fall through UFM. After he had told about his plans I told my parents about the three sessions I plan to lead. After that Ben, my eight year old son, told about the birdwatching class he will lead.
>
> It's quite an organization that can serve as an umbrella for three generations' very different educational interests (creative writing, child rearing, birdwatching)! The span of ages just in one family is seventy-four years. All of us had participated in UFM offerings before; none of us had led any classes until now. This conveys what UFM means to the community.[6]

People from all walks of life teach at the free university. Businessmen teach at the free university—sometimes skills they have learned in their own business, sometimes a hobby or avocation. Housewives often teach in free universities. Professional artists, such as painters, dancers, and poets, teach in free universities. High school and college dropouts teach in free universities; sometimes they teach college-level subjects. College dropout Jim Hatch, a record-store clerk, taught "The Mysterious Maya," a course about the Maya Indians of Mexico, at the Cincinnati Free University. Occasionally, professors in colleges and universities will teach, though often in fields other than their professional ones. A chemistry professor at Kansas State University teaches a course on sundials.

STAFF

The typical free university staff person is young, has little or no professional training in education or administration, stays with the free university for fewer than three years, and is motivated primarily by a desire to create or operate a service or educational organization, rather than to have a job or gain a salary.

In fact, most free university staff people are not paid, and those that are—even in the richest free universities—are paid less than the median average income for Americans.

The NCES study showed that 1,250 persons held administrative positions in free universities and learning networks in 1978 and that most, 73 percent, were nonpaid and most, also 73 percent, worked part-time.

Of the 1,250 staff people, 337 were paid, and 155 of them worked full-time. These 155 full-time paid people worked in sixty-six organizations, about a third of all free universities. Among the sixty-six organizations, thirty-five had one full-time employee, and thirteen had two. The other eighteen free universities had from three to thirteen full-time paid staff people.

Staff members paid full-time are apt to be younger than forty, college educated, and dedicated to their work. There are as many women directing free universities, including some of the largest in the country, as there are men. Of the ten largest free universities in the country, women are currently directors of five. The largest free university staff in the country, at times totaling twenty-five full-time and part-time paid people, is University for Man in Manhattan, Kansas. It is headed by Sue Maes, who has been director for ten years.

Full-time paid staff are becoming older and are more likely to be married and to own homes. Although free university leaders were mostly in their twenties five years ago, many are now in their thirties.

Recently, several people in their late fifties have joined free university staffs.

The question of staffing in free universities is one of the most critical factors for any free university.

While the free university organization is dependent upon sound and lively leadership on the staff, the free university is unable, as the data show, to reward its staff in sufficient material ways over a long term. This factor has been one of the greatest concerns for free university leaders.

FEES AND BUDGETS

Free universities have always remained committed to offer classes at the lowest possible charge. This has been at least half due to educational philosophy, and probably half due to necessity. Initially, many free universities in the mid and late sixties were started as no-fee organizations, although one of the first free universities, Midpeninsula Free University, charged a $10 fee and was the forerunner of the independent fee-charging model of today.

It is a mistake to assume that the "free" university is no-cost. The word *free* has instead referred to structure, freedom to teach and learn, and independence, as in "free enterprise."

However, it is remarkable, given both the free universities' difficult financial position and a prevailing attitude against the "free lunch," that half the free universities in the country do not charge a fee to participants to take a class. This means that there is no registration fee and no fee to cover teacher time. The no-fee free universities, though, do add a fee for materials for those classes that need them, such as courses in arts and crafts, cooking, and wine-tasting.

Almost all the no-fee organizations are campus-based or rural small-town free universities. They seemed to have survived the often repeated remark, sometimes phrased as a belief and sometimes as a fact, that people don't appreciate or learn as much if a course is given without a fee. There are also claims that the dropout rate is higher among no-fee organizations, suggesting that participants don't value the experience as much. Despite all these claims and beliefs, however, there have been no conclusive studies done to show that these claims are, in fact, valid. Dropout rates among no-fee organizations do not seem to be appreciably different from those of fee-charging organizations.

The impetus for the no-fee organization often comes from the community at large. This is especially true for small rural free universities, where small-town residents are not used to, cannot see the rationale for, or cannot afford paying for courses. In these communities, for example, community college courses, priced at $20 or so, draw limited numbers of students, filling only a handful of courses. But no-fee courses in the same communities draw hundreds of participants and can fill twenty to fifty classes with participants. The other half of the free universities in the country charge either a registration fee or both a registration fee and a teacher fee. The impetus for charging a fee also comes partly from educational philosophy and from necessity.

Fee-charging free universities often profess a belief in free enterprise, in independence from any government subsidy (which must in some shape or form sustain the no-fee organization), and in the insistence that independent teachers must be able to make a living, or part of one, from the sale of their valuable services.

Necessity for fee-charging free universities is simply survival. Without government support, fees are the only regular way to gain income. Fees are in the form of registration fees, which go to the organization for administration and operating expenses, and often teacher fees, which go to teachers.

Fees charged by free universities range from $1 to $40 per class. Some offer more than one class for one registration fee, and some particularly expensive courses, such as hot-air ballooning or private flying lessons, go above the $40 mark.

Free universities maintain that they are the most cost-efficient adult educational organizations in the country. Nationwide, including fee and no-fee organizations, an average of $10 per class is the cost of a participant's partaking of one free university class, whether paid for by fees, grants, or donations. There is not another educational institution offering classes to the general public that can demonstrate such figures.

Even the nation's most expensive free university is more reasonable in cost than its local competitors. The Community Free School in Boulder, Colorado, which charges an average of $29 per class, the highest in the country, did a study comparing its fees with those of other local adult learning providers, including the recreation department, university continuing education, and another independent school. In almost all the class areas studied, including dance, language, yoga and photography, the Free School had lower fees based on a per-hour average.

Using the NCES data, University for Man in Manhattan looked

at all Kansas free universities and the cost to the public. The study included some twenty-five free universities in Kansas, of which only one, Wichita Free University, charged a fee to learners. The study found that the average cost per participant for a class was just $7, taking all costs together—cost to the individual learner in the form of a fee, cost to government, donations, grants, fund-raisers, and all other sources of income. If a national technical assistance grant was subtracted, leaving only operating budgets as the actual cost, that figure of cost per class dropped to $5. The figures were obtained by dividing the total free university budget in the state by the total registrations, for an average cost per participant per class.

The low cost to learners and government has helped free universities in several ways. Lower fees have attracted learners who would not normally attend adult learning opportunities for higher prices. They have also helped free universities with the competition in adult learning. And they have helped promote free universities as a new model for adult learning, as legislators and others become increasingly concerned about the high cost of post-secondary education.

In years past, the no-fee and fee-charging free universities debated the merits of each system. The argument today has subsided into a mere strategy of figuring what works. There seems to be no discernable trend favoring either no-fee or fee-charging organizations. While more independent fee-charging free universities are starting in metropolitan areas, there are an equal number of small-town free universities starting without fees.

While free universities are pleased to have such low fees, they are not as happy with their low budgets. Total budgets for 150 free universities in the NCES study came to less than $3 million. The sixteen largest free universities accounted for around three fourths of that total, leaving over half the free universities with budgets of under $1,000 a year. Free universities receive their income from five basic sources—money from affiliated institutions, registration fees, contracts and grants, donations, and benefits. By far the major sources of income are money from affiliated institutions and registration fees.

Staff salaries lead the expense column for free universities, with catalog printing and other advertising also ranking very high in expenses, since free universities put a good deal of money as well as time into their catalog production and distribution. Teacher fees rank third, with as much as 50 percent of the income of large independent free universities going to teachers. Facilities and other expenses fall far behind in expenses; free universities hold down their costs by having little overhead.

Taken together, the figures show a growth in the stability of free universities and in the number of participants. And there is a diversity of people participating in free universities that just wasn't there ten years ago. There are more participants, from a broader societal spectrum, and they view the free university very positively. From an institutional point of view, free universities are not challenging our major educational institutions. As *Newsweek* put it, "They're not going to put the Big Ten out of business."[7] But from an indigenous point of view, from where the average citizen stands, it is a remarkable development that has sprung up from local people themselves, without any major governmental funding or enabling legislation. That free universities have grown, even without a financial foundation, to become one of the major providers of adult learning in the country is worthy of note. Beneath those statistics and data are a concept and a joy about learning that is admired, popular, and contagious. That joy of learning is reflected in the variety of classes that free universities offer, which we will explore next.

Chapter 4
Courses Unlimited

To leaf through a free university catalog is to walk through a cafeteria of ideas, for free universities offer a smorgasbord of classes tempting the reader to taste them all. There are appetizers, like space colonization; there are meat-and-potatoes courses, like home repair or time management; there are side dishes, such as self-hypnosis or winter camping; and delightful desserts, like square dancing or European travel.

Just reading the course catalog is enjoyable and stimulating. A couple in Boulder, Colorado, avidly read the free university catalog for months before they took a course, saying,

> During the year we lived in Boulder, my wife, Sarah, and I always had the current issue at home. We picked them up primarily as a source of interesting reading material. I read such articles as, "Einstein Sought God's Thought," "Oil Merchants Versus Man and Sea," "Positive Energy Makes the Garden Grow." Then, early this year, we graduated from articles to course descriptions, and thence to some courses.[1]

There are few boundaries in what is taught and learned in a free university, and the types of courses offered span the range of knowledge and interest of mankind. Because anyone may walk into a free university office and offer a course on any topic, the resulting courses combine popular topics and individualistic ideas.

There are courses on new ideas, such as these two:

Neurolinguistic Programming: A New Approach to Personal Change

Students in this course will learn the basic distinctions necessary to an understanding of Neurolinguistic Programming as a method of human change. It has proven over the past five years to be a useful method of expanding one's ability to learn almost any new skill. Leader: Jonathan Rice, PhD, a licensed marriage, family and child counselor. (University for Man, Monterey, Spring 1980)

Pre-Columbian Welsh Colonization of the Florida Coast

Did the Welsh really colonize North America 300 years before Columbus? Are there Welsh words in the Cherokee language? Did Columbus use the Welsh maps in his travels to America? A look at some evidence!

A geologist by profession, Dr. Walters has probed far back in the traces of the Welsh in North America in the 1100s. (University for Man, Manhattan, Fall 1979)

There are courses on problems confronting people in different stages of life, such as this one:

Do I Choose Motherhood?

As the biological clock ticks away, causing a sense of urgency, many women decide to re-examine their decision to bear a child "before it is too late." This class sheds light on what remains a hazy, mystical area to many women. There is no right or wrong in this class. (Class Factory, Houston, January–February 1980)

There are fun courses, such as "Panning for Gold" or "Social Kissing" (both at Class Factory, January–February 1980) or

A Pillowfight

Grr! Hold it Horace! First, we make some rules. Then we get down to the nitty gritty. Pillow warfare—almost as good as the primal scream. Go ahead, beat your classmates to a pulp. We can start a craze bigger than disco. (Denver Free University, Winter 1980)

There are even courses that aren't courses. These "spoof" courses, like a course on nihilism held in a vacant lot, keep learners entertained and on their toes. Usually there is a tipoff as to their fictitious nature with a class time at 4 A.M. or a date such as January 35. Nevertheless, report free university leaders who hold such spoof courses, some people always register for them anyway. Here are listings for two of the better spoof courses:

Take Care of Me
   Class one: Massage me. Learn from others how to massage effectively, with me as your perpetual subject to practice on. Class two: Listen to me. Everyone could use more practice in the art of listening. I'll also help teach you the virtue of patience as I moan incessantly about what a lousy life I have. Class three: Give me money. It's easy to say you're someone's friend, but I will give you a chance to test your commitment in an area that really matters; your willingness to give them money.
Course fee: Free
Materials fee: $100 for Class 3
Time, place: Ongoing, your place.
(Denver Free University, Winter 1980)

Tax Collecting for Fun and Profit
   Enjoy the pure delight of watching people squirm while you cash in on the biggest growth industry in the country—tax collecting. Here's a business that requires almost no overhead and yet succeeds during booms, depressions and wars. Most people already spend up to 40 percent of their income every year with enterprising tax collectors, and this figure is rising rapidly. Learn the sure-fire way to get a piece of everybody's pay check—be a tax collector!
Donald C. Salamander
6 Saturdays 11:45 p.m.
Place: To be announced.
(Indianapolis Free University, Summer 1977)

The National Center for Education Statistics (NCES) study shows that approximately 20,000 classes are offered by free universities every year. It reports 19,361 for the year 1978, with an average of 13.5 persons taking each course.
   Four broad subject areas constituted more than half the courses

offered by free universities, according to the NCES survey (see the table on p. 63). The leading category is the visual and performing arts, with 3,861 classes offered nationwide. These are courses like dance, disco, and painting. Courses on home living—what NCES terms home economics—are second, with 2,936 classes. They include Korean cooking and home wiring. In the third most popular spot are recreation and leisure courses, numbering 2,124. They include sailing and playing chess. The fourth most popular courses are arts and crafts courses, which NCES maintains fall into their engineering and engineering-related technology category, with 2,120 courses. They include macrame and dulcimer building.

But there are courses in free universities in every other NCES subject category, showing the wide range of courses offered in free universities. There are also more than 1,000 courses which don't fall into any category.

The NCES subject categories, designed for formal education, do not fit free university course topics in several areas. What NCES labels Military Science in free universities is probably gun safety courses. Agriculture is probably home gardening, and Engineering is mainly arts and crafts courses for free universities.

Why are free university courses so different? There are several reasons. The first is that whatever skill or knowledge someone has, there is someone else who would like to learn it. Adult education professor Lloyd Korhonen has said, "Give me a topic and I will find twelve people who would like to learn about it." Another is the free university view that "it only takes two to make a class." Because most free universities do not need to guarantee a minimum number of students for any particular class, as few as one student can make a class (the other one is the teacher). And if the learning experience is worthwhile for that one person, then it is a worthwhile class. "We have been trapped by formal schooling into thinking that thirty people make a class," says one free university staffer. "But qualitatively, there are no minimums on learning." A third stimulus for the wide range of courses found in free universities is the basic philosophy that anyone can teach. Inherent in that philosophy is that anyone can teach any idea he or she wants, as long as it is legal. Thus, there is little or no administrative censorship of ideas. A fourth reason for creative and innovative courses is the irreverent and intentional disregard for academic disciplines and categories of classes. By consciously re-

Class sections in free universities by subject:
United States 1978[2]

Subject	Total Sections Offered	Percent of Total
Agriculture and renewable natural resources	538	2.8
Arts, visual and performing	3,861	19.9
Business	532	2.7
Education	304	1.6
Engineering and engineering-related technology	2,120	10.9
Health care sciences and technology	1,263	6.5
Home economics	2,936	15.2
Personal services and occupations	65	0.3
Language, linguistics and literature	1,382	7.1
Law	174	0.9
Library/museum science	33	0.2
Life and physical sciences	358	1.8
Mathematics	72	0.4
Military science	21	0.1
Philosophy and religion	1,780	9.2
Physical education and leisure studies	2,124	11.0
Psychology	103	0.5
Public administration and social services	48	0.3
Social science and social studies	553	2.9
Interdisciplinary studies	19	0.1
Other and not reported	1,075	5.6

structuring their subject areas in the broadest terms, such as Play, Skills, and Ideas, free universities encourage divergent and creative thinking in teachers who want to experiment with ideas and topics.

The subject areas in the catalog reflect the learning trends of the times, but they show a reckless disregard for traditional disciplines. Here are two examples of subject areas from different free university catalogs.

University for Man, Manhattan, Kansas

Play	Kids
Self	Tours
Skills	Fine Arts
Earth	Crafts
Community	Foods

Denver Free University, Denver, Colorado

Holistic	Practical	Personal
Health	Children's	Growth
Body	Courses	Potpourri
Spirit	Self Directed	Dance
Language	Living	Music
Arts & Crafts	Playing	Theater
	Social Issues	

In fact, some free university courses absolutely defy traditional disciplinary categories. Where would you put these?

"Swimming and the Effortless Effort of Zen" (Milwaukee Free University, 1972)—Religion, Recreation?

"Media for Social Change" (Sundry School, Houston, Spring 1980)—Sociology, Journalism?

"Decisions, Decisions" (Communiversity, Rochester, New York, Spring 1980)—Psychology, Management?

Although there are no restrictions on what can be taught in a free university setting, trends and generalizations can be made about the nature of the courses. The subject matter is determined primarily by the needs of the adults taking these courses. Because most free university participants are college educated, there are few credit courses or topics usually associated with credit college programs. It is hard to find sociology, psychology, or biology, although a good many courses are sociological, psychological, and biological in nature. Because most free university participants hold jobs, there are few vocational courses. There are few courses in refrigerator repair, cosmetology, or certified public accounting. That does not mean that free university courses are not job-related, for Joseph Rippetoe, doing research for University for Man, Manhattan, found that a surprisingly high number of people in surveys indicate that they take free university courses for work-related reasons. But there are not many vocational training courses. Because most free university learners are busy, courses tend to be narrow in scope. Thus, one won't find many advanced calculus classes running for twenty-six weeks in a free university. But these are generalizations based on learner needs. Ten years from now, if the public wants it, there could be training in advanced calculus or in becoming a beauty-shop owner.

To follow the public's interests, free universities have begun to chart course trends. Although some fads, such as disco roller-skating (popular in late 1979) may be popular in one area of the country and either not make it to the other end or experience a time lapse, course trends do not vary much by geography. What is popular in a big city is just as likely to be popular in a small rural town. Rural organizers were a little surprised to find that rural residents were interested in more than just tractor repair and macrame. Instead, they found a desire for such urbane topics as biofeedback, stress management, and yoga.

Although course trends do not seem to differ by geography, they do vary over time. Course trends in free universities appear to change slowly but definitively over a two-to-three-year period. Subject categories do not disappear, nor do they dominate the catalog, but there are rises and fadings of subject popularity. The pacesetting courses in the past fourteen years were:

1966–1968   Political topics
1968–1970   Cultural life-style topics
1970–1972   Environmental concerns
1972–1974   Women's issues
1974–1976   Interpersonal relations
1976–1978   Personal growth (spiritual)
1978–1980   Self (practical)

There are also topic trends. Holistic health, dance, and solar energy are recent trends.

There are always courses which, through the years, have had relative consistency in the free university offerings. Fine arts, cooking, music, recreation, and arts and crafts appear in just about every catalog.

In addition to their stable offerings and currently popular courses, free universities pride themselves on the number of "idea and thought courses" in their catalogs. Much of adult education focuses almost entirely on purely practical or recreation classes—the macrame and auto repair courses—and leaves citizen education, social issues, and other important topic areas almost untouched. But the humanities constitute almost 20 percent of all offerings—courses in language, philosophy, literature, comparative religion, and law.

Social-issues courses, while downplayed and almost ignored by most adults, are still a part of most free university offerings. Courses in nuclear-power issues, world hunger, local community development, Latin America, and other topics are available.

The range of courses, the unusual topics, and the occasional flair for the social event make the free university catalog lively and constantly changing. As United Press International noted,

[Free university] classes continue to thrive off the regular academic trail across the nation. . . . These are not your usual courses, usual students, usual universities. The 'schools' are for working and nonworking people who want to learn something, anything, of value in the world of work, play or enrichment.[3]

Part II
Where We've Been

If a teacher wants to teach something he must think it worthwhile; and students want either to learn something particular, or find out what they want to learn. This is enough for a school.

Paul Goodman

Chapter 5

Free Universities on Campus: The Sixties

A look at the history of free universities, both for those who are familiar with them and for those who are not, lends a better understanding of where free universities are now and their potential for the future.

For those not familiar with free universities, this history is important in gauging one's view of them today by where they were ten years ago. All organizations and institutions evolve from certain circumstances—time frames, settings, and social climates. Free universities have always sought to break out of their historical context, not to be trapped by the image, atmosphere, or constraints of their past. They have tried, and fairly successfully too, to periodically renew their orientation in light of the present rather than past realities. This is largely because the free university has prospered by responding to the current needs and desires of the population it serves. Some institutions can chart their courses almost independently of the pace and trends of society at large. Our universities maintain their essential characteristics throughout the years, regardless of whether the American society is rural, urban, or suburban, at war or at peace, in a recession, or stirred by ecological considerations. While free universities have prospered by responding to the current educational needs and wishes of the population, they have also been dependent on those wishes, and so dependent not only on the present population but on the past population as well. The history of free universities reflects society at that time.

Our society is also probably guilty of being fairly ahistorical in its view of itself. We tend to look at the present as permanent. From the present we project backward, viewing the past as an extension of the present, only not so good. Despite our preoccupation with the future, future shock, and futurecasts, we are unable to see the future except as an extension of the present, only better. It would help to keep in mind, particularly when looking at free universities of today, the thought, "But it has not always been this way." It should not be surprising that many elderly persons are both learning and teaching in free universities. But it was not long ago that the slogan about teaching old dogs new tricks was taken as gospel, and it has not always been this way. It seems quite natural to see a thriving community education program in small rural villages in Kansas, with neighbors sharing their skills, talking about homemade beef jerky and Swedish culture. But it was only three years ago that an Iowa postsecondary study commission declared that lifelong learners were most likely to be urban dwellers,[1] and it has not always been this way.

By looking at the history of free universities, we can see more clearly the relevance of the present free university. We can also see the potential for the free university of the future and will be less likely to dismiss the model for its present limitations when we can see the metamorphosis of the past free university. Who would have, or could have, looked at the free university in 1970, a small organization on a college campus patronized by students in their late teens and early twenties, and imagined that ten years later free universities could thrive in rural communities with farmers and townspeople, or could compete in the big city and enroll thousands of participants from all walks of life? A look at the history of free universities is also a catalyst for realizing the potential for the future. It helps us not only to understand the free university of today but also to realize that the free university of tomorrow may not always be this way either.

Free university leaders are also caught up in the history of the present. There is no history lesson taught to new free university staff people. Few of the originators are left to recall the old days, and no leatherbound books on the library shelves preserve and document past deeds, thoughts, and motivations. Yet the history is important to those in free universities. It is relevant to free universities that offer their courses free and to those who charge, to those that are older and to those whose reference point is the seventies or eighties. Free universities survive not by going along with history but by creating it. Free university organizations have had to survive by their wits, by being one step ahead of the game rather than playing it. Throughout the history of free universities, no financial spigots have been turned on by government. Furthermore, ideas have been co-opted by other educational institutions as quickly as they have been conceived by free universities. One will find few conservative participants in free universities, longing for the good old days.

Although free universities differ, there is a common historical thread that somehow spins around and becomes part of the same web. There is a tendency for free university people to view their situation as unique, unlike any other organization or town around. That fiercely individualistic localized viewpoint is one of the stronger aspects of the character of the local free university person. But it also has its weakness. Free university people have a great loyalty to their own towns. They usually come to the free university from a community and leave the free university not for another city but to stay in the community. They see their program as meeting peculiarly local needs. That spirit is encouraged by the free university structure. There are no national norms, no standards, not even common terminology. Each free university has a distinctly local name. Who would know that Open University in Washington, D.C., is similar to the Forum in Winter Park, Colorado; or that the Experimental College in Northridge, California, is similar to the Phillips County Community Education program in Phillipsburg, Kansas? There are few free university folks interested in cloning free universities from city to city.

So if free university leaders want to be as relevant to society's learning needs tomorrow as they are today, it helps to know how they have come to where they are now. For both the reader unfamiliar with free universities and the reader who has had some knowledge of them, the history of free universities is not only entertaining but instructive as well.

A SHORT HISTORY OF ADULT EDUCATION

The history of free universities has evolved both from higher education and from adult education. Free universities were generated by college students and faculty and were first started on college campuses. But philosophically and in the manner in which they were created, free universities had more to do with adult education than with higher education. While during the sixties they would follow events on campus, in the seventies they would reflect the trends in adult learning. And in the eighties, as higher education moves closer to adult learning, we may see those tracks converge.

The history of adult education in this country is less well known than that of formal schooling, both elementary and higher education. Although adult education has been quite active, involving millions of adults at various times, it has been an undercurrent in society rather than a visible and talked-about movement. In many ways, the history of free universities has followed a similar pattern characteristic of other great adult learning movements in this country.

Adult education has developed very differently from formal schooling. Historically, adult education programs have arisen to meet specific needs, not as part of an overall general design of education for the country. Its development has been episodic, not consistent, reflecting its origins in the community rather than in large structured institutions. Adult education has survived when attached to other agencies, and in fact, its status within those agencies has been secondary to the primary mission of the agency. While Cooperative Extension, churches, and libraries, for instance, are some of the major adult educators in the history of our country, their main concerns are to promote agriculture, religion, and information, respectively.

A typical adult education movement in the United States arises spontaneously out of a perceived need. It is localized and, even if it is a national trend, is decentralized in structure, looking more toward the local community than its own organizational structure. It is often run by volunteers and lay citizens rather than by professional educators. There is often no permanent funding, and the movement may remain uninstitutionalized and even die after a decade or more, having fulfilled a need in American life.

Adult educator A. A. Liveright distinguishes between adult education and elementary and secondary education in the United States in terms of the federal government's role,[2] and from that, a broader comparison between the characteristics of formal schooling—public schools, colleges, and universities—and adult education can also be drawn:

Formal Schools	Adult Education
Operated largely by public agencies	Operated mostly by private and federal interests
Few but large systems	Small and multiple organizations
Traditional approaches to education	Innovative approaches to education
Programs planned as a response to a perceived societal need and growth	Programs usually a response to a local need
Development consistent	Development episodic
Education primary mission of the institution	Education secondary mission of the institution
Program perceived as indefinite	Program has a given lifetime, often dies

There are examples of these characteristics in adult education throughout the history of our country. During colonial times in America, apprenticeships were a common way for young men and women to learn a trade. Although organized to some degree, an apprenticeship was essentially an agreement between two people. The apprentice would agree to work for his or her "teacher" for a given length of time and in return would be trained in an occupational skill. Benjamin Franklin is sometimes referred to as the father of adult education in this country. In 1727 he formed in Philadelphia a weekly discussion group called the Junto. Subscription libraries, the predecessors of today's free public libraries, were started in colonial times. In those days, people paid a subscription for the privilege of using a library, with the fees going to purchase new books. The primary educational institution of those times was the church.

Between the Revolutionary War and the Civil War, other adult education movements arose. The lyceum movement, which flourished between 1826 and 1839, was a popular one. It was started by Josiah Holbrook and comprised a series of lectures and town forums offered in circuit fashion throughout the small towns of New England and later extended to other parts of the country. Public libraries and museums started during this time, and mechanics' institutes were instrumental in providing training—the

Cooper Union and the Lowell Institute being two famous ones. Such voluntary associations as the YMCA blossomed, leading de Tocqueville, a French commentator of the time, to note that America was a land of volunteer organizations.

The time between the Civil War and World War I was a transitional period, with the country moving from an agricultural economy to an industrial one and people moving from rural settings to increasingly urban ones. Cooperative Extension was started during this time, as were a multitude of correspondence courses. Perhaps the most intriguing movement of the time was the chautauqua movement. It was started on the shores of Lake Chautauqua in New York State as a residential summer church school. Soon it became popularized, and its range of study broadened to include cultural, artistic, political, and even scientific endeavors. With speakers, plays, music, and demonstrations, summer learners were both entertained and informed. In due time, other chautauquas were established, and then traveling chautauquas, using circus tents, were sent throughout the East and Midwest. Millions of people would attend a chautauqua in its heyday, listening to the great speakers of the time, outstanding musicians and vocalists, and other performer-educators. Although the movement died in the mid-1920s, its spontaneous birth, fresh and innovative style, and orientation to the general public have made it an exciting example of adult learning in our history.

Since the 1920s, much adult education has been institutionalized —in labor unions, churches, Cooperative Extension, the military, business, and industry. But much of it still arises spontaneously at different times to meet local needs, sometimes startling professional educators. The moonlight schools of Kentucky were started by a woman who saw the need to teach reading to adults. Being a public school teacher, she opened up her school at night so adults could attend. They were called moonlight schools because the adults could only come on moonlit nights when they could see their way to the school. The Highlander Folk School in Tennessee, started in 1927 by Myles Horton, remains to this day a testament to the craving that adults have for linking learning with their own social condition. For more than fifty years, Highlander has provided a place where poor mountain people, blacks, labor leaders, coal miners, and others could come and learn from each other. Some of the recent great social movements have been spurred on by this unique adult learning center.[3]

It would take a decade after the start of the first free university in the early sixties for free universities to become heavily involved in adult learning, and almost another five years to understand that transition. But the history of free universities has in many ways, both philosophically and operationally, been within the tradition of adult education in this country. The elements of exciting grass-roots organization, of local initiative of creative and innovative responses to adult learning needs, found in the early libraries, lyceums, and chautauquas of the nation, would also be evident in the free university movement as it developed.

Although it would take free universities ten years to recognize their participation in the history of adult education, it was clear from the beginning that free universities were part of the higher education scene. Free universities were started within ivy-covered walls, often a reaction against those very walls, and they would later be described as having changed those walls—or at least made them more flexible.

FREE UNIVERSITIES ON CAMPUS: THE SIXTIES

Dissatisfaction has been a great social mover, and during the early sixties there was increasing dissatisfaction over the college scene, a scene which took shape in the previous decade. The colleges of the 1950s were quiet places with eager and intense, but silent and apathetic, students, bent more on gaining security than on social awareness. They had been sold on the American Dream— one of increasing material prosperity, acceptance of societal values, and an uncritical outlook on the world. College life was one of stability, seasonal shenanigans, and a strict adherence to the values of white, middle-class, male-dominated America.

In *Bring Your Own Bag*, Jane Lichtman outlines the major contribution of the 1950s in setting the stage for the educational volcano that was to erupt in 1964:

> It was primarily in the realm of the arts that students of the late 50's foreshadowed those of the 60's. Albert Camus, J. D. Salinger, Thomas Wolfe, D. H. Lawrence, William Faulkner, and Ayn Rand were popular campus authors. Jack Kerouac initiated the Beat Movement with *On the Road* in 1957. At the end of the decade, a few European films were shown but Hollywood firmly dominated the college scene. As the 50's passed

and the McCarthy influence waned, students began to move away from apple pie American chauvinism to a deeper questioning of their own values.[4]

That questioning of values would be catalyzed not so much from lectures, readings, and discussions within academia as from events outside it. The decade of the 1960s began on a note of positivism, enthusiasm, and idealism that Americans could change their world, both internationally and domestically. Lichtman writes,

> The new decade plunged students into off-campus activity. John F. Kennedy formally entered the presidential arena the first day of the decade. By the end of the year, he was elected. His reign brought a period of intense youthful idealism. John F. Kennedy challenged the college students to become involved, to enter the newly created Peace Corps, to "do for your country." He promised that good intentions and hard work could accomplish miracles. Even the moon would be reached, he vowed, by the end of the decade. Students accepted the challenge and became involved in community, national, and international affairs. They tutored in the Harlems and Fillmore districts of the nation. They flocked to Mississippi for the summers to register voters. They picketed stores with discriminatory racial policies. They marched on Selma and on Washington. They worked to ban the bomb and they cried out against capital punishment. They caught the action, the vitality of the period, and moved with it.[5]

But if students moved to the calls from national leaders, they also responded to cries from ordinary citizens. And those cries were not so positive in tone. One month after John F. Kennedy declared his candidacy for president, on February 1, 1960, four black engineering students sat in at a Greensboro, North Carolina, Woolworth store counter reserved for white people. While there had been sit-ins and demonstrations previously, this one marked the entrance of college students into the civil rights movement, an entrance which would have a profound impact not only on civil rights but also on the students themselves.

Lichtman noted the distinction in inspiration and initiation, which again ties into the history of adult education rather than higher education:

The sit-ins and the freedom rides were unique because they were spontaneous outbursts by local people rather than massively organized political actions. The actions came before the organizations and were not run by the "experts" but rather by locally affected people. Free universities are part of this tradition.[6]

During the next few years, black students would be joined by white students in demonstrating against discrimination. By the summer of 1964, the sit-ins would turn to teach-ins, and the freedom rides into Freedom Schools. The occasion was the Mississippi Freedom Ballot, a movement organized by Bob Moses in 1963 to sponsor an unofficial ballot in the state of Mississippi in which all citizens could vote. Although its immediate political impact was slight, it did serve to bring to the attention not only of Mississippians but also of the country that elections in Mississippi in 1964 were not free and that blacks could not vote.

As part of the Mississippi summer, Freedom Schools were formed, and 250 college students—primarily northern, primarily white—came south for the summer to involve 2,500 people in a variety of learning experiences. Some involved preschool children, some school children, some youth, some adults. Some involved teaching, some discussing, some singing—all learning. Staughton Lynd, a prominent intellectual activist of the time, was asked to describe them. He answered, "Our approach to curriculum was to have no curriculum and our approach to administrative structure was not to have any. . . . So my answer to the question: 'How do you start a Freedom School?' is, 'I don't know.' And if people ask, 'What were the Freedom Schools like?' again I have to answer, 'I don't know.' "[7]

The Mississippi summer of 1964 was important not only for civil rights but also for educational innovation. For the need of the moment had prompted a response, at first unstructured and not too cohesive, but built on local people learning and sharing from each other. Although 250 students was not many, some of them would return to their college campuses to start their own Freedom Schools, turning them into free universities. While the college students had contributed their summers to Mississippi (several had given even their lives), Mississippi gave in return. Paul Lauter and Florence Howe in their book *The Conspiracy of the Young* write,

And of course Mississippi gave even more to the volunteers. Our experience in the freedom schools—in learning to teach by asking, in discovering radical connections between school and life—led us to raise some fundamental questions about the quality and nature of our own northern schools. It was no accident either that many of the leaders of the student rebellion at Berkeley that next winter were Mississippi veterans, nor that among the most prominent demands of the Berkeley students was that education at the University of California become more relevant and humane.[8]

While the Freedom Schools of Mississippi provided those few college students with a foundation for action after they returned back home to school, the philosophical cornerstone had been laid two years earlier in a town called Port Huron, Michigan. There, college people met at a convention of the newly formed Students for a Democratic Society (SDS) and developed a statement outlining the conditions, problems, and potential for what would come to be known as the New Student Left. From it, SDS activity, civil rights, free universities, and many other campus movements of the sixties began. It is an important statement, not only for the picture it portrays of society in 1962, but also for some of the changes and some of the similar conditions between that time almost twenty years ago and today.

The Port Huron statement began

We are people of this generation, bred in at least modest comfort, housed in universities, looking uncomfortably to the world we inherit.

Our work is guided by the sense that we may be the last generation in the experiment with living. But we are a minority—the vast majority of our people regard the temporary equilibriums of our society and the world as eternally-functional parts. In this is perhaps the outstanding paradox: We ourselves are imbued with urgency, yet the message of our society is that there is no viable alternative to the present.[9]

But the statement was a doomsday one, for it also reiterated values and noted the possibility of student action, by saying

In the last few years, thousands of American students demonstrated that they at least felt the urgency of the times. They moved actively and directly against racial injustices, the threat of war, violations of individual rights of conscience and, less frequently, against economic manipulation. They succeeded in restoring a small measure of controversy to the campuses after the stillness of the McCarthy period. They succeeded, too, in gaining some concessions from the people and institutions they opposed, especially in the fight against racial bigotry.[10]

And finally, the Port Huron statement provided some positive values to replace those that it deemed destructive. Although free universities were not mentioned by name at this point, the philosophical comments were ones that free universities embraced:

Men have unrealized potential for self-cultivation, self-direction, and self-understanding, and creativity. The goal of man and society should be human independence: a concern not with image or popularity but with finding a meaning in life that is personally authentic; a quality of mind not compulsively driven by a sense of powerlessness, nor one which unthinkingly adopts status values, nor one which represses all threats to its habits, but one which has full, spontaneous access to present and past experiences, one which easily unites the fragmented parts of personal history, one which openly faces problems which are troubling and unresolved—one with an intuitive awareness of possibilities, an active sense of curiosity, an ability and willingness to learn.[11]

The Port Huron convention and the summer of 1964 in Mississippi were two of the more striking events that contributed to a growing student movement on college campuses around the country. In the fall of 1964, several students returned from the Freedom Schools in Mississippi to their home college, the University of California at Berkeley. They were to catalyze those thoughts about educational reform into action.

Returning to Berkeley, students became increasingly aware of their limited role in determining their own education. They began to speak, to gather, to demonstrate, to march in what became known as the Free Speech Movement, whose most eloquent speaker was Mario Savio. The university administration responded with citations against the leaders of the protest, and when this happened, 1,000 students marched to the administration building, Sproul Hall, and took it over.

It was in the spontaneity of that action that the first free university was born. It was without name, structure, catalog, or organization, but it symbolized the praxis of thought and action on which the first free universities were based. Michael Rossman, one of the Free Speech Movement leaders, described it this way in *Center* magazine a few years later:

> In that building, during the fifteen hours before the police arrived, the nation's first free university was established, with a dozen classes, some conducted cross-legged atop the civil-defense disaster drums stored in the basement. Chaplin movies were shown. A Chanukah service was read, followed by the traditional folk dances. Instrumentalists and singers performed in stairwell niches....[12]

The free university, like many that would come after it, and many activities that free universities would engage in, was a burst of energy born of the moment, responding to very real—if temporary and local—needs. It showed from the beginning that learning did not have to be authorized, credited, and structured before it could happen, and that citizens could learn from each other. As Robert G. Greenway noted in his article "Free U's and the Strange Revolution," "the 'proclamation of freedom' was rooted in an action. They didn't sit down and laboriously plan a future 'free university' to begin at some future time. They started doing it right then and there, out of the joy and frustration in their guts."[13]

Within months of the spontaneous birth of the first free university at Sproul Hall in December 1964, the Free University of Berkeley would emerge as the first nationally recognized free university in the country and would start offering organized classes.

THE EARLIEST FREE UNIVERSITIES

The three earliest free universities in the country were all started in the Bay Area in California within two years of each other. They all gained national attention for their activities, but each one had a distinct structure different from the others, a slightly different reason for being, a different plan for achieving educational and social change and for securing its own future stability. The Free University of Berkeley, the nation's first, quickly moved off the campus and established itself as a community center, creating the model for free universities sponsored as part of a larger community agency. The Free University of Palo Alto, which would join forces with The Experiment at Stanford to become the Mid-peninsula Free University, became a leader of free universities that were independent and separate organizations, existing as financially self-sufficient organizations in the community. And the Experimental College at San Francisco State University was the first free university to begin and remain on campus, becoming the model for campus-based free universities.

Free University of Berkeley

The Free University of Berkeley (FUB) appeared sometime in 1965 after the takeover of Sproul Hall in the fall of 1964. Various accounts put its initial session at later dates, but *The Nation* mentions FUB—as it quickly became known—in an article in the summer of 1965, along with a fledgling free university planned in Gainesville, Florida, and the Free University of New York.[14]

FUB's purpose was calmly but openly stated on page two of its early catalogs. "The Free University is a promise and a protest. It promises a new focus for our intellectual concerns. It rejects the Educational Establishment which produces proud cynicism but sustains neither enthusiasm nor integrity."[15]

Within a month of its formation, it moved off the Berkeley campus and rented a building in the community along with another alternative organization, the Free Church. From its community center base, FUB during the next seven years would not only offer a wide array of intriguing classes but spin off scores of projects as well, many of them growing out of classes. There would be a newspaper, a radio station, community businesses, alternative schools for children, law and architecture collectives, and a free clinic. As FUB grew, it became the hub of community activity.

In its early years, from 1966 to 1968, FUB catalogs did not display the color, exuberance, and abundant artwork that later catalogs would. In the beginning, FUB catalogs were fairly traditional, with little or no art and little rhetoric about educational change. In the spring of 1966, FUB would offer twenty-four classes and enroll 750 people. For its three sessions in 1967, it offered eighty-one courses, probably enrolling between 1,000 and 2,000 participants.

The courses were all taught by volunteers, many of whom had traditional academic credentials, and most of the classes met in one building. Although FUB was the first free university, it did charge a fee of $10 per course. Welfare recipients could take classes for no charge. It is unclear just who coined the term *free university*, or whether it came from the Freedom Schools of Mississippi or from the Free Speech Movement, but despite a public impression to the contrary, the definition of a free university never meant that courses were offered for no cost. A later catalog would characterize FUB in this way:

FREE U IS

FREE form ...   YOU can teach
FREE space ...   YOU can attend
FREE thought...   YOU can participate
FREE forum ...   YOU can initiate
FREE the people.

YOU[16]

During the first two years of free university courses, political and social change courses were the dominant classes. Many free universities were started to offer this kind of course, which was not offered on campus. Some of the courses were intellectual overviews on political subjects with readings, bibliographies, and guest speakers. Other courses were designed to incorporate action as part of the learning process. Some of the early political and social change courses at FUB included "A Marxist Analysis of the Week's News," "Psychology for the Left," and "How to Win an Election Without Selling Out." There were courses in Marxist theory, black history, anarchism, the draft, farm labor struggles, and revolution.

But even in the years 1966 to 1968, when political courses were the trend, they never constituted more than half of all the courses offered. In 1967, FUB offered eighty-one classes, forty-one of which were political in some way, and forty of which were definitely not political. Some of the nonpolitical courses included "A History of Scientific Thought," "The Early Chaplin and His Contemporaries," and "Living in the Woods." Others included the arts (such as ceramics, piano, and modern dance) along with courses on drugs and psychedelic experiences, literature, and music (particularly jazz and the blues). Between the Fall 1967 and Spring

1968 sessions, the number of political and social change courses dropped to around 15 percent. After 1967, they would never again constitute more than a small minority of the classes in free university catalogs.

The political and social change courses were quickly replaced by a wide variety of courses that continue to reflect the unlimited diversity in course topics in free universities. Many courses would continue to be intellectually progressive. There were "The Decline of Western Culture," "The Negro in America," "Lenny Bruce," and "Starting a Rural Intentional Community." But there were also courses on Japan, stone carving, poetry, group dynamics, and local ecology.

In 1969, FUB abandoned its rather respectable but plain approach, and the catalog erupted in an explosion of color and creativity. For the remaining years of FUB's life, its catalogs would become a place for experimentation with course descriptions, ideas, art, and projects. Many drawings decorated the catalog pages; course descriptions became less academic and formal, and instead sought to attract the attention and impulse of the learner. FUB made initial attempts at developing catchy course titles, which would later become a science in free universities. Topics such as "Infinity: Can You Ever Get There?" and "Degapping the Generations" appeared. A page of the catalog would be devoted to listing names, phone numbers, and addresses of other community organizations, and activities. Course descriptions would be typed in designs, circles, and other nonlinear ways. Enrollments jumped, and in the summer of 1971, more than 130 courses were offered, compared with 30 per session four years earlier.

But problems also set in, along with success, for the nation's first free university. Rent increases, a city denial of a building permit, financial woes, a loose decision-making structure, and too many nonpaying participants all gave the Free University of Berkeley management headaches they were unprepared to tackle. Decisions were made at biweekly meetings open to any member of the free university—and anybody could join—so there was no tight administrative structure. FUB had to move out of the building it shared with Free Church in 1969, the same year the city denied FUB a building permit. The number of participants claiming to be welfare recipients, and who thus did not have to pay class fees, went from 15 percent to 40 percent in 1969. In 1972,

FUB collapsed at the age of seven, a ripe old age for free universities in the sixties.

Midpeninsula Free University

The Midpeninsula Free University evolved as a model for the independent free university and was also to gain national attention, particularly through its magazine, *The Free You.*

In began when the Free University of Palo Alto and The Experiment, a free university at Stanford, merged in 1966 to become Midpeninsula Free University (MFU), the first free university independent of a college or university.

The MFU quickly drew up and published its Manifesto, which would be included in every issue of the catalog. In the Manifesto, MFU asserted that "the American education establishment has proven incapable of meeting the needs of our society. It often discourages students from thinking critically, and does not afford them meaningful training to help them understand the crucial issues confronting mankind today." It said, "A revolution in American education is required to meet today's needs, and a new type of education—a free university—must provide the impetus for change."

The Manifesto affirmed a set of beliefs:

That freedom of inquiry is the cornerstone of education.

That each individual must generate his own most vital questions and program his own education, free from central control by administrative bureaucracies and disciplinary oligarchies.

That education aims at generality rather than specialization and should supply the glue which cements together our fragmented lives.

That education is a process involving the total environment, which can only occur in a total community, in which each individual participates equally in making the decisions which importantly affect his life.

That the most revolutionary thing we can do is think for ourselves, and regain contact with our vital centers.

That the most important questions which confront us must be asked again and again and answered again and again, until the millenium comes.

That the natural state of man is ecstatic wonder.
That we should not settle for less.[17]

That statement, one of the most concise and poetic to come from the early free university movement, would be reprinted in catalogs all over the country.

By fall of 1967, MFU had expanded to nearly 140 courses. Some famous people of the day taught, including singer Joan Baez, guru Richard Alpert, philosopher Herbert Marcuse, and activist David Harris. But internally, MFU was facing the same dilemma that other free universities had—how to be a radical organization, create social and educational change, and respond to changing learner interests all at the same time. In his history of MFU, Dennis DuBé writes,

> The encounter between political activism and personal liberation continued as these different elements utilized the free university's democratic governing structure as a forum for their confrontation. The period saw a see-saw battle among the factions, and annual elections for the school's director became the battleground.[18]

By 1968 the courses had shifted from politics to self-liberation, with encounter groups, meditation, and gestalt. Yet the free university organization remained outwardly political and began a print shop, magazine, and other ventures. In 1969 MFU instituted a $10 fee per student to support the organization, but even so, the free university and its other projects began to lose money. By 1970 it had worn itself out and closed after a four-year history.

What MFU left was the legacy of an exciting free university, a colorful catalog, and the establishment of a model for other independent free universities to follow.

Experimental College at San Francisco State

The third early free university differed sharply from FUB and MFU. The Experimental College, or EC, at San Francisco State, remained within the academic setting and saw its mission as operating not outside the traditional university but within it. EC would soon become the model for most other campus free universities, the predominant type of free university during the sixties.

By 1965–66, the academic year in which EC was created, the regular credit system at San Francisco State, like that at other colleges and universities, had been formalized to the point of stifling student choice and faculty initiative. For most undergraduates, classes at the university were not intimate discussions with twelve students and a professor, but massive lectures with hundreds of students, a professor behind the lectern, and legions of graduate students providing the real contact with students. Just the demographics of higher education in the sixties were ponderous. The decade saw college student enrollments more than double, from 3.2 million to 7.3 million students in 1970. And almost half those 7 million students were in the 200 largest universities, each having more than 10,000 students.[19] But EC was the product not only of demographics but also of a rigidity in curriculum.

Many of the higher-level courses were unavailable to most students because of a series of prerequisite courses that had to be taken first. Some prerequisites even had prerequisites, making learning a long chain of inner doors to be unlocked. At San Francisco State, general education courses were required of all freshmen and sophomores. These courses were reportedly despised by students and faculty alike and used as "an academic obstacle to weed out students who were unwilling or unable to put up with the requirements of the institution."[20] But the students were not the only ones harnessed by the academic system. Faculty members also were constrained. It took a year or more for faculty to get new courses approved. So it was in the fall of 1965 that Cynthia Carlson, a graduate teaching assistant, began to offer noncredit seminars to teach students to think critically.

That experience led to the formation of a committee of students and administrators to look into making the curriculum more relevant, or at least a little more flexible. One of those students was Jim Nixon, the founder of the Experimental College. "I was always fascinated by the relationship between theory and practice,"[21] he said of his initial motivation. The formation of EC was distinctly different from the start of either FUB or MFU. Although they were born of confrontation and of rejection of the educational powers, Experimental College was not only condoned but also approved of, at least initially, by the administration at San Francisco State. In fact, some of the EC courses would be available for credit under a special-studies number in the university catalog.

The Experimental College chose an inside route based on pragmatic and strategic concerns. The EC founders wanted a "college within a college, assured of resources and student constituency, and with a concrete political objective."[22] That political objective was to change higher education, or at least San Francisco State. One reason for staying within the university structure, filled with administrative ties, faculty resistance, and potential for co-optation, was that EC could be funded by the university itself. The next year, when Jim Nixon was elected associated student body president, riding the crest of the EC favor, he was able to get $24,-000 of student government money allocated for Experimental College.

But EC was not, at least in its formative stages, an organization without a radical purpose. "We wanted to create a situation in which students could become revolutionaries," recalls Nixon, "and that meant dealing with every aspect of their lives."[23]

The first session of Experimental College began in the spring of 1966, and its twenty-two seminars drew 444 students. Its first session also had a few headliners for instructors. Well-known alternative educator Paul Goodman was hired by the students to teach a course; famed pacifist Ira Sandperl taught "Nonviolence in a Violent World;" and black student activist Jimmy Garrett offered a course on urban action. EC had two slogans that it hoped would reflect its plan for both making EC successful and changing the university. The first was "Blackmail them with quality." With sterile lectures being the normative learning experience on campus, EC wanted to offer creative, exciting, educational experiences that would not only be stimulating but also of high quality. The second slogan, "Anybody can teach a course," was aimed at breaking down the authoritative relationships in the university and the idea of the student as mere consumer of knowledge. The pyramidical structure of regular college courses, with prerequisites keeping out more students than they let in to higher-level courses, would crumble if anyone could teach any subject that he or she chose.

The strategy fostered by the "Anybody can teach . . ." slogan was successful. Not only at EC, but also across the country the slogan "Anybody can teach . . ." became associated with the free university, and the concept was widely employed.

But the first slogan made no such dent in the university. Although EC could provide high-quality classes, that quality had no power to blackmail the university. EC organizers thought that if they could provide quality classes outside the regular curriculum, the situation within the academic classroom would have to change and adopt those reforms. EC could produce quality classes, but it could not blackmail anybody with them. It became apparent that the university was not moved by quality. A more insular institution, the university left students little choice but to take its prescribed courses, leading to a degree and a job, whether those classes were of high quality or not.

Thus, after only one semester of operation, the Experimental College faced a problem of direction in the summer of 1966. It could develop a coherent political strategy for redefining the education priorities of the college, and thus attempt to change directly the regular credit curriculum, or it could expand its already successful attempt at educational innovation and devote energies to new course topics, new processes in learning, teacher-student interaction, and educational experimentation. It could not do both. It could not, at the same time, work to change Sociology 203 in the regular classroom and set up an experimental "Interpersonal Relations" experience to develop new educational practice. The second direction won out.

In the fall of 1966, EC bloomed in terms of numbers. More than seventy courses were offered for that term, with 1,200 students participating, almost 15 percent of the student body, according to one estimate. But the radical and intellectual orientation of the first semester was replaced by a "do your own thing" philosophy in the course topics, as zen basketball and astro-psychology became the popular course subjects.

By 1967, EC had tapered off, at least in the eyes of its founders, who had hoped widespread change at San Francisco State would result from their efforts. Instead, while thousands of students flocked to it to take intriguing offbeat courses, EC posed no threat to the administrative structure that it had hoped to shake up. The authors of *An End to Silence,* a book about San Francisco State in the sixties, remarked, "Originally conceived of as a vehicle to effect institutional change within the traditional college, the Experimental College had developed into an institutional safety valve for the very college it had hoped to revolutionize."[24] And a disillusioned Ian Grand, the last EC director, commented, "For the most part, the Experimental College became an educational playground for bored or alienated students, and as such, it absorbed, ironically, much of the discontent it had hoped to crystallize for political purposes."[25]

But if the Experimental College at San Francisco State didn't live up to its founders' expectations, it nevertheless created a free university model that was to be replicated on 100 or more college campuses for the next five years as other students designed ECs for their own campuses and took up similar views about educational change and EC's role.

Experimental College set the pattern for future campus free universities. It sought, and sometimes received, administration approval for its existence and its programs, and even funding. It attempted to bring faculty, students, and administrators together to work for educational change. And it viewed its ultimate goal as the transformation of the traditional university, not the establishment of an alternative and separate institution.

There would be variations on other college campuses as the EC model and name spread during the next five years. Some experimental colleges would clash with their administrations, while others, like Dartmouth's Experimental College, would be so approved and co-opted by the administration that little student dissent could take place. Many other campus free universities would also see their mission as direct change in the university, while others would see their role as a supplement to the university— adding to it rather than changing it.

If the Experimental College at San Francisco State did not achieve much change in the university, it did succeed in establishing a sound model for free universities. EC laid sound educational objectives as its principles, gained student-government support, gained national recognition, and ran its courses effectively.

OTHER EARLY FREE UNIVERSITIES

Early free universities, from 1966 to 1968, were also set up in other cities, and nationwide media devoted a certain amount of attention to the growing movement.

In 1965 there was a short-lived free university newsletter, and the free university appeared as an important topic for debate at the SDS national convention in the summer of 1965. SDS's romance with free universities did not last long, but SDS organizers did set up about a dozen free universities in the next year or so, "in that brief period of unity between political activists and educational reformers," as Paul Lauter and Florence Howe describe it.[26] In fact, SDS began the first debate over the term *free university* even before the first free university. SDS favored dropping the term in favor of "free educational atmosphere," and the basic concern was whether or not the atmosphere of the free university was more important than the subjects discussed.

Two free universities that were essentially radical political centers were the New School in San Francisco and the Free University of New York (FUNY), which captured a bit of national publicity. Both were started not by students but by professors who were disenchanted with the traditional university, and both were started as separate, off-campus organizations. They did not particularly endorse the concept that anyone could teach. When confronted with the question of whether conservative columnist William Buckley could teach at FUNY, FUNY founder Allen Krebs hedged and talked about limited classroom space and the need for "constructive" social thought to be taught at FUNY.[27] But these schools did not pretend to be open forums for all points of view. Their organizers were disturbed that traditional academia would not offer subjects on socialism, Marxism, Cuba, or leftist political thinking, and they wanted to fill that information gap in society.

Other early free universities on campuses included those at Gainesville, Florida; Seattle, Washington; the University of Michigan in Ann Arbor; the University of Minnesota; Princeton University; Bowling Green State University; the Free University of Pennsylvania at the University of Pennsylvania in Philadelphia; Notre Dame; the University of Houston; Brooklyn College; the University of Utah; and Whittier College. Lauter determined that five free universities were set up in 1965, ten in 1966, and thirty-five in 1967—or fifty total in the first three years. Many of them would last only a year; some would not survive the planning stages. The infant mortality rate among the early free universities was high.

THE NATURE AND RECEPTION
OF THE EARLY FREE UNIVERSITIES

On the whole, it is difficult to separate political action from educational reform during the first three years of the free university movement. The founders of the first free universities wanted both positive social change and educational reform. Some saw this happening by offering political and radical courses. Others saw it happening by allowing anyone to offer a course. Although the media often highlighted those free universities that were leftist in orientation, those free universities that were overtly political in course content did not last long.

Instead, the free universities that survived were more likely to be those that accepted all points of view, even if the founders and organizers of the free university were themselves radicals. Even in early free university catalogs, one can find courses on Bible study and traditional Christian views.

The courses were a product of the times and of people's interest in learning about and teaching those subjects, rather than of the free university's administrative notion of what should be offered. As interest in political courses waned around 1968, they were dropped in significant numbers from the free university catalogs.

Political courses continued to be offered, of course, and course organizers combined blatant frankness about their subject with coy overtures to the potential learner. A particularly intriguing course description ran in the El Paso Free University catalog in 1971:

> REVOLUTIONARY ORGANIZING, TERRORISM AND SABOTAGE. . . .
> Ron Vincent
> Tues. & Thurs.; Evenings
> Student Union Building

> Workshops and discussions cover everything a budding radical needs to know, from how [to] print leaflets to how to blow up a bank—how best to use words or weapons. Stress developing on well-rounded radical leaders with an understanding of issues, skill in communications, able to affect opinion. And with the technical ability to deal with institutions by any means necessary.

> Persons felt to be politically unreliable may be dropped. Enrollment by permission only. (Sign up anyway!)

> Any weapons and/or infernal devices will be supplied for those unable to supply their own. People with a 'violence' hang-up may take only the nonviolent parts. Occasional weekend of special 'workshop' excursions.[28]

The course description was slipped in between a course on "Rock 'n' Roll and Pop Culture" and one on dressmaking and shirt design.

The reaction of the media to the early free universities was a mixed one of cautious approval and disdain. Howard Junker, writing in *The Nation* in August 1965, lent his tentative support: "Crucial, then, in the evaluation of the experiment . . . is the simple fact it has been set up. . . . Now that students know how to organize themselves, the notion of a Free University will spread. . . . Freedom, at least to learn and teach, is sometimes available for the asking."[29] And *Life* magazine, participating in a class at FUNY in 1966, was startled to find that "more than 150 people showed up. Not 150 beatniks, but 150 real people, with coats and ties and dresses."[30]

But *Newsweek* was not impressed. Its editors thought that some of the basic ideas were "hardly new," having their roots in medieval times or in German universities. They complained that "many free university courses are as cliché-ridden as the universities they criticize." The article went on to predict the movement's demise.

New School for Social Research president John R. Everett is quoted as saying, "I doubt the free universities serve any serious academic purpose. I suspect it's a protest without a clear understanding of what they are protesting against." And *Newsweek* ended its report with its own dour guess: "Practically all the schools report plans for enlarged curriculums and student bodies this spring, but it's doubtful that total enrollment will exceed 3,000."[31]

The tenor in the early free university was one of seriousness and purpose very much like the feeling with which the decade had opened five years earlier. There was a sense of protest but also one of positivism. Early free university leaders believed they could radically change higher education for the better.

The philosophy of the early free university was strident and rhetorical. It demanded change in the regular university and postulated basic theories of learning and teaching. It also carried with it a basic idealism, whether in America or in free universities, that education could be converted from an elitist, hierarchical, and regulated process to an egalitarian, open, and free-thinking exchange between students and teachers.

The emphasis in early catalogs was on course content, not process. One participant at an early free university remembers,

"Many of us, I believe, had no particular interest in unconventional instructional techniques. We simply wanted a quick background briefing on Vietnamese history—a subject that regular history courses seemed to miss. . . . I took conventional lecture notes."[32]

But while the early free university was mostly serious, it also was punctuated with humor, a trait free universities would embrace even more in later years. The humor began with the Free Speech Movement, when protestors sang such carols as "We Three Deans" and "O Come, All Ye Mindless." The religious spirit extended to a free university credo, written in early 1966, ending, "All true artists, all true teachers, all true men and women and children, are students in the free university. The free university always has been, is now, and ever shall be. (Drink the *fourth* [emphasis added] goblet of wine.)"[33]

By the end of 1967, the free university critique of contemporary higher education had been laid out, followed by its own philosophy of what learning and teaching should be. Four models for free university structure had been developed: the community center (Free University of Berkeley); the independent free university (Midpeninsula Free University); the campus free university (Experimental College–San Francisco State); and the radical free university (Free University of New York). Although monumental educational change in higher education would not quickly ensue, the concept behind the slogan "Anybody can teach a course" would provide a basis for widespread change in learning that would extend far beyond the university walls.

A CULTURAL EXPERIENCE

In the next four years, from 1968 to 1971, free universities would blossom on college campuses around the country. They would enroll, despite *Newsweek*'s projections, an estimated 100,000 participants a year. They would be referred to by the media as "The Jivy League," "Shadow Schools," or "Do It Yourself Colleges." Catalogs would be colorful, artistic, and occasionally outrageous; invitations to participate would be sweeping. "Expand! Experience! Be!" one would shout.[34] Concern over process would equal or sometimes surpass interest in subject matter. Affective learning would replace cognitive thinking in many classes. Teachers would become facilitators or conveners; students became participants.

Political courses would be superseded by cultural courses dealing with changing life-styles, alternative ways of living, and culture. A concern for changing outside society or the university
would be redirected toward changing one's own life-style, local
community, and culture.

By the spring of 1969, course catalogs became large enough to
warrant subject categories. Ignoring traditional disciplines like
English, biology, and sociology, free universities developed their
own interdisciplinary topic categories. The Washington Area Free
University (WAFU), a consortium of seven area free universities,
had these categories in its Spring 1969 catalog: History & Political
Science, Economics and Social Sciences, Language, Philosophy
& Religion, Good Trips, Medicine, the Arts, Media, Encounter,
and Projects. The Midpeninsula Free University ran its table of
contents as Arts, Crafts, Education, Encounter/Sensitivity, Philosophy, Play, Politics, Whole Earth Studies, and Community/
Special Projects.

Process was beginning to become more important. As one free
university staffer later insisted, "Just by taking a free university
course, even if it's in macrame, you're thumbing your nose at
the system. The process—that's the revolution, not the content."[35]
And while many courses still had readings and bibliography attached, the teach-ins had changed to be-ins and happenings, and
some courses were more experience than cognition. A participant
at the Midpeninsula Free University remembers,

> There's one class I'll always treasure. It was a one-session,
> Midnight to Sunrise, Greet the Full Moon, and Bread Baking
> class. I went to a party with my husband and planned to stay
> up all night for the class. I talked two men at the party into
> coming with me. We arrived at the class a little late and a little
> boisterous and this very soft-spoken man greeted us and took
> us to his downstairs apartment in Palo Alto. We ground grain,
> prepared dough, and baked bread all night. By morning we were
> eating fresh bread and honey and drinking tea. I'm so glad we
> showed up because we were the only students he had.[36]

In 1968 the number of new free universities jumped to forty-
six, according to Lauter. Another seventy-five or so would be
started in the next three years.

Many were started after campus leaders attended one of several workshops on free universities sponsored by the National Student Association, which heralded the free university concept during the late sixties. A national conference of free universities was held in 1968. Most of the larger free universities in the country today were started during this time. The Experimental College at the University of Washington, Seattle, was started in 1968. It is now the largest in the nation, enrolling more than 28,000 participants a year. The University for Man in Manhattan, and the Wichita Free University, both in Kansas, also were started in 1968. The Denver Free University and the Community Free School in Boulder, Colorado, followed in 1969. And the Free University at Penn State and the Center for Participant Education in Tallahassee, Florida, were begun in 1970.

As the decade closed, some of the early free universities died and new ones were started, more often than not in the Midwest rather than on the coasts, where free universities were first born.

The period from 1968 to 1971 was one of controversy. Internally, free universities struggled with their ultimate purpose and political change. They wondered whether free universities had any impact on higher education. They criticized each other and tried to develop cohesive organizations in a changing time. Externally, the press was not uncritical. Traditional educators either attacked the free university concept or tried to co-opt it. Yet it was also a time when many of the free university educational hallmarks were pioneered. The courses in personal growth led both to a learner-centered orientation in course offerings and to a preoccupation with the process of learning, not just its content. Course catalogs became the free university's message as well as its medium, reflecting in courses titles and colorful art the kind of joyous learning being advocated and offered.

Some of the changes in higher education were even attributed to the impact of free universities. In fact, formal higher education would install numerous changes in its operations to make it more flexible and student centered. But even if the free university movement had died at the close of the sixties, it would have provided an exciting story in the history of education, as well as some changes in higher education.

The end of the first phase of the history of free universities was signaled by a premature obituary in the *New York Times*. The article marked the end of the period, which actually ran from

1964 to 1971, in which free universities would flourish as student-
and campus-oriented organizations.

With the catchy headline "No Grades, No Exams—And Now,
No Schools," *New York Times* education writer Fred M. Hechinger proclaimed the free university movement dead. "As colleges
prepared last week for another term, it was clear that the free university movement was running out of steam," he wrote in August
of 1971. Speaking of free universities in the past tense, he went
on, "As informal unstructured counter-universities lacking central
purpose, the free universities were largely exercises in dilettantism.
At their most serious, they differed little from well-run extracurricular activities on the traditional campuses. While the lack of
requirements and direction at first may have looked like utopia,
it eventually turned into lack of motivation and cohesion."[37]

What Hechinger was seeing, however, was not the demise of
free universities. Although he did correctly perceive a diminish-
ing of the fervor of free universities on campus, what was actually
happening was not the demise of free universities, but the shifting
of orientation from students to the community at large. Although
it would take almost another seven years to gain its full impact,
the growth and effect of the free university movement on the
general public at large would far outdo its influence on the college campus. It was time for the era of lifelong learning.

Chapter 6

Free Universities in the Community: The Seventies

TRANSITION

The period from 1971 to 1976 was a difficult time for free universities. It was a period of transition, in which the free university would reorient itself away from a limited audience of young students on campus and toward the community and general public at large—a change that would have long-term effects both on free universities and on lifelong learning.

The early seventies was a period of doubting for free universities. The *New York Times* had just declared free universities dead, and even those people running free universities believed it. It would take two years, until 1973, just to discover that the movement had not completely faltered. The philosophy of free universities, rooted in "Anybody can teach, anybody can learn," was doubted. It would take half a decade for the general public to prove its interest by taking free university classes and for traditional educators to recognize the educational practices of free universities as sound. And there were doubts about survival. Many free universities had died in infancy, and there were no easy answers to the question of financing free universities.

The doubts were reinforced by the myths that developed about free universities. Some of those myths:

97

Free universities die within a few years after they are founded.

Free universities were all started in the sixties: They're not starting anymore.

Free universities are for students on campus who want to learn about radical politics.

Free universities are loosely managed, unaccountable, with no controls or structure.

Free universities are dying or on their way out.

Events on campus and in society did not help the free university's dilemma. On the college scene, the numbers of college students started to level off or decline. The post–World War II baby boom was ending: there was no need to go to college just to avoid the draft; the economic prosperity of the sixties no longer provided surplus money for families to send all their children to college; and there was a greater emphasis on getting a well-paying job. Students on campus were becoming more materialistic and more bent on getting degrees and jobs than on liberal arts education. They rejected the customs, behavior, and favorite pastimes of the previous generation of college students—including free universities.

The attitude on campus was neither positive nor change oriented. While the decade of the sixties started with a youthful presidential campaign and a civil rights sit-in, the decade of the seventies began ominously when, on January 1, 1970, a few students flew a light plane over a munitions plant near Madison, Wisconsin, and tried to drop a bomb on it. The decade of the seventies, both on and off campus, would turn downward, from dismay and disharmony to distinterest and disillusionment.

Society as a whole was not much more upbeat. It would wrench its way through Watergate and never quite completely recover a national sense of pride or positivism. The recession of 1974–75 would particularly hurt free universities, whose fragile financial condition seemed most stable during prosperity and especially precarious during recessions.

During this time, for example, the Experimental College at Northridge, California, carried this notice in its catalog: "Although the Experimental College is funded by the Associated Students of California State University, Northridge, there still is not enough funding for smooth management and certainly not enough for innovation, growth and emergencies."[1] The number of new free universities started during the recession, for instance, was fewer than in the periods before and after it. Only sixteen new organizations were started in 1972, just three in 1973, and only eleven in 1974. The doubting and hard times were reflected in the free university national conferences, which were begun again in 1973. There great arguments took place with righteous Chevy Chase overtones of "I'm a free university and You're Not." There were heated discussions about whether or not to charge fees, whether to be independent or to be attached to a university, and whether to accept or to refuse government money. Although all those positions would eventually be justified, it was unclear then whether all, or any, were right.

The "technology" of the free university operation during the early 1970s did not differ significantly from the techniques used in the sixties. In fact, because of rising costs in printing, some of the four-color catalogs that brightened the scene in the late sixties had to be scrapped for plain black on white. With increasing frequency, odd-shaped sizes, such as the large poster shape or the index-card-size catalog, gave way to standard cost-efficient sizes. While some free universities switched to typesetting to make their catalogs look better, many remained a basic typewriter operation. One free university catalog, in expressing gratitude to its production staff, made a point to offer "specail thanxs to the typsit."

But the undeniable bright spot in the free university picture of the time was enrollments. They continued to climb. In her book on free universities, Jane Lichtman reported in 1972 between 120 and 200 free universities in the country. They enrolled an estimated 150,000 participants, up 50 percent from the 100,000 estimated in 1968. By 1976, that participation would hit almost 200,000. The course trends in subject matter did not stagnate either. The cultural classes of the late sixties gave way to ecological, environmental, and whole earth studies; then to women's studies; and then to a trend toward interpersonal relations. Courses in politics were steadily decreasing. By the mid-seventies Community Free School director Dennis DuBé, tongue in cheek, would sigh, "Yes, we haven't seen a Communist around here in years."

Free universities looked around to see where those enrollments were coming from and found that an increasing number of participants were coming from the community rather than from the campus. Slowly and unconsciously, free universities began to orient themselves toward the community. Some free universities moved off campus; more were started in the community, unaffiliated with any college or university. Those that remained on campus did more publicity in the community, sought teachers from the community, and actively recruited participants from the broader community.

This was done without acknowledgment or overall plan but as a reflex response to a need in the community for more and varied learning. Patti Pruett, a middle-aged housewife who started Communiversity in Macomb, Illinois, said, "First we did it; then we labeled it."[2]

What was happening was a whole transformation of postsecondary education in the United States—a transformation that is still taking shape and whose implications are only beginning to be understood. It was called adult education, adult learning, continuing education, and finally—adopting the term developed in western Europe, where the phenomenon was one step ahead of the United States—lifelong learning. No one knew precisely what it was, as one can see by the many names given it.

But there were some sound reasons why it was occurring. One was again simply demographic. The post–World War II baby boom children were in college in the sixties; by the seventies they were out. Their appetite for learning had now shifted from the academic arena to the community. America in the seventies became a mobile society. People now were changing jobs twelve times, including four completely different career changes.[3] They were moving from city to city, and they were changing the structure of the family as well. More and more single people lived alone, more unmarried couples lived together, more elderly lived by themselves. Increasing technology and knowledge meant that facts and figures of five years ago were now obsolete. Professionals had to be retrained periodically to keep up with developments in their own occupations. As many more middle-class people earned college degrees, their educational needs shifted from credit offerings to noncredit offerings in more practical areas, like job-related topics and personal growth and development, and practical items, such as buying a house or fixing a car. Learning habits became more personal, more useful, more practical.

Free universities seemed perfect settings for these learning needs to be satisfied. Free universities offered classes in living rooms, churches, and other informal atmospheres, so the learning was not stuffy or sterile, as in the traditional classroom. New topics emerged quickly, and free universities were changing their course offerings each session in response to new ideas. The learning was low-cost, usually took place at night, did not interfere with work, involved no tedious homework, and was short-term. Its narrow topics got to the point.

The new phenomenon of lifelong learning and appealing to the general public called for a new look and some changes for free universities. Courses needed to appeal to the working person and to be held in the community. Catalogs needed to be attractive, respectable, and distributed throughout the community. Good public relations at the local level became more important.

From that period evolved three different models of free universities in response to the changing learning trends in society. Although their antecedents went back to the first free universities— Free University of Berkeley, Midpeninsula Free University, and Experimental College—the successful building of the models was not completed and proclaimed until 1976.

The campus-community free university would remain associated with the traditional university, but its orientation would encompass the community as well as the campus. By the mid-seventies a majority of participants at these free universities were coming from the community. The double foothold—on campus and in the community— meant that the free university could draw from both town and gown elements not only its participants but also its funding. These free universities would tap student government, college, and community funds as well. Sometimes, if the free university received substantial support from the student government, higher fees were charged to the community. At other free universities, the student government support meant that the free university would not have to charge fees. The Free University at University Park, Pennsylvania, is one such free university, and it enrolls more than 8,000 participants a year. Experimental College at Seattle charges fees and actually returns money to the university.

The dual base also meant that some free universities could remain medium-sized and still become stable organizations, unlike independent free universities, which must expand or falter. University for Man in Monterey and the Baltimore Free University are two good examples of free universities that have remained small but viable organizations over the years.

A second free university model was pioneered by Jim Killacky and Sue Maes at University for Man in Manhattan, Kansas. In a state with almost 600 towns of fewer than 2,500 people, Maes and Killacky were challenged to take their successful free university into small towns of Kansas where there were few, if any, opportunities for adult learning. In late 1975 they began a four-year effort to establish locally run free universities in small rural communities around the state.

The third free university model that was developed during this time was the independent fee-charging free university. Led by the Community Free School in Boulder and the Denver Free University, both in Colorado, independent free universities sprang up in urban areas of the country outside the university sphere of influence.

The history of the Boulder Community Free School (CFS) is typical of the ups and downs of independent free universities during this period. CFS was originally called Unincorporated University and was located on the campus of the University of Colorado at Boulder. After a faulty start in 1968, it was renamed CFS and started classes in September of 1969. By 1970, CFS wanted out of the university and moved off campus, arguing that "independence from the university was the only way the Free School could promote true individual and academic freedoms."[4] After a brief period in which the free school was the vortex of activity not just for classes but for community projects as well, CFS fell dormant because of staff turnovers, a deep financial debt, and low morale. But the Free School was reenergized in late 1972 when Honora Wolfe, Dennis DuBé, and Will Schaleben took over the school.

They were able to lease Highland Elementary School, which brought a burst of life to the Free School. The numbers of students and classes skyrocketed, more people joined the board of directors, and the Free School's income situation was improved. Artists rented studios in the Free School building, and soon a leatherworks, a jewelry workshop, and a recording studio were operating, bringing in more students for the Free School.

The studios and classes began a series of projects that were started by the Free School. Poetry readings, the making of an environmental film, and activities in cable television were initiated. The Free School's dance classes blossomed, and by 1978, some eighty classes in dance were offered. A special coordinator was hired by the staff to coordinate the dance program. Classes in holistic health also grew in the mid-seventies, resulting in the formation of the Healing Arts Center by Honora Wolfe.

In 1976 the Free School tried to buy its historic elementary school but was unable to match a more lucrative purchase offer and moved into a church a few miles away. The move did not affect the Free School's growth, however, and by the end of the seventies, the Free School was one of the five largest free universities in the country, boasting a budget of more than a half million dollars a year.

While DuBé was building the Free School, the Denver Free University was also expanding, and together they produced a model for an independent free university that could survive by charging fees to its participants. Given a metropolitan population base and a reasonable number of relatively young, middle-class residents, the independent free university could succeed.

Independent free universities grew in other cities as well. In Indianapolis, in Washington, D.C., in San Francisco, in Tucson, and in Toronto, free universities began to enroll not just a couple of thousand participants—as in the heyday of the campus free university in the late sixties—but 5,000, and later more than 10,000, participants a year.

But the new independents learned a few lessons from the past and were determined to construct workable organizations built on financial and managerial skills. They did not want loose structure, group decisions, or a carefree attitude about income and expenses. Instead, management—much maligned and dreaded by earlier free university people—became a necessity. It would not be until 1977 that Robert Lewis and Dennis DuBé could offer at a free university conference a widely attended seminar on management skills, but the impetus for those concerns was evident in the formation of the independent free university model.

One such place where management was essential was in Oakland, California, near the home of the first Free University of Berkeley. Here free universities and countercultural institutions had come and gone so often that people were skeptical of any new organization that appeared on the scene, feeling that it would soon meet its demise as others had, in a quagmire of disorganization, disillusionment, and disorder. In fact, while fifty-five free universities have been started in California, only twelve currently exist.

Bart Brodsky, founder of the Open Education Exchange in Oakland, documented its beginning:

> The Open Education Exchange started June, 1974, with the counsel of the board of directors of the Berkeley Institute and a pledge of $100. Student registration was modest, yet a number of classes were very successful, and income from student registration covered continuing operational expenses.
>
> If this seems more like a financial report than a statement of philosophy, it is done so in recognition of the disastrous record of "community" enterprises. Social inertia imposes a curious dualism whereby community interest and fiscal management rarely go hand in hand. One instructor disappointed with our first catalog remarked, "The old Free University of Berkeley had a 32 page catalog with lavish graphics." I replied that the old Free University folded because it couldn't pay its bills. My friend noted, "Yes, their catalogs did get skimpy near the end. . . ." The point is that, although we are a non-profit institution, we will remain unapologetic about being a money-generating corporation.[5]

While financial mismanagement was the downfall of many a free university, national impact and concern reached their heights when another Bay Area free university disintegrated, with alienated teachers and a reputed lawsuit, in 1976. Its very name causes older free university people to shudder. Befitting of such a satanic tale, no other free university has taken the name—Heliotrope—since.

Heliotrope began in 1968 as a bright and promising independent fee-charging free university. The name Heliotrope came from plants whose flowers turned toward the sun. The early years saw Heliotrope grow like the other Bay Area free universities. Their catalogs were attractive and colorful. The courses were current and popular. Unlike some other free universities, Heliotrope gained some national publicity. A course on "Howling at the Moon," held in the evening on a grassy hillside in Berkeley, drew television crews, a couple of hundred aspiring howlers, and plenty of press notices.[6]

But Heliotrope was soon to acquire a reputation more as a money-making organization than as an educational one. An entrepreneurial pamphlet distributor published a booklet on how to start your own freestyle university, and using Heliotrope as an example, noted that profits could be made from one. When Heliotrope closed its doors in 1976, it left behind a good many disaffected and disillusioned teachers and participants. The news of the collapse of Heliotrope reverberated around the nation's free universities, and other free university leaders were disturbed by Heliotrope's reported profit-seeking, its eventual mismanagement and poor reputation, and the effect that its demise might have on their own reputations.

But by 1976, free universities had bounced back from their premature obituary in the *New York Times* in 1971. Their educational philosophy had been proven, three types of successful free universities had been developed, and perhaps most importantly, the free universities' target population had changed and expanded to include the general public as a whole, opening up new audiences and challenges in lifelong learning. Also, by the mid-seventies, the locus for a majority of free university activity had gone inland from the West and East coasts, where it had been in the sixties, to the Midwest. Kansas and Colorado became the leading free university states. Major free universities were located in such unhip, uncosmopolitan Midwestern cities as Kansas City, Missouri; Indianapolis, Indiana; Tulsa, Oklahoma; Wichita, Kansas; and Carbondale, Illinois.

By 1976, free universities had survived several death notices, doubts about their own philosophy and ability to manage their organization, and a recession. In 1975, the number of new free universities starting came out of the doldrums and hit twenty-four for the first time since 1970. More than twenty would start every year after, as free universities moved into a period of expansion.

EXPANSION

The year 1976 was another pivotal one for free universities. Not only would it mark the start of a period of expansion for free universities, but it would also be in 1976 that free university leaders would come to realize what had happened in the previous five years. During the early 1970s it was not readily apparent what the phenomenon of lifelong learning meant for free universities, what the decline of student activism and the counterculture indicated, or even what unique contribution free universities could make to adult education.

It was time to make a distinction between those free universities looking back and those free universities looking forward. For those looking back, either to an exclusive campus orientation or to the youthful counterculture, there were few prospects for growth or vitality. But for those looking forward to the concept of lifelong learning and appealing to the broad general public, there was promise indeed.

The recognition of that concept for free universities was elucidated by Community Free School director Dennis DuBé at the 1976 national free university conference in Louisville, Kentucky. There a skeptical National Public Radio (NPR) education reporter interviewed DuBé and others for a program on "Options in Education." Part of the NPR transcript reads

WENDY BLAIR (NPR): And so far the best definition we've heard comes from Dennis DuBé, who runs one of the most successful free universities in the country.

DENNIS DU BE: It's easy to tell us by what we aren't than what we are. The free universities, as a whole, have been, I think riding on a wave of nostalgic hippy-ism, or some imaginary leftism coming from the early attempts in California back in the Sixties. And there are a lot of things about free universities which are almost vestigial in the sense of how people who do free universities think about themselves and think about the function they're trying to fulfill.

JOHN MERROW (NPR): Well, that says to me, anyhow, that there's really not that much of a future for free universities. If most of them are largely recreation, largely vestigial, largely kind of middle-class rebellion that exists at the sufferance of the university itself, then the places like your institution are going to be few and far between in the future.[7]

Former free university leader Lona Jean Turner, in her analysis of that interview, outlined the importance of DuBé's comments, both one that Merrow missed and one that DuBé missed as well.

DuBé's comment about the vestigial nature of free universities is one of his most interesting, and one that Merrow failed to react to. As Merrow summarized DuBé's comments, he refers to free universities as "largely vestigial." But if I understand what DuBé said, it goes something like this: the people who do free universities today think about themselves and the function they're trying to fulfill in ways that are quite different from earlier, nearly vestigial views of what free universities were and what they did. This is not the same as saying that free universities are "largely vestigial." What is vestigial about free universities is a cultural image—the free university as a place where rich kids go to learn how to weave baskets, to overthrow the system, to make love, not war. This image of the free university is not simply vestigial, but *dead as an image*. The free university itself not only lives but continues in its unique contribution to community education in America.[8]

Turner then attempts to turn a backward-looking definition of free universities into a forward-looking one:

Though it may be easier ". . . to tell us by what we aren't than by what we are," it is increasingly important to stop defining ourselves in negative terms. Free universities, for all their diversity, must begin to define themselves positively as educational outreach systems that differ in significant ways from other such systems. In order to do that we must look at our history and development, recognizing that what DuBé calls "nostalgic hippyism" or "imaginary leftism" of the sixties did contribute to our beginnings, but we must remember that free universities have grown and prospered and changed, and continue to do so, into what is rapidly becoming the late seventies.[9]

Turner felt that four essential and unique features of free universities also weighed heavily in making free universities a popular notion with the general public in the seventies:

1. Free universities' protection and upholding of the First Amendment right to free speech, the educational implication of which is that any person should be able to teach anything he or she desires.

2. The interrelation between learning and citizen action, and the belief that learning should not be isolated from action but be the basis for it.

3. The attempt to meet locally defined needs. Turner notes that free universities attempt to meet community-defined needs rather

than create community needs and then supply the "necessary" programs.

4. The search for a sense of community. Turner says that urban and rural free universities alike function as social networks, connecting people who have similar interests and, possibly, similar values and goals.

Those characteristics underlying free universities and their purpose, Turner held, provided the continuity from the free universities' years on the college campus to their future in the community. Free universities still had some attractive external features—low cost, interesting courses, and informal atmosphere. Together the underlying principles behind free universities and their approach to learning would make free universities even more popular in the late seventies than they had been before.

The last half of the seventies was a time of growth, expansion, and stability. Free universities had not become institutionalized by any means, but they had become an acceptable alternative to both the public and more traditional educators. The numbers of participants continued to grow, especially in the large free universities, where enrollments topped 10,000 and even 15,000 participants a year in some of the larger free universities. The type of participants expanded from the young and college-educated to include middle-aged and older adults, professionals and business people, housewives and rural residents. Free universities also became more diversified. "Skills exchanges" formed, concentrating on practical and, later, vocational skills, downplaying thought and more academic courses. Different kinds of organizations sponsored free universities—a YMCA, a church, a library. Free universities gained some measure of stability. Three major sources of income—fees, sponsoring organizations, and local fundraising—combined to provide free universities with options for sustaining themselves. While still dependent on the personal commitment of their staff, staff turnover no longer threatened the organizations' existence.

The late seventies was definitely a positive time for free universities. Organizational concerns replaced philosophical or survival ones. Management, staff salaries, funding, publicity, marketing techniques, training, board and staff relations, all moved to the center stage as workshop topics and general needs.

The late seventies also saw the slow but steady growth of a

national organization for free universities and later learning networks, the Free University Network.

It started when Sue Maes and University for Man hosted a national free university conference in Manhattan, Kansas, in 1973 —the first of what became annual gatherings. The next year, the national organization was formed in Boulder, with three broad purposes: 1. to help people and communities start free universities, 2. to assist existing local organizations, and 3. to promote alternative education at the national level.

Begun at the Community Free School in Boulder, it soon moved to UFM in Manhattan, where it set up headquarters. It eventually expanded its activities to include a newsletter and publications, annual regional as well as national conferences, national publicity for free universities, some research, and occasional technical assistance.

Run by a board of directors composed of free university leaders elected by region, in 1978 the Network asked a number of respected educators to serve on a national advisory board. They were Sandra Cooper of the American Library Association; Jane Lichtman from the American Association for Higher Education; Fran Macy of the National Center for Educational Brokering; Denis Detzel of the McDonald's Corporation; futurist and consultant Ron Barnes; Roger Sell from the Western Interstate Commission of Higher Education; and adult educator Malcolm Knowles.

The Network also provided a national forum in which to debate and analyze the movement's changes. In the mid-seventies, it was an arena in which to debate the philosophy and structure of the "ideal free U." In the late seventies, it was a way to accept and even learn from different kinds of organizations. It also served to keep the increasingly different organizations together in one organization and to demonstrate the benefits of learning from operations different from one's own.

The end of the decade came with a cover photo on the magazine Lifelong Learning: The Adult Years, illustrating a young man teaching an elderly woman how to play the guitar at a free university. It was symbolic of the broader scope of free universities as well as the increasing recognition that free universities were enjoying.

Chapter 7

The Rural Story

In 1975 there were only one or two free universities in small towns, but Jim Killacky and Sue Maes of University for Man in Manhattan, Kansas, felt that the free university model was perfect for small communities.

At that time Kansas had several free universities, but all of them were on college campuses. The Wichita Free University, Neosho River Free School in Emporia, Free University in Lawrence, and the Other Term in Lindsborg appealed mainly to their campus constituencies.

University for Man was already a leader in the campus-community free university model. UFM was started in 1968 by a group of students and a humanities professor, Len Epstein. Although only seven courses were held that year, the program was strong enough to host the first national gathering of free universities. Sue Maes, then a student, became director of UFM while it was still in its infancy. After her graduation, she received a position in the Division of Continuing Education at Kansas State University to help foster UFM. Maes got started with UFM by attending its first course, "Man in the Year 2000." "It was over my head," she recalls, "but I enjoyed it." By helping Epstein host the first national gathering of free universities the next year, she was engaged in the national scene from the beginning. As a college free university, UFM was absorbed by campus issues. By national standards, however, UFM was hardly radical. A *New Yorker* article in 1971 on Maes presents a rather tame image of UFM, noting that it "has been supported by both the administration and the students of K-State from the start."[1]

By 1973, though, UFM began to shift its orientation from the campus to the community. By then, the war and other campus issues were winding down. An increasing number of community people were attending UFM classes, and that began to be reflected in its finances as well. Student government monies were cut because of the increased nonstudent participation, and UFM sought community money for its work, initially asking the local United Way for support.

The fervor of changing higher education had also waned a bit. "The energy generated from the free university concept found a new direction and a home in the community," Maes says.[2]

By the mid-seventies, UFM's participation included a good many community residents. It was receiving some support from the community, and its staff included nonstudents who were older than the college students on the staff in UFM.

In the next six years, UFM would grow to become one of the five largest free universities in the country, enrolling approximately 12,000 participants a year. About half now come from the K-State campus and half from the community of Manhattan, a city of 30,000.

Run from a large old fraternity house leased from the University Endowment Association, UFM has a staff of twenty-five people, the largest in the country, about half of them full-time and half part-time. On the staff are work-study students at Kansas State, college graduates in their twenties, free university veterans in their thirties and forties, and older citizens.

There are four divisions in the UFM organization. The campus-community staff puts out the brochure and its 300 class descriptions three times a year and works on special local events, like a weekly radio show, an international affairs lecture series, festivals, and social events. The outreach staff works with communities throughout the Midwest in setting up and running free universities, putting out a monthly rural community education newsletter, hosting conferences and workshops, and traveling to towns to visit programs and provide technical assistance. The appropriate-technology staff is UFM's most recent venture, specializing in weatherization and helping people conserve energy. In the summer of 1980 a $50,000 solar-heated greenhouse was added to the UFM facilities, where horticultural therapy programs for senior citizens and the handicapped will take place and appropriate-technology demonstrations will be presented.

The fourth division is the development office, a one-person office resulting from UFM's success and dependence on writing grants to create and sustain its many different projects. Those sponsoring agencies are on the local, state, and national levels. In the spring of 1980, for instance, UFM listed funding sources as Kansas State Division of Continuing Education, Student Government Association, United Way, state Comprehensive Employment and Training Act program, two federal education agencies, an independent clearinghouse in Washington, D.C., the state arts commission, the state economic development department, the U.S. Department of Energy, and the Kansas Farmers Union Green Thumb program.[3]

Like other free universities, UFM has spawned a number of community projects that have become independent or semi-autonomous, including a drug education center, a food cooperative, a community gardens program, a farmers market, and an alternative school for children.

One of these projects was a telephone crisis line, and one of its founders, Jim Killacky, a graduate student at K-State, joined the UFM staff in 1973. Killacky brought a sociological perspective, and a rural folksiness and charm that would fit in with small Kansas towns. Himself a native of a small town in Ireland, Killacky came to the United States at age seventeen and eventually became a student at Kansas State.

In 1974 Maes and Killacky conducted a series of humanities forums in small towns surrounding Manhattan. From those discussions about the future of the towns, local residents became interested in the UFM program and in seeing it replicated in their towns. As a result of that interest, UFM applied to an agency in Washington, the Fund for the Improvement of Postsecondary Education (FIPSE), for a grant to start free universities in small rural towns in Kansas. But federal attention was focused on urban areas, and the application was turned down. "What do we have to do?" asked Killacky at the time. "Burn down a small town?" But the next year the grant was awarded, along with a grant from ACTION for twelve VISTA volunteers to serve as coordinators in the small towns. Six towns were selected for the first year, three in north-central Kansas—Abilene, Clay Center, and Marysville—and three in northwestern Kansas—Norton, Oberlin, and Hoxie.

Although free universities had never been developed in a small town, Maes and Killacky started with the basic UFM model. UFM offered classes for no charge, received local funding, and had an advisory board of prominent local citizens. Those elements would remain in the rural free university. Before the VISTAs arrived, there was a good deal of groundbreaking to be done. Killacky in central Kansas and a UFM colleague in northwestern Kansas began to talk to local people about the UFM concept and the potential for a program in their town. A survey had been sent out, and almost twenty towns had responded with interest, from which the first six towns were chosen. But a survey is one thing; starting something is another.

In the next few months, Killacky would spend hours visiting with local people, explaining the concept, gaining their trust, and convincing them this was not another outside federal poverty project that would pull up roots as soon as the federal money spigot was turned off.

Talking with local people often involved more conversation about wheat, weather, and sports than about free universities. At one porch sitting, Killacky talked with a potential advisory board member about farming for forty-five minutes and finally asked her, "Well, Mrs. Arnholdt, would you like to be on our community education advisory board?" "Oh, I'm not Mrs. Arnholdt," the woman replied. "The Arnholdts live at the next farmhouse down the road."

With the formation of advisory boards and the support of some local citizens, the programs took shape. They were usually called community education programs because the term *free university* might have negative connotations. When the VISTAs arrived, they completed work on the first class session. The next year, six more towns were selected, while the first towns picked up their funding for the program from local sources. In Abilene, the city recreation department took over the program and integrated it with its recreation classes. In Clay Center, the county provided direct funding for the project. In Norton, local funds and CETA funds ran the program.

When the project ended, an amazingly high percentage of the towns continued funding of the programs. Five years later, ten of the twelve original programs are still in existence. Among them are some of the more active community education programs in the state, such as Rooks County Community Education, TREE program in Wakeeney, and Clay County Community Education.

What was even more important than just their physical existence was that other towns heard about the programs and wanted to start their own. Within the next two years, another twelve programs were started around the state. No longer did UFM have to seek out towns and sell the free university idea; now people were asking for assistance in starting their own program.

One of the original towns, Hoxie, was the smallest of the twelve towns, and the program did not survive there. UFM staffers speculated that a community education program could not make it in towns of less than 3,000 people. So when people in the town of Olsburg, located just twenty miles north of Manhattan, and with a total population of 170 people, asked for assistance in starting a free university, the UFMers were hesitant. But they traveled to Olsburg and met with six or seven local residents, many of whom had taken courses or even taught at UFM in Manhattan. It was suggested that people in Olsburg could take UFM courses in Manhattan, but they wanted their own program.

The group was led by newcomers to Olsburg, Barb and Jay Nelson and Pat and Ken Embers, and some old-timers, like Gerry Westling and his wife Lois, who ran the post office. Although Mr. Westling was skeptical at first about the program, he lent his support.

Two weeks later, a community interest survey was sent to townspeople to announce a town meeting on the program and to solicit ideas for classes. That Sunday, Gerry stood outside the Lutheran church in Olsburg and passed out the surveys to churchgoers as they entered. An announcement from the pulpit explained the survey. After the service, Gerry collected the surveys at the front door as people left. In one hour, he had a 100-percent response rate from a third of the town.

Later that month the town meeting was held, with almost forty people attending—about one fourth of the town—including little children and their grandmothers. Course topics were suggested, ranging from Irish poets to making beef jerky, and people volunteered to teach and help out on the steering committee.

Those humble beginnings led to the formation of the Olsburg Rural Educational Opportunities (OREO) program, which is now one of the more active programs in the state and has earned the distinction of being the world's smallest free university.

Since then, more than fifty classes have been offered a year, with enrollments far exceeding the population of the town, as rural residents from the surrounding area join in. Not only classes but also projects have been sponsored by OREO. An oral history of Olsburg was begun, and six members of the community, all more than eighty years old, were invited to be on a panel. "You could see their eyes light up three weeks ahead of time," remembers Barb Nelson. The programs were taped, and a book coinciding with the town's 100th anniversary was printed. A speaker on death and dying, himself close to death with a terminal disease, was brought in for three days of seminars, talks, and church services. A summer flea market was instituted so that local people could sell their garden produce and handicrafts. With each seller paying OREO $4 for the booth, the project earns its $300 yearly budget at the annual flea market.

When UFM organizers went back to Olsburg six months later, amazed at the project's success, they asked the people of Olsburg why they wanted a free university. "We wanted to meet people," was one of the primary reasons. In a town of 170? Even in a town of 170, society has divided newcomers from old-timers, the young from the old, so that people did not have opportunities to mix. The OREO project provided that social setting in which people could not only learn and teach but also interact socially and work on building a better community.

It has also brought people of different age groups together. When a fifty-five-year-old man taught blacksmithing, Barb Nelson's twelve-year-old daughter Sarah signed up for the course, much to the surprise of her mother.

What effect has the OREO program had on Olsburg? In testimony before the Kansas legislature, Barb Nelson said,

> Our OREO program has many benefits. An increased awareness of community, an opportunity for people to get to know others in situations other than the traditional means such as churches, public school, or 4-H. OREO crosses many lines and

has become an event promoting community development and an elimination of barriers. Craft courses have inspired new directions. Courses in exploring the local area have created an interest in the past. A course in poetry reading has opened new means of communication. A medical series has brought doctors into discussions with people to a mutual benefit. A volleyball game, a jam session, Christmas caroling and a sing-a-long, all bring folks together to enjoy an event.

Community education is needed as a means of increasing community spirit. We are not talking about economic development. We are talking about community development on cultural and educational levels in communities who desire it. It is non-competitive, nonbureaucratic, people-oriented programs. Community education is worthwhile. With it the spirit of the community will be promoted and expanded; without it, rural Kansas will not die, it will languish.[4]

By 1979, twenty-five free universities were active in Kansas, enrolling more than 31,000 participants a year. All but the Wichita Free University charged no fees to the learner, believing that their success was attributed in large measure to offering classes to everyone regardless of ability to pay. "We're open to everyone in the community," said Mary Clare Dwyer of the Rooks County Community Education program. The no-fee aspect of the UFM model also meant that many more courses could be offered than would be cost-efficient if fees had to support the classes. While nearby community colleges can offer three to five successful classes for a fee of $20 per person, the community education program can offer twenty-five classes, involving hundreds of people and stimulating new ideas.

New ideas in rural Kansas? While the UFM organizers had feared courses in small towns would be the stereotypical tractor repair and macrame, that did not prove to be the case. The Norton County program offered the "Life of Willa Cather," the famous novelist, including a trip to her home in Nebraska. People to People in Dighton offered courses on new farming techniques. The Clay County program offered a course on "Comparing the Sixteenth and Twentieth Centuries."

Not only did community education stir up new ideas, but it brought out hidden talents as well. Skills and knowledge that local residents did not know were present came to the surface. In small towns, where financial, economic, and physical resources are scarce, and people may be hours from a college or university, the human resources in the town are valuable. The community education program helped discover more of them. In Tampa, Kansas, a town of 200, Mark Roberts approached Killacky and told him that he wanted to teach creative writing for the Herington community education program. He told Killacky that he had written twenty-two novels and scripts for such television shows as "Mission Impossible" and "Star Trek." Killacky decided to check his claims out and asked local leaders in the community about Roberts. No one knew of Roberts, or his writing skill, until Jim asked the post office clerk. "He keeps me in business," the clerk confirmed, "with all his manuscripts coming and going to Hollywood." Previously unknown in his own community, Roberts taught a highly successful creative writing course to twelve enthusiastic participants.

The UFM rural model also proved to be cost-effective for the community and the state.

By early 1979, the programs were so successful that more towns wanted technical assistance from UFM than it could provide. An eighteen-minute color film was made to show to local townspeople, and a *Rural and Small Town Community Education* manual was written. To provide more towns with the technical assistance in starting a program, state legislation was suggested.

THE FIRST FREE UNIVERSITY LEGISLATION

There is a Kansas tale that state legislation takes at least four years. The first year the bill is introduced, but doesn't get read. The second year the bill is read. The third year the bill is read and discussed. The fourth year the lawmakers say, "Haven't we seen this before?" and take some action.

So it was inconceivable that anyone, from astute political observer to state legislator, would have guessed that it would take only ten weeks for free university legislation to go through two committees, pass both state houses, and be signed by the governor, and for an appropriations measure to be introduced and acted upon.

The idea came about when Gary Griffiths of Clay Center, who helped start and fund the Clay County Education Program, and who was on UFM's state advisory board, suggested that UFM see state representative Jim Braden, a Republican from Wakefield, in Clay County, about state support.

In January of 1978, UFM had worked with the Associated Students of Kansas in presenting an "Eggs and Issues" breakfast on community education for the Kansas legislators, but other than that, the free university staff had no knowledge about the lawmaking body or the legislative process. That point was made clear when the UFMers visited Representative Braden in the state capitol and asked to talk about their idea. The representative had only five minutes, and the free university people were interrupted for three of those five minutes by an influential lobbyist. As the representative dashed down the hall to his next meeting, UFM quickly learned that the time to talk was *not* during the legislative session.

During the summer and fall, UFM considered various possibilities, using to a great extent the wisdom and experience of Lou Douglas, a retired political science professor who was donating a year of his time to work for UFM. Similar community education legislation in other states was researched, but none focused on private nonprofit groups such as UFM's free universities. Using some of the language of other legislation, but substituting some very different substantive concepts and direction, a rough idea was put together.

The UFMers met with Braden, who became very interested in the concept, and decided on some specifics:

1. The money would be only to start new programs, not maintain them, as Braden wanted no part of ongoing state support. The vitality, he said, was in local control.

2. The legislation would be specific to the UFM rural model for free universities—volunteer teachers, advisory boards, local initiative, classes with citizen teachers coming from the community.

3. The term *community resource program* was chosen to designate the idea. There is tremendous confusion and overlap in adult learning terms nationwide, and *community education* as a term was already confusing, with community colleges, public schools, and others all claiming it. The term *free university* was deemed a little misleading for these rural noncollegiate activities. Also, the idea of community resources appealed to both UFM and Braden

as both descriptive of the human resources in a small community and promoting the overall community development of that town, which they both felt the rural free university did. The new term was also appropriate, as this legislation would be unique, describing a Kansas approach to lifelong learning and community development.

4. UFM wanted the legislation, if passed, to be administered by the Kansas Department of Economic Development, not the state department of education. The economic development department was accustomed to working with community groups, and UFM felt that the state department of education would reorient the program toward public schools to the exclusion of community groups.

In January, Braden introduced the legislation, and it was referred to the house education committee. There, several small-town supporters, including Gary Griffiths of Clay Center and Barb Nelson of Olsburg, who came with her infant son in a knapsack on her back, testified before the education committee. After a brief skirmish with public school officials who wanted the legislation to be administered by the state department of education, the committee approved the legislation.

The house voted on the bill 100–25, and the bill went to the senate. There UFM also testified, and the senate committee approved the bill as well. The full senate then voted 31–7 in favor of it. A week later the governor signed the bill, making it law.

In the appropriations session later in the month, an appropriation of $37,500 was approved for the first year. The entire legislative process took less than ten weeks, and it astounded and surprised just about everyone.

Newsweek magazine later interviewed UFM and Braden and came to small towns as part of a national story on free universities, initiated by the legislation's passage. Kansas State president Duane Acker presented UFM's first "Grassroots Education" award to representative Braden at UFM's annual summer meeting. Later UFM hired Clay County Education Program coordinator Bev Wilhelm to head up its technical assistance efforts under the act. And one year later, eleven community groups had been funded by the legislation to start new free universities.

Chapter 8
Philosophy

Whether shouted stridently from a student podium in the early 1960s or casually mentioned in passing during a rural town meeting in the late 1970s, the philosophy of the free university has provided the foundation of the movement. That philosophy has been the *raison d'être* for many a dedicated free university administrator unrewarded in other ways. One of the great victories for free universities is that their philosophy has been accepted as sound practice by the general public and many traditional educators.

The philosophy behind free universities has been the occasion for joyous optimism, for desperate moans, for student pleas, and for confident faith in people. It has often been played down and has continually been debated. Occasionally it has threatened rifts between free universities, but it has always remained at the core of the free university operation.

Although the philosophy behind free universities has never become an unchallenged dogma, it has been the standard shield against charges that free universities are just another organization offering noncredit classes.

To understand the philosophy behind free universities, one can begin with a set of ideas agreed to by almost all in free universities. From there, the philosophy diverges into various viewpoints on the role of education, change, and human nature itself. That discussion is still going on—at times muted, at times vociferous.

The most commonly accepted definition of a free university was formulated by the Free University Network in 1977. It is "A free university is an organization which offers noncredit classes to the general public in which 'anyone can teach and anyone can learn.'"

Other definitions do not contradict the Network's. Jane Lichtman, in her work on free universities, wrote, "A free university is a community learning center that connects people who want to teach or learn with the resources to meet their needs."[1] Michael Rossman says that it is "a cooperative association of voluntary learning groups investigating a broad curriculum in a variety of old and new styles."[2]

But if the philosophy has been important to free universities in the past, it will also be central to their future.

The need to maintain a unique philosophy is still justified. As free universities continue to grow, people are going to ask what is so unique about them. A lot of organizations offer noncredit classes. What is so different about free universities? The answers are important.

The three core concepts behind free universities, those which are professed by the most free universities with the least disagreement and that constitute the basic uniqueness of free universities in adult learning today are discussed below.

The responsibility for learning rests with the teacher and the participants. Free universities promote self-directed learning. They do not guarantee learning. Learning is not a consumer product.

This philosophical tenet has many ramifications.

One is both philosophical and structural. It is Lichtman's definitive statement about being a learning center that connects people who want to teach or learn. Free universities are a linking system, not an institution as such. An institution takes responsibility—makes demands and in return delivers—whether it be a product or services. But a linking mechanism can make no such promises. It is a neutral passageway like a telephone line with no control or claim over the quality of content transmitted. The only guarantee is that the linking system will be operable and neutral.

This concept of a linking mechanism with little or no responsibility over what is taught and learned does not stem from a lack of concern over the learning process or a careless attitude about quality. Indeed, it is precisely that intense interest in what is taught, and how, that led free universities to this neutral, but at the same time, inquisitive and intensely concerned position.

The linking mechanism position has, of course, met with a great deal of resistance conceptually from people and organizations used to institutional modes of behavior. But it has also gained a measure of respect and acceptance. That acceptance has extended even to the Internal Revenue Service, which has made two guidelines supporting this contention. The first IRS statement is a definition of organizations that are free universities, even though the IRS does not name them as such. In the definition, the IRS refers to an "educational clearinghouse" which acts as a go-between for teachers and learners. In the second, the IRS makes allowances for teachers of free universities, again, without specifically naming free universities, to be independent contractors rather than employees of the organization. This is important to free universities, from a financial as well as philosophical standpoint.

A second ramification is the free university's support of the notion of self-directed learning. If the free university is not responsible for the learning, then it must be up to the learner and teacher. The free university places heavy responsibility on the learner for his or her own learning. This brings up the recurring argument about whether people know what is good for them, and free universities definitely come down on the side of "yes," or at least that people *should* know what is good for them. As consumers, learners ought to be able to distinguish a good class from a poor one. If they cannot, how can they judge an automobile, a mate, a political candidate, a value? The consumer education movement in health, products, law, and other services has been an unwitting ally in this contention. If a learner does not know when he or she is learning, is he or she learning? If a person cannot distinguish a good class from a poor one, how can that learner develop any competency in the content of the actual class?

This battle is a long one and is far from over. Some educators are attempting to promote mandatory continuing education for professionals.[3] This could be easily extended to the general public. This movement is based in large measure on financial greed, but its premise lies in a contention that people do not know what is good for them and thus must be made by law to return to the classroom. It is a dismal picture for any believer in human freedom and growth: to think that one could be sixty-five years old—having been through compulsory schooling for eighteen years in public education, six years in college and graduate work, and twenty years in mandated professional training—but never have been in the position of being able to determine his or her own learning. This contrary position rests in large measure with the idea that people are always deficient, never knowledgeable enough, never capable enough on their own.

This brings us to the free university view of human nature, which is a stubbornly positive and naive one. John McKnight, professor at Northwestern University and longtime friend of learning networks, uses the old water glass analogy to explain it. Traditional institutions look at the half-empty water glass, representing people as learners, and point to the fact that the glass is not full and there is much emptiness there. Free universities and learning networks, on the other hand, look and say, "Yes, but there's a lot of water there." The difference is not one of perspective but of reinforcement. For if we reinforce the deficiencies, by grades, progress reports, or escalating degree requirements, we associate learning with being inadequate—at least in people's minds. But if we reinforce what is there, we do not deny the need to learn more, but we proceed from a position of self-confidence and pride about one's own knowledge. This is an important self-motivator to learning. If a person with no credentials and no formal education nevertheless recognizes that he or she has a good deal of skill and knowledge, then that person can comfortably deal with learning more, knowing that he or she does have some knowledge.

The opposite reaction occurs when we emphasize the negative. Counselors of minority women discovered this negative attitude when they asked the women about their formal schooling. Many women would say, "I don't have an education," although they had high school diplomas. Twenty years ago they would have been proud of that high school diploma and would have said that they did have an education. Today, the educational ante has been upped again, and by the time these women, or their daughters, have a college degree, "an education" will have been upped further. That emphasis on the negative, on "not having," affects not just minorities, not just those with no or little formal education, but all of us.

Free university leaders look at young children, full of curiosity and inquisitiveness, as witnesses to the innate self-directed motivation to learn.

Free universities throughout their history have been trumpeting the joys of self-directed learning. Robert Greenway wrote at the start of the seventies, "Courses organized in the freedom of free universities often reflect a sense of ecstatic wonder, this 'new' rediscovery of being alive, of having a 10-million-year storage of life-wisdom in our blood. We have lost the IDEA OF HOW RICH AND INFINITE OUR CAPACITIES REALLY ARE!"[4]

John McKnight follows up with another analogy.

Mark Twain once said, "If your only tool is a hammer, then all problems look like nails." Society has a great commitment to tools that don't work that well. Many systems just don't work and require that people be nails, not screws, bolts, or whatever they naturally are. Learning networks were a better hammer. Now I see learning networks as doing something different— they're not a hammer, but a new tool. Schools (the hammer) see people with deficiencies that need to be corrected. Learning networks see people with skills and knowledge to share. Learning networks are meeting needs.[5]

Anyone can learn. As this book is being written in the early 1980s, the concept that anyone can learn is not particularly startling. But just ten years ago, when a series of restrictions barricaded many a college course, and when the adage "You can't teach an old dog new tricks" was in style, the concept was a challenging one.

On college campuses, so-called advanced courses were protected from students by a number of prerequisite courses. Off campus, adult classes were few, and social attitudes were geared against continued learning. "I have my education," was a typical comment from an adult, as if "education" were a packaged and obtainable quantity. The view that most adults could not or did not want to learn was widely held. Part of the reason for this was that knowledge was, and still is in many quarters, seen in a hierarchical way. There are steps that lead up the knowledge pyramid, and one cannot move to the next step without having reached a lower one. Like a pyramid, the room for climbing the knowledge pyramid narrows the further up one gets, so that only a few are allowed to reach the top. Each step is controlled by someone who has reached a higher level. Magic keys are unlocked to a higher knowledge step only to those selected. The others must fall by the wayside. Grades, entrance exams, graduate degrees, all are used to regulate the traffic up the knowledge pyramid, to weed out those not eligible to climb higher, and to distinguish those who are allowed up.

In contrast, free universities adhere to an outlook that regards knowledge as horizontal.

It does not deny the rigor or depth of knowledge, skill, or training needed to conquer a given body of knowledge, but it does say that the entrance point to knowledge can be anywhere and that anyone should be able to learn anything at any point.

An underlying assumption is that gatekeeping knowledge denies an individual a basic right to learn. Where would we be if Lincoln had been denied his attorney's license because he did not have a law degree, if Edison had been denied his light bulb patent because he did not have a degree, if Mark Twain had been prohibited from publishing his books because he didn't have a degree in English? How many geniuses, potential inventors, creators have been stunted because of restrictions in our access to knowledge today?

A corollary is that everyone should keep on learning. Not only can the unwashed learn, but those who have considerable expertise and knowledge by whatever standard should also be keen to the opportunity to learn more, even from those—and sometimes especially from those—who are less learned. When the attitude sets in that one knows enough and can't learn anything more, then perhaps that person's knowledge is already obsolete.

One free university staff person ran into an elderly man who showed up early for the decoupage class. "Are you the teacher or a learner?" asked the staff person. "Well, I'm the teacher," replied the old man, "but I'm always learning more too." It is that attitude which epitomizes the ideal learning attitude.

Anyone can teach. Perhaps the most controversial and problematic tenet in the free university faith is that anyone can teach anything.

From the first, free university philosophy has been that anyone should be welcome to teach a course. This article has been the most important one in the free university creed and, not unexpectedly, also the hardest one to follow.

But the philosophy is at the heart of what makes a free university different and—more than that—unique in American education today.

"Each one of us has some knowledge, skill, idea, or experience that someone else would like to know," goes a typical rural free university refrain. That sentiment expresses the worth of the individual, the belief that each one of us knows something that someone else would like to know. With the unlimited number of topics adults want to learn about today, and the increasing knowledge of citizens today, that idea is readily accepted, even in conservative communities where the belief in the individual is strong.

But the idea that anybody can teach goes beyond mere invitation to citizens to share their skills. It says that anyone should be able to teach *anything* he or she wants to. (Most free universities would add, "anything that is legal.") To sustain such a radical notion, free universities point directly to the U.S. Constitution.

Free universities maintain that the First Amendment's guarantee of freedom of speech is provision enough to allow any person the right to teach any idea or thought he or she desires. If a person has the right to speak his or her views to another person, why not to a group? If it is a group, why not call it a class? Says one free university, "In the true spirit of American democracy, citizens have a chance to offer their views, however unorthodox, to other citizens."

Attorney Lori Andrews, in her research on the legality of teaching self-care health classes, found some court decisions that seem to justify this stance:

For example, in Martin vs Struthers, 319 U.S. 141, 143 (1943), the Supreme Court noted that "the authors of the First Amendment knew that novel and unconventional ideas might disturb the complacent, but they choose to encourage a freedom which they believed essential if vigorous enlightenment was ever to triumph over slothful ignorance."

In Griswold vs Connecticut, 381 U.S. 479, 482 (1965), a doctor and Planned Parenthood director were convicted of aiding and abetting in the use of contraceptives in violation of a Connecticut statute by giving information, instruction, and medical advice to married people as the means of preventing conception. In reversing the convictions, the Court noted that "the State may not, consistent with the First Amendment, contract the spectrum of available knowledge. The right to freedom of speech and press includes not only the right to utter or to print, but the right to distribute, the right to receive, the right to read, . . . and freedom of inquiry, freedom of thought, and freedom to teach. . . ."

The right-to-teach argument was successful in a Colorado case regarding a health course. In Hurley v. People, 99 Colo. 510, 63 P. 2d 1227 (1936), a layperson conducted a school for healing, offering a 72-hour course dealing primarily with posture. Although the trial court found him guilty of the unauthorized practice of medicine and chiropractic, the Colorado Supreme Court reversed the lower court's decision. They held that a Colorado citizen has a constitutional right to teach any branch of learning that is not inherently injurious or harmful to the public health, safety or morals and to charge for his services.[6]

The free university's main weapon against chicanery, ineptitude, or hidden agendas on the part of teachers who may not be offering constructive classes is that of honest course descriptions. "If a person wants to teach a German class and knows only ten words of German, fine," says one free university staff person. "We'll put in the catalog description that he only knows ten words but is willing to teach them."

Free university instructors who have not been honest in their qualifications have not been allowed to teach again. If students complain about their teachers, the classes are investigated by the free university. If the complaints are borne out, the teachers are not allowed to teach again.

Many a free university administrator has heard the inevitable question, "What if someone wants to teach brain surgery?" Aside from the fact that no one in the fifteen-year history of free universities, with an estimated 200,000 classes and more than a million learners, has yet tried to teach brain surgery, the question is answered in several ways, depending on the free university. Some would say sure, as long as it isn't practiced; some would refuse to allow such a course; some would balance the course with one taught by a medical authority on brain surgery; others would try to blunt the approach by suggesting that the teacher question current surgery techniques or be on a panel discussion with doctors; some would make very clear the teacher's qualifications.

John Merrow, in his National Public Radio program on free universities in 1976, carried that theme to its extreme in an interview with Meredith McElroy, director of the New Orleans Free University:

MERROW: Suppose I came and said, "I'd like to teach a course in auto mechanics?"

MC ELROY: Terrific. We've been needing somebody to teach auto mechanics for a long time. . . .

MERROW: But the point is— I don't know anything about auto mechanics, and you didn't ask me if I knew anything about it.

MC ELROY: Well, if you don't know anything about it, then you shouldn't be asking me to teach a course in auto mechanics. People don't volunteer to teach things they don't know anything about.

MERROW: You're willing to take that on faith.

MC ELROY: Yeah. Because they don't do it. It's never happened.

MERROW: Somehow there's a kind of marvelous naiveté there. I could just walk in and say, "I'd like to do anything. . . ."

MC ELROY: A person doesn't want to get up in front of a bunch of people and make a fool of him or herself.

MERROW: Let me try another example: Suppose I want to teach a course in Indo-Psychotherapy, which is a new form of Western Semi-Consciousness to elevate your mind.

MC ELROY: I really feel like all of this is sort of hokey. I don't know if that is. . . . I feel like you're making things up that don't make any sense.

MERROW: Well, I am because of what you said—where the teachers are coming from.

MC ELROY: You're not asking me if you can teach a Free University course. You're trying to make up hokey things, and that's not what people do when they come to offer Free University courses. They're sincerely interested in sharing what they know.

MERROW: Suppose I'm sincerely interested in sharing what I know, but I don't know very much. That's really where I'm at.

MC ELROY: Then you can share it. And if you don't know very much, and you want to share what you know, and you think there might be other people who might be interested in the same thing, and some of them might even know more than you do, then you can offer a Free University class, and say in your description that you know something about this and you want to know more, and you want to tell people what you know and who know less than you, and have other people come in and share what they know, too. Then you can do that.

MERROW: Now, I can see where that would work very well in macrame and making stain glass windows or in auto mechanics, but it seems to me that there are some very real areas of a curriculum where that could be downright dangerous.

MC ELROY: I don't see any danger. I don't see any danger in the free exchange of knowledge.[7]

The rationale behind allowing brain surgery to be taught is not mere dogmatism. It rests in a proven and tested belief that some uncommon ideas may eventually lead to some positive and enormously beneficial developments.

Whole categories of classes branded as unorthodox or just plain wrong by traditional institutions have been allowed in free university catalogs. Free universities sense that, while out of ten crazy ideas, nine may be no good, that tenth idea may turn out to be something important to society. If we quash all ten ideas, which we would have to do because we don't know beforehand which idea will prove accurate, we quash creativity, imagination, and in the end, all social progress.

Thus, in the early 1970s free universities allowed courses on legal matters to be taught, breaking the sanctity of the law office. Later a national wave of books and activities teaching the lay person legal matters swept the nation. In the mid-1970s free universities offered an increasing number of holistic health-care courses. They were branded ineffectual and improper, with such crazy notions as acupuncture, foot massage, reflexology, and iridiology. Self-care is now increasingly recognized by traditional institutions as important and useful. The same goes for free university courses in alternative sources of energy, at first called ridiculous and now applauded by everyone from the president on down.

The well-established notion of quality control usually comes up as well. How does a free university guarantee that its courses aren't all poor quality? Well, it doesn't. But the free university also maintains that no other institution can guarantee or define quality either.

Robert Pirsig, in his book *Zen and the Art of Motorcycle Maintenance*, has an amusing introduction to that perplexing question. The hero of his story is a college professor in the state of Montana. Every so often his dean would walk past his desk and tell him, "I'm so *happy* you're teaching *Quality* this quarter. Hardly anybody *is* these days." After several repeated comments to this effect by the dean, the college professor asks himself, "What the hell is Quality? What is it?" and then proceeds for the next seventy-seven pages to try to define quality, to no avail.[8]

What is quality? Who determines quality? How does an educational administrator *know* whether or not someone is qualified, since the administrator cannot possibly grasp the depth of knowledge needed in a variety of topics—from auto mechanics to interpersonal relations? What is quality to one person might not be to another.

If we knew what quality was, it would not be very difficult to install it as a permanent feature of the educational institution. But the standards for quality in more formal educational institutions, based on post-baccalaureate degrees, are no more valid—and most free university leaders would probably argue a good deal less valid—than learner feedback.

The ten-word course in German is not too far off the mark as an actual example. Although many people would consider the course poor quality, it may be just the right course for someone going to Germany for two weeks and wanting to know just ten words of German.

Many people have had painful experiences with college language courses, reading nineteenth-century poems one word at a time with a dictionary, not learning how to get to the train station, and feeling tense and uptight about their language deficiency later on. In contrast, Communiversity in Kansas City offered a course in conversational German—in a bar. The course emphasized conversation, even poor conversation, and the deliberate use of the informal tavern atmosphere encouraged a feeling of looseness, of willingness to make mistakes, and thus eliminated tensions.

OTHER IDEAS ABOUT LEARNING

In addition to these three fundamental ideas in the free university philosophy, there are a host of others of no little importance.

Informal structure. Free universities are relaxed, enjoyable, and informal. There should be as little interference as possible with the experience of people interacting with people. By keeping the structure informal, the free university is able to maintain flexibility, responsiveness, and its primary educational mission of linking learners with teachers.

Credentials as meaningless. Free universities tend to regard credentials as meaningless except as artificial guideposts for formal educational or career advancement. Since free universities are not involved in either formal education or career advancement, they do not see a need for credentials. There does not appear to be any substantiated, intrinsic value in credentials. They serve to separate people, weed out, and provide gaps in society, but these distinctions are not very helpful to society as a whole. There is no need to reinforce a black teenager's feelings of defeat and hopelessness by pointing out that he or she does not have a college degree, an apprentice certificate, a union card, or membership in an honorary professional association. In a society built on credentials, it is difficult to pursue this tenet of noncredentials too far. Yet free universities have been successful in turning down both threats and temptations to credentials. Association with credits, degrees, continuing education units, and other forms of artificial educational measurement have not been undertaken by free universities.

The free university rationale for noncredit, uncredentialed learning has been backed up by some positive practical reasons as well.

Studies by the Carnegie Commission on Nontraditional Study in 1972 showed that more than half the adults surveyed indicated a desire for noncredit learning, as opposed to credit courses, at any given time. Undoubtedly that figure has either remained above the majority line or increased since the early seventies. By offering noncredit learning, free universities are responding to the wishes of a majority of the adult-learning public.

The community as a learning environment. The average community is a desolate wasteland of noncommunication, an area of superficial, false, or needless little tidbits of facts. The learning environment is dull and unstimulating; redundant billboards portray simple objects for purchase, and neon signs blast out trivia or advocate consumption.

We see little in our morning walk, gaze at few exciting posters or billboards, pass no storefronts encouraging production rather than consumption, overlook what few art objects may lie in our path, and rarely stop to talk to a friend about economics, philosophy, or music.

In addition to seeing the community as the ideal learning environment and striving in many small ways to make the community more of an educational utopia than it is, free universities also highlight existing learning resources in the community. Since most of us spend most of our lives in the community and not within the halls of a university, our learning takes its cues from the community environment. That environment can and should be more stimulating, and free universities see themselves as promoting this kind of integration of learning in the community.

Linking knowledge and action. It is becoming increasingly difficult to maintain that knowledge is neutral or should be. It is also harder to see why knowledge should not be linked to action. Organizations can be as fair as possible in presenting all sides of an issue, but in fact we have few neutral institutions in our country. By separating knowledge from action, an informed citizenry is discouraged from participating in our society. Free universities see themselves as providing forums in which positive constructive action can evolve, and while free universities often do not sponsor that action, they definitely promote and encourage classes to turn into projects and discussion into development.

Process over content. Although free universities value the kinds of courses they offer, the primary accomplishment, in terms of educational value to the learner, is in the process of learning in an independent and self-directed way. If learners experience learning "under their own power," the importance of that motivation and self-direction will be evident, regardless of the subject matter involved.

Low-cost and/or free education. Free universities strive to make their learning as low-cost as possible, not just for marketing reasons but because learning should not be a consumer product, another item with a price tag, or an expense available only to those who can afford it. If lifelong learning is to be plentiful, it must be affordable.

Responsiveness to the community's characteristics. Free universities are different, but each free university is local in nature, decentralized, and intent on responding to the characteristics of the community it serves. Thus, there has been little or no standardization of educational practice in free universities. The free university's mission has been to look inward to its own community. Rather than trying to make the community conform to its wishes, the free university has responded to the community.

Education for social change. Since the beginning of free universities, in the hearts and minds of many free university people, there has been the element of education for social change. Education has usually been used for some greater purpose in our society. For free universities, that greater purpose has usually been a better society—one more responsive to human needs, to the poor, to the ideals of a democracy, to the development of the poorer nations on Earth and international understanding. Within that broad framework, free universities have fostered and welcomed a variety of approaches to positive and constructive social change. Free universities have not embraced any particular causes, ideologies, or political or economic views, but they have encouraged others to express their views and to explore ways in which to promote prosperity, social equality, and progress.

As is the case with many religious and philosophical faiths, the faithful do not always practice what is preached. Throughout the history of free universities, there has been much discussion and controversy over the worth of each one of the philosophical points. Many free universities restrict teachers in one way or another—some as strictly as in traditional institutions, some in only minor ways. Others censor course topics, no matter who teaches them. Wine making is taboo somewhere, witchcraft not allowed somewhere else. No political or religious courses are allowed at Open University in Washington, D.C. On the other hand, the Baltimore School in Baltimore "reject[s] all political courses that promote capitalism or any form of authoritarianism."

But that is the character of free universities—localized, decentralized, autonomous. There are no state regulations, accreditation associations, or other external forces to force standardization of philosophy upon free universities. So some free universities will continue to stress that all courses must be free of charge; others will contend that individual instructors have a right to charge; others will maintain that any course should be offered; others that only "quality" courses must be offered.

Promoting the free university philosophy has varied through the years. In the early years, the promotion was strident, loud, definite, and contrasting. In the early 1970s, it was underplayed, not yet accepted as true even by free universities. As the concepts have gained more legitimacy, they have again come out in the open, but with more confidence and less shouting. Having gained a place in the educational world, free universities are more apt to state their philosophy in the catalogs confidently, but without capital letters.

EDUCATIONAL THEORISTS

The free university movement has not been without its educational theorists and occasionally even a hero. Free university people themselves have rarely delved into educational theory, concentrating instead on putting theory into practice. But they have drawn on educational theorists and, along the way, may even have influenced them.

In the 1960s free universities drew upon the writings of Paul Goodman and Carl Rogers to support their philosophy. Goodman, with his books *Compulsory Mis-Education* and *Growing Up Absurd* in the mid-sixties, helped the free universities with their critique of higher education. Goodman was hired by San Francisco State's Experimental College to teach for a semester and said, "I'm invited to be on the staff of every free university in the land. I wish I could, but I don't have the time."[9]

Rogers was instrumental in helping change free university learning, and much adult learning as a whole, from a purely cognitive teacher-to-student process to an affective and more equal experience. Rogers, a counselor and psychotherapist, moved from his theories of client-centered therapy into nondirective teaching, using the same principles of self-determination and learner orientation. Rogers asked, "If in therapy it is possible to rely upon the capacity of a client to deal constructively with his life situation, and if the therapist's aim is best directed towards releasing that capacity, then why not apply this hypothesis and this method in teaching?"[10]

In the early 1970s free university people were quick to embrace the writings of Ivan Illich and Paulo Freire. Illich, with his stunning analysis of the formal school system, *Deschooling Society*, published in 1971, provided an analysis not only of formal schools but also of ways in which free universities and learning networks could be formed in the community. Illich suggested neutral channels for teacher-student interaction, which he called "learning webs." As a direct result of a visit to Illich's center in Cuernavaca, Mexico, Denis Detzel and Robert Lewis started the Learning Exchange in Evanston, Illinois, based on Illich's theory. Illich not only provided a critique of education in general but moved theory into the area of adult learning, assisting free universities in that transition from campus-based service to a community orientation. Illich was a popular if infrequent speaker at alternative-education conferences in the United States and occasionally visited the Learning Exchange on trips to Chicago.

While Illich provided an analysis of educational structures, Freire concentrated on the learning process. Having established a highly successful technique of involving poor people in teaching themselves to read in Brazil, Freire, in *Pedagogy of the Oppressed*, sparked a good deal of interest and attempts at application by free university people. Freire's work provided further confirmation that the free university method of encouraging learner participation, responsibility, and sharing was on track.

By the late 1970s the shift in educational theory from higher education and schools to adult learning had been completed, as free university people discovered the works of Allen Tough and

Malcolm Knowles. Tough startled the formal education world in 1971 with his pioneering study into the way adults learn, which showed that most adults do engage in consciously planned and completed learning projects. They do so usually without the help of formal classes, by relying on books, friends, peers, and other independent modes of study. Tough's work thrust the concept of self-directed learning into the forefront of education, an idea and ideal that free universities could easily applaud. Tough also challenged free university people, telling them in a 1978 conference to look closer at their own classes and to do more in turning the control of learning over to the participants, to provide other resources to learners, and to inform the public about other learning resources as well.

With his work on andragogy, the adult learner, and self-directed learning, Malcolm Knowles gained the attention of free university people in the late seventies. Knowles was a pioneer in the adult education movement of the 1950s and 1960s, working in many nonformal adult-learning organizations as well as in the formal institutions of education. Well known to the adult education world before free university people discovered him, Knowles's words and writings helped put the free university movement in historical perspective.

There have been other educators who have contributed to free university thought and practice as well. Margaret Mead, with her single statement, "My grandmother wanted me to have an education, so she kept me out of school," endeared her to free university people. Jonathan Kozol, with his book *Death at an Early Age* and later his work in alternative schools and adult illiteracy, is known to many free university people. Miles Horton, founder of the Highlander Folk School, provided an example and a challenge to free universities. John Ohliger added his critique of mandatory continuing education. John Holt's work on teaching led to later efforts on helping parents and children grow without schooling. Ron Gross continues to develop his concept of free learning, independent learning, and amateur scholarship.

PURPOSE OF THE FREE UNIVERSITY

Although almost all free universities would agree on a philosophy concerning learning and teaching and the role of education in philosophy, they differ among themselves on the purpose of free universities as organizations. Some of those different purposes, past and present, are these:

1. To transform higher education.

2. To supplement the traditional university and provide a place for innovation and experimental concepts.

3. To provide a place for radical political thought to be expressed and promoted.

4. To change society.

5. To help individuals change and grow.

6. To sustain the counterculture.

7. To be an alternative self-supporting institution.

8. To provide lifelong learning opportunities to adults.

9. To link knowledge and action.

10. To preserve the First Amendment freedom of speech and allow citizens the right to teach or learn any subject they want.

Since the beginning, their philosophy has been one of the most exciting aspects of free universities. Today the philosophy of learning and the purpose of free universities in society are still widely discussed and debated, and the subject remains one of controversy and intrigue.

The philosophy behind the free university model is critical to understanding the basic operations of the free university and its key to success as a provider of adult learning. With a view of the history and philosophy of free universities, we can now move on to a look at the practical side of running a free university.

Part III
How We Do It

Not only has the organization of the Denver Free University revolutionized education in Colorado, the course content reflected what people wanted to learn long before traditional educational institutions updated their curriculum.

Patricia Calhoun

Chapter 9

How to Start
a Free University

Just as anyone can participate in a free university and anyone can teach in a free university, anyone can start one. Professionals and lay people alike have started free universities, sometimes within an existing institutional framework and sometimes independently.

In Tulsa, campus minister Thad Holcombe started a free university, Praxis Project, as part of his campus ministry in 1969. Praxis is still thriving today.

In Champaign, Illinois, YMCA program coordinator Anne Colgan wanted to reach more people. She had run a free university while in college and turned the idea into Communiversity, a self-sustaining YMCA program for the entire community.'

In Westmoreland, Kansas, housewife Carol Threewit convinced her church the idea would be good, and the local Methodist church initiated the Westy Community Education program, now receiving broad community support.

In San Luis Obispo, California, college administrator Ed Lunn wanted a program for both students and, eventually, community people. He started Smorgasbord, a campus free university.

In Brooklyn, New York, educator Shirley Rausher thought the idea would promote more community spirit in her "small town." Later her son Mark joined the effort, and the Brooklyn Skills Exchange became a family enterprise.

In Boston, student Chris Larned started the Free University at Boston College.

Free universities are started by directors of continuing education, senior citizens, young people, businessmen, county extension agents, librarians, professionals, and ordinary citizens.

While the process of starting a free university has changed over the years, the basic ingredients have remained the same—an office, a telephone, and human energy.

Most free universities used to start spontaneously, and some still do. Interested people get together, round up some teachers, and publish the first catalog. After that, they consider the long-term aspects of planning, finance, and organization.

The process of starting a free university has become more structured, however, in the last few years. More people are starting them with a long and thorough planning stage, sometimes lasting up to a year or more. During that time, the needs of the community are assessed. Other models are researched, practical information is gathered, and conferences are attended. A planning committee is usually formed, other educational providers in the area are visited, a board of directors or advisors is selected, and then structure and organization are designed. Long-term finances should be thought through and civic and community leaders approached for their support. Finally, attention is gained from local publicity and media people, and teachers are recruited for the first session.

Money has been and continues to remain a secondary consideration in starting an organization. The primary investment is human energy. Whether that energy is spread among several people or concentrated in the coordinator, the time, thought, and energy investment needed to start and maintain a free university is great.

Free universities have been started in all types of communities and institutional settings. They are in urban areas, as is the Indianapolis Free University; in suburban areas, like the Class Factory in southwestern Houston; and in rural areas, like the Choctaw Community Education project in Choctaw, Oklahoma. They are in large cities, like the New York Network for Learning in New

York City; in small towns, like the Olsburg Rural Educational Opportunities (OREO) program in Olsburg, Kansas (population 170); in college towns, like University Park, Pennsylvania; and in middle-sized towns, like Duluth, Minnesota. They are in liberal communities, like Orpheus in San Francisco; and in conservative towns, like Praxis Project in Tulsa.

Each local organization fits the community and its characteristics. There are large, small, and medium-sized free universities. There are free universities with budgets of a half million dollars and with budgets of $300 a year.

MONEY

Money is usually a prerequisite to any enterprise, profit or non-profit. Although the financial aspects of free universities are just as important as they are in any other operation, large amounts of money are not needed to start a free university. Most free universities have started with very little money. As little as $100 in a smaller community or within an institution, and $500 for a larger city, is enough to start the first session. More of an initial investment would aid the operation greatly, but there are few cases of large amounts of capital being invested in a free university at the beginning. So the benefits of a large amount of money are not well known.

The initial investment is almost entirely for the first catalog and miscellaneous starting costs. From the first catalog on, enough money should be generated each session to provide for the next catalog to be printed. Some initial expense items are usually donated and can be obtained free in many cases. An office can be borrowed from another service or community organization—likewise a phone—and lawyer's fees for incorporation can be requested for free. What the initial investment does not take into consideration is staff time, which during the first year is considerable. That time is not likely to be reimbursed during the first year. Some organizations start out of existing agencies and host institutions where the time is taken from other professional duties. Others start with volunteer energies, where a host committee, housewives, and other volunteers agree to provide the person-power during the first year. Some organizations acquire a grant or service position for the coordinator. VISTA workers and CETA positions have been instrumental in starting many free universities. Some people work nights and weekends after a regular job to get the free university operation going until they can be paid for the work. Some people work as volunteers, expecting that within a year the free university will have generated enough money or grants to provide a paid position for them.

For a year or so, the free university is likely to provide only enough money to print the next catalog. After a year, the free university should be returning enough money to pay a coordinator, depending on the size of community served. By the end of two years, the free university should be financially self-sufficient.

One possible reason large amounts of capital are not invested in free universities is that the return is likely to be only nominal. Free universities, with some exceptions, do not make a lot of money. It could take two to five years to recover enough money to pay someone for the time invested during the first year. With a few possible exceptions, free universities have not proven to be large profit-makers.

Essential cost items in starting a free university are stationery, incorporation papers, office supplies, first catalog printing, and postage. An office and telephone service may be obtained by donations from sponsoring organizations or other community-minded agencies.

The major question mark is staff time. Staff time can come from volunteers, existing paid staff, or recipients of grants.

THE COORDINATOR

Perhaps the major factor in whether the free university will succeed is the coordinator, or primary leader. That person will need to have a sense of vision, commitment, and good management skills. Although anyone can coordinate a free university, the task is not easy.

Free universities depend largely upon leaders for their existence. It is important that the coordinator be a person committed to the free university and lifelong learning. If a free university director leaves, the entire organization could fold for lack of another competent leader.

A free university needs two to three years of steady, consistent commitment from one or more leaders. If the initiator leaves within that time, another person has to take over in a smooth transition.

Free university leaders can be either professionals or ordinary citizens. Most of them have not handled an adult learning program before. Their commitment is usually more toward the free university as a service or community organization than as a business or means to professional advancement in education. Because most leaders have not had previous experience in managing adult-learning programs, those skills must be learned in a rather serious and studied manner. Publications, manuals, conferences, and training workshops are all used by new free university coordinators to acquaint themselves with free university operations.

TIMETABLES

There are three initial periods to get the free university off the ground: planning, the first sessions, and stabilization.

Planning averages six months, but can range from two months to one year.

The first sessions are the first four sessions, usually one year of operation. During this time the program's image is established, it is introduced to the community, and operational bugs are worked out of the system. The first year is the toughest for the organization. The first session requires a good deal of start-up time and planning. The first group of teachers is the hardest to recruit, and the registrations for the first year may not live up to expectations. Then, too, while the first session may be a successful and optimistic one, many free universities experience a second session that has lower enrollments than the first one. This has happened so many times that its cause probably relates to a general rule of thumb rather than individual inadequacy, but the free university must be able to survive and muster additional strength to make it through any particular session that may have reduced enrollments.

It is also during the first year that some vital statistics can be analyzed. After three to four sessions, the enrollment data are sufficient to be measured. The number of catalogs printed, number of classes, number of registrations, income from fees, refunds, and net income will all be important in establishing a trend for future enrollments and expectations. The catalog-to-student ratio—the number of catalogs that it takes to enroll one student—and the average number of students per class are two important statistics. Those figures should tell the young organization what to expect when the number of classes is increased or decreased and how to increase or maintain the number of enrollments.

A sound plan for future stabilization is the key to keeping the free university alive. Although it is not difficult to start a free university and get the first session together, it is considerably more difficult to maintain a free university. Between the first and second years, the young free university determines its future direction, including structure, organization, finances, and staff.

Patience is also a virtue during the stabilization time for free universities wishing to expand. During the first year, when the free university is establishing itself, working out functional details, planning, and trying to gain recognition in the community, it is unlikely that enrollments will skyrocket. In each locality, the gestation time between when the free university is ready to expand and when enrollments start increasing differs. In Indianapolis, when the free university was seven years old, enrollments were still around 2,000 participants a year. Then they started doubling. The next year they were 4,000; the following year, 8,000; and in 1979, they hit 15,000. The Class Factory in Houston, on the other hand, began expansion quickly after its formation. Founder Donna Gerdin enrolled just 118 participants the first session in 1977. In 1978, enrollments were around 1,000. In 1979, they started upward during the middle of the year and reached 2,000 participants a session, or an average of more than 10,000 a year. Catalysts for growth include a concentrated effort on the part of the free university to expand and community recognition. That recognition may take time to crystallize, but once it does, it provides the free university with attention and a familiarity that can create momentum in growth.

WHY THEY FAIL

New free universities continue to fail, though not at the rate they did at one time. Failure can be attributed in large measure to the fact that they are community organizations that rely on the strength and acumen of individuals and in part because they are like all other small businesses.

Probably around a third of all new free universities are unable to continue. This proportion is much better, however, than the failure rate for all small businesses—reported to be close to 80 percent.

The leading causes for failure of new free universities follow.

1. Inadequate planning. Free universities started without planning, without a community-needs assessment, without support from community leaders, without interaction with other educational and social service agencies, or without a group of advisers and volunteers are going to have a tough time gaining that support and interest later.

2. Coordinator or key person leaving. The most critical time for any free university is when the primary leader leaves. If that happens during the first two years, it is doubly important that another competent individual take over in a smooth transition, assuming the duties immediately after, or even before, the first coordinator departs. The new person must be provided with the necessary skills and training to pick up where the other coordinator left off without a fatal interruption.

3. Not enough time devoted by key individual(s). Free universities take time, usually ten to twenty hours a week at least, to get going. If it is a successful free university, with more than 1,000 participants, it will take even more time. In the beginning, the coordinator will need to devote a good deal of energy to the project, and other volunteers, board members, and advisers also will need to contribute their time in the initial stages of development.

4. Lack of management skills and training. Even simple volunteer organizations nowadays require skilled leadership and management. Management skills are not obtainable only by corporate executives or in business school. Developing procedures, keeping records, conducting meetings, and delineating tasks and expectations are all possible in any organization.

5. Lack of financial accountability. Free universities, even small ones, involve money. Financial accounting is essential, not only at the beginning but at all times in later growth. Large free universities can collapse within months if a critical financial error is made or if unforeseen expenses build up. Financial accountability is not just keeping expenses within income but also developing contingency plans for unexpected or foreseen financial changes and keeping accurate records and up-to-date summaries.

6. Inability to provide for coordinator's salary support. Even a successful free university may not be able to provide salary support for its coordinator, and at some time almost all free univer-

sities require a part-time or full-time paid coordinator. Planning when and where to get the resources to reward the coordinator with a paid position is critical. Admittedly, this is not always controllable and is susceptible to external forces, especially in small and medium-sized communities unable to sustain a free university on fees alone. In these places, some good free universities die because of inadequate funding. But the various types of schemes used to finance free universities mean that free universities do not have to rely on any one source of income. There are fees, federal funds, grants, donations, affiliation with other institutions, and local fundraisers—all of which are possible in almost any community and can be employed in various measures at different times. Several sources of income can be combined to sustain the coordinator, and thus the free university.

7. Institutional restraints. Free universities operating within other institutions may find that institutional restraints prohibit the growth and development of the free university. The free university needs flexibility, some degree of independence, and the ability to experiment and establish new trends and norms. Some institutions may want the free university to serve only its members and not the general public. Others may want all activities held in institutional buildings. Some may require all activities and personnel to be approved by higher authorities. At times, these institutional restraints can be dealt with or even used to the free university's advantage. At other times, the free university leaders will need to explain to institutional officials how the free university can benefit the larger institution, how and why the new procedures are needed, and to seek to remove any institutional restraints that may cripple the free university.

Few free universities fail because of competition from other adult-learning programs; few because of outside pressures or nonacceptance by the community. None have been reported failing because there was no need for a free university.

PROFIT VS. NONPROFIT

Almost all free universities in the country are incorporated as nonprofit organizations or are affiliated with nonprofit institutions. There are many advantages to nonprofit status for both practical purposes and image. If the community views your organization as a not-for-profit operation, people will be more apt to lend a hand, to donate time and effort and see it as a community service. There are practical reasons for being nonprofit as well. Nonprofit organizations can receive grants or individual tax-deductible donations after the organization receives its tax-exempt status from the IRS. Nonprofit organizations can receive public-service air time on radio and television, and this free advertising can be worth hundreds or thousands of dollars a year. Nonprofit organizations are eligible for a special bulk postal rate for mailing out catalogs—a rate roughly half what commercial enterprises pay. For most free universities, it is more profitable to be nonprofit.

But as free universities enroll more people and take in more money in fees, especially in the larger cities, some free universities are being organized as for-profit organizations. The Class Factory in Houston, the Learning Exchange in Sacramento, California, and the New York Network for Learning in New York City are three such organizations. There are at least three reasons why free universities are incorporated as for-profit organizatons.

1. To maintain control over the organization. A nonprofit organization is controlled by a board of directors rather than an individual.

2. To have the option of selling the organization at some future date for a profit.

3. To gain investors and raise capital and still retain control of the organization. A free university can offer 49 percent of its stock to one or more financial backers, who put up the needed capital to get the free university off the ground. While the backers may make a profit on their investment, the originator of the free university still retains 51-percent control of the organization.

Although the number of free universities organized for profit remains small, there is more interest in this type of free enterprise now than five years ago.

A GENERALIZED APPROACH

Before outlining some differences in starting a free university in a rural setting, in a big city, and within a sponsoring institution, there are some general perspectives and approaches that anyone starting an organization should be aware of. Although each situation differs, there are some common elements of planning. In *How to Start a Free University,* Greg Marsello writes, "No two free universities are exactly identical, and your free university, although it may be modeled after another one, will not be a Xerox copy. Each community has different needs and wants. I must stress that your background work is very important, so make sure you have thought out the structure of your free university and you have made contacts with people in your community to find out if they would support the free university."[1]

Marsello offers a checklist of important decisions and considerations in planning the free university:[2]

_____ Community needs defined
_____ Target audience selected
_____ Educational philosophy identified
_____ Structure determined
_____ Fee structure selected
_____ Core of staff people ready
_____ Personal commitment present
_____ Name agreed to
_____ Office location chosen
_____ Phone hours covered
_____ Incorporation initiated
_____ Short-term money raised
_____ Long-term financing planned

Community needs defined.   No matter what one's own personal enthusiasm and interest in the project, the free university must meet a community need to succeed. By acquiring a clear idea of what needs exist in the community, the new organization can orient itself toward those needs and better explain its existence and mission. In Pawnee Rock, Kansas, the small town of 400 had lost its public school, and residents wanted an educational institution to call their own and bring people together. In Baltimore, the elderly community around Johns Hopkins University had few low-cost programs. In Denver, people new to the city needed a way to meet other people in a learning situation. By better understanding the community's needs, the free university can sell itself better.

Too often formal educational institutions attempt to define community or individual needs and then set out to meet them. "First we create the needs, then we fill them," says one cynical educator. Free universities cannot afford to pretend that they can create needs. Community needs can be determined or confirmed in several different ways—by talking with local people, with community and civic leaders, with journalists, and with church leaders. Sometimes formal surveys help. Finally, a town meeting, community meeting, or group meeting to discuss the community and its needs is a way to brainstorm about the free university and its role in the community.

Target audience selected. It is easy to say that the free university is open to everyone and that you are trying to reach the general public. In reality the way you structure your organization, where and how you direct your publicity, what you offer and how, will determine what audience responds. So if you are trying to reach a particular audience, or several audiences, you need to plan in terms of reaching that audience. The typical adult-learning audience is mostly young, college-educated, professional or working, earning a middle-level income, living in an urban or suburban area. If you want to reach out beyond this typical group, you will need to reorient your program. Geography must be considered as you locate your office, distribute your catalogs, and direct your publicity. You will also need to get representation on your board from the various geographic localities you are trying to reach. Some target audiences include men, elderly, youth, blue-collar workers, blacks, Hispanics, housewives, and rural residents. The Clay Center Education Program, located in a rural county of 10,000 people, nevertheless drew mostly from the city of Clay Center, population 5,000. To reach rural residents in small towns and villages outside Clay Center, the name was changed to Clay County Education Program, the offices were moved into the county courthouse, classes were set up in rural areas, and catalogs were distributed countywide. The president of the board came from a small town outside Clay Center. Through those efforts, almost 50 percent of participants now come from outside Clay Center. In larger towns, it is even more important to target your audience; without that conscious effort, it is unlikely that you will reach a broader public.

Educational philosophy identified. Not all free universities share the same philosophy. In fact, there are great differences among them. Whatever the educational philosophy and the ultimate purpose of the free university are, they should be clear to the staff and organization. Getting it down on paper is not a bad way to clarify one's thinking and present ideas for group discussion.

Structure determined. The structure is important and should be determined before the first session. Is there a board of directors or board of advisers? Is the program affiliated with a sponsoring organization, or is it independent? Is there a staff, a paid coordinator, a volunteer committee, or a steering committee? The locus of policy- and decision-making should be clear.

Fee structure selected. There are various ways to set up your fee structure. Many free universities have no fee at all. The courses are open to anyone without cost, except for materials. These free universities are sponsored by host institutions or receive monies from local sources. Some free universities have a registration fee only. This fee goes to the free university for its expenses. In some free universities that fee is token; in others it runs from $4 to $10. Some free universities have a registration fee that covers all the courses a person takes in any one session; others impose the fee for each course. Some free universities have both registration and teacher fees. This is set up in one of two ways. Either the free university sets the total fee, usually between $10 and $30, from which the registration fee is taken; or the teacher sets the course fee, from which the free university takes a portion (usually 50 percent).

Core of staff people ready. Without a staff, or one or more people with time to do the actual work, the free university cannot move. The staff needs to allot a given amount of personal or professional time to devote to the project. The core group should also form a board of directors or board of advisers. The board is one of the most important aspects of the young free university. The board can help the organization become legitimate and accepted and get publicity and possibly funding, and it provides valuable suggestions about the operation. Although some free universities use their own staff or close acquaintances for the board, more free universities have reached out to community and civic leaders to provide a broader base. Businessmen, professors, ministers, social service agency heads, and media people are all potential candidates.

Personal commitment present. Whatever the plans and well-designed mechanics, personal commitment is necessary to put them into action. Board members and staff must be ready to devote some energy, time, and maybe money, to put the organization in business.

Name agreed to. The name should be identified with the community you are serving and should be more folksy than formal. The term *free university* is often not used in individual names nowadays because it evokes false impressions of being without cost, which it may not be, and of being a university, which may not relate to many people who have not been to college. Names like community education program, open university, skills exchange, and communiversity better express the free university idea.

Office location chosen. The site of your office will have a certain effect on associating the free university with the surrounding neighborhood. Free universities starting from institutions have used the institution's offices; others have used churches, community centers, and community organizations. Some have rented office space, and others have started out of the coordinator's home. Especially in the beginning, it may be advantageous to obtain the office and possibly telephone service as donations. At the start, when financial resources are least, it is often better to put those resources into your first catalog and other expenses.

Phone hours covered. One sure way to irritate your potential students and teachers is to generate publicity, have people call, and have no one to answer the phone. That leaves people wondering whether the operation is really running, and if so, why is it so disorganized that no one can answer the phone? Answering the phone is a full-time job, however. If you have one coordinator, that person cannot be answering the phone and be out in the community organizing the free university at the same time. Some ways to get the phone covered without devoting your whole day to it are these:

1. Use another organization's office in the beginning and use their phone answering help.

2. Get a phone answering service.

3. Install a taped message machine that at least lets people know when you will be in.

4. Reduce your office hours to a couple of hours a day or a few days a week, thus leaving yourself time to do other things.

5. Get volunteers to answer the phone.

6. Have the calls automatically transferred to other numbers where volunteers, a shut-in, or a friend can answer the phone while at home.

Incorporation initiated. If your free university is sponsored or associated with another institution, you may not need or want to incorporate as a separate organization. But several free universities associated with larger institutions have incorporated separately, giving them greater freedom and ability to apply for grants that the host institution is not eligible for. If you are not associated with a larger organization, you should incorporate. If it is for nonprofit status, you file incorporation papers in the state in which you will operate. The filing fee is less than $100 in most cases. You will need a board of directors to incorporate as a not-for-profit organization. The second step is to file the bylaws, detailing how the organization will be run, with the secretary of state. A third step is to file for tax-exempt status with the federal Internal Revenue Service. There have been few problems with free universities receiving tax-exempt status, though the process may take up to a year to complete.

Short-term money raised. Short-term money should be raised to get your first session going. That amount may be between $25 and $1,000, depending on how many catalogs you want to print and how many classes you have. Short-term money can be raised by fundraisers, individual donations, and borrowing. If your free university is associated with another institution, that institution should be willing to put up the money.

Long-term financing planned. A realistic long-term financing plan should be made before your first session. Where will the money come from to run the organization? How soon can you hire a paid coordinator, at what rate, and for how much time? Free universities are fortunate in that there are a variety of ways to raise that long-term money, including course fees, grants, and local sources of support, such as city or county money. Combinations of sources are quite popular and reduce your dependency on any one source. Catalog advertising, annual arts-and-crafts sales, and the selling of free university diplomas are other ways to supplement income.

The planning stage of the free university, whether it is two months or a year, should be as complete and comprehensive as possible. Once the free university is operating, there will be little time for thinking, brainstorming, and planning. There will only be time to wish you had done more of it.

STARTING AN INDEPENDENT
FREE UNIVERSITY

The procedures for starting a free university in various situations differ. Independent free universities most often are found in larger metropolitan areas where there is a population base great enough to support a free university on fees.

The urban independent free university is most like a small business or free enterprise organization in society and, with good management, can rise to be one of the major providers of non-credit adult-learning courses in the entire city.

One or more people can start an independent free university in an urban area. The members of the board of directors for the independent free university should be chosen for their individual expertise and their contribution to community acceptance of the organization. Although an urban free university is unlikely to get the total support of the city, community and civic leaders on your board can provide the legitimacy needed for a new organization.

The money needed for the first catalog will be much greater for a big-city free university. You may print anywhere from 10,-000 to 30,000 catalogs the first time, which involves some investment.

If you are located in one of the three largest cities in the country —New York, Chicago, or Los Angeles—you may want to target a particular neighborhood within that metropolitan area.

The metropolitan environment and the dependency on registration fees for income mean that good management skills will be needed to plan, start, and expand the independent free university.

Budgets will need to be drawn up, projecting income and expenses. Some marketing expertise will be needed to distribute the catalogs and select the target population for the program. Aggressive publicity techniques need to be employed to gain recognition in a large city. The first few catalogs should look professionally done in order to establish a credible image. More than any other kind of free university, the independent free university is like a small business, and it needs to be run efficiently.

THE RURAL FREE UNIVERSITY

Anyone may start a rural or small-town free university, but at some point the community and civic leadership of the town will need to support the free university for it to succeed.

To earn that support, a group of interested people should meet and discuss the learning needs in the community and how a free university would benefit the town. As many people as are interested should be invited to the meeting. People in such professional education roles as the school principal, Cooperative Extension agent, and librarian should be invited. Community leaders, such as ministers, bank presidents, lawyers, and newspaper editors, should also be invited. People from various segments of the population, like an older person, someone from the Hispanic community, or a high school student, should be welcome. At this meeting, people can talk about community needs, and free university brochures from other small towns can be passed around. A film on rural education can be ordered from University for Man in Manhattan, Kansas. Although no decisions need to be made, this initial kickoff meeting will provide some interest and support for the idea.

Immediately after, civic leaders who were not able to attend the meeting should be sought out and told of the discussion and possibility for such a venture. Most community leaders enjoy knowing about a project as soon as possible, and there will be more support for, and less fear of and caution toward, any project explained to civic leaders at an early stage. The president of the chamber of commerce, school officials, the mayor, county supervisors, leading businessmen, and the newspaper publisher are all important people to talk to about the project. You will want to get their suggestions and even support for the idea at this early stage.

Even though only a few interested people may have come to your first meeting (it doesn't have to be large), a larger second meeting will kick off the project. The larger meeting should have a notice in the paper, and all interested people should be welcome to attend. Sometimes a town meeting can attract people with a potluck supper or cookies and punch. A church or school should be willing to host the event. It is at this time that the concept of the free university is explained. A successful technique used in many group meetings is to follow up that explanation by asking each person in the room to name three things that he or she would like to learn and one thing that he or she could teach. The list can be put on a blackboard. While people will find it easy to tell what they would like to learn, many will try to maintain that they don't know anything well enough to teach. This is where the free university philosophy is tested and proven, as neighbors "tattle" on their friends and relate skills that they know their friends have. With all the topics on the blackboard, you may find that you already have enough class topics and teachers to start your first session.

Either before the larger meeting or right after, a steering committee should be formed to add structure to the project. Participants at the meeting should be invited to join it. Depending on the size of your community, your organizational structure can evolve in any one of these three ways:

1. For very small communities (fewer than 1,000 people), a volunteer steering committee probably will be the only committee necessary. These people get the course leaders, print the brochure, and run the free university as volunteers. A budget of $100 to $300 is large enough for this kind of free university.

2. For towns of more than 1,000 people, you probably will want an advisory board composed of civic leaders and people who will do the work. The board can range from five to eleven people. Working with the advisory board should be a volunteer or paid coordinator who contributes time to the project every week. In areas of fewer than 2,000 people, this may be a volunteer or someone who is paid a nominal sum, like $500, for coordinating an entire session. This is the case with People to People in Dighton,

Kansas, where the population of Lane County, 2,800, is not large enough to support even a quarter-time paid coordinator. So the coordinator is paid approximately $500 to coordinate each session.

3. For towns or counties of 5,000 to 10,000 people, a half-time paid coordinator is usually required, and that person reports to the board of advisers or board of directors. A yearly budget of around $5,000 can be raised from local sources. In these larger small towns, volunteers can be sought by the coordinator to assist with teacher recruitment, provide art for the brochure, help raise money, and perform other tasks.

In a small town the free university will want and need support from the entire community. Thus, it is important to illustrate how the new organization will benefit the community, will not compete with existing programs, and will provide a basis for development, pride, and spirit in the community.

INSTITUTION-SPONSORED
FREE UNIVERSITIES

Institutions sponsor free universities both in small towns and in big cities. Colleges, libraries, Cooperative Extensions, recreation departments, social service agencies, community centers, and YMCAs all sponsor free universities.

While the implementation of the free university within an existing institution should follow institutional procedures, use existing channels, and seek approval from top officials, some features of the free university should be kept in mind.

1. The more support you have from the highest institutional authority, the better. Do not be afraid to promote your program idea with boards of directors, the institution's executive director, or even patrons and supporters of the institution. As the free university is a communitywide project, it should seek input from all levels in the institution. The more friends the free university has at the top, the better its chances for total institutional support.

2. The free university should have as much autonomy within the institution as possible. Free universities have flourished partly because of flexible guidelines and partly because they are seen as

separate community service organizations. A fairly free hand in running the project will allow the free university to grow. A separate board of advisers, without power but with ideas and suggestions, is positive. A separate name, oriented toward the community rather than the institution, is helpful. A YMCA program in Champaign, Illinois, for example, is called Communiversity rather than YMCA Classes, and St. Thomas College in Houston runs Courses à la Carte.

3. The free university should be open to the general public, not just to institutional members. The free university is a way to bridge gaps, to reach more people, and to bring in new people to the institution. If it has a limited audience, it will be narrow and rigid in scope.

4. Benefits should be explained to the institution. The free university is not a charitable project but a valuable one for the institution sponsoring it. Although the free university itself may not be a money-maker, it can be financially self-sufficient and bring in publicity and other positive benefits to the organization. For instance, while St. Thomas College in Houston has only 1,200 students on campus, it has thousands more participants in Courses à la Carte, a valuable recruiting and publicity tool for the college. Make a list of benefits to the host institution sponsoring the free university and promote these benefits at meetings, in letters, and in conversations with institutional officials.

5. A professional staff member is the best person to be in charge of the project, even if the time allocated to the free university is only one of his or her duties. With a paid coordinator on staff, the program is guaranteed continuity and future existence. Volunteers, students, and others associated with the institution should be actively sought out as staff, steering committee members, or helpers. The program cannot run by itself, without staff commitment. Sometimes a new full- or part-time staff person can be hired, and sometimes the free university can be part of a larger program position.

Chapter 10

Keys to Success

The philosophy behind free universities goes a long way in explaining their popularity among adults today. But there is a pragmatic side, and some utilitarian answers, as to why free universities succeed. The answers are both interesting and valuable to practicing adult educators.

Free universities in the past have been characterized as counter-institutions or alternative organizations. Increasingly, that notion is being replaced by another, the notion of a model. The free university represents a vision and a model, not an institution.

The vision of free universities is contained in their philosophy. The model is the practical side, the functional aspect. To borrow from a dictionary, a model is a plan; a standard to be imitated; a style or design. A "model refers to a representation made to be copied."[1]

Free universities are not institutions—at least not now. Institutions have a stable funding base. They have some standardization. They do not depend upon individuals or leaders. Free universities are too diverse to qualify as institutions.

The functional components of the free university model are workable, feasible, and cost-efficient. They can be adapted, either singly or collectively, by other educational organizations.

The practical aspects of the free university are transferable to other adult-learning situations. The composite picture may add up to a free university, but any adult-learning situation could use the individual features that make free universities so successful.

There are many reasons why the free university model works, but there are three major factors contributing to the success of free universities:

1. The administration is streamlined and fairly simple.

2. The free university has a well-developed and positive image in the community.

3. The program is responsive to course trends and changing public interests.

All three aspects are important to educational providers today. As lifelong learning has become the trumpet of learning in the 1980s, the scene has shifted from curricula, institutions, and campuses to the general public. Tailoring a program to meet the needs, or at least the interests, of the general public is the key to a successful learning program today.

Let's look at those three elements of the free university operation—administration, image, and responsiveness—and how free universities use each to their advantage.

ADMINISTRATION

The free university strips educational administration of its trimmings, trappings, excesses, records, and ceremony and brings the handling of noncredit classes down to a simple procedure. The basic outline of the process is to collect course descriptions, publish and distribute the catalog, and register participants. There may be a thousand details in between and during those steps, but the basic operational outline of the free university model is fairly simple.

This process varies little from the smallest of free universities to those that are ten years old and handling half a million dollars.

In the largest of free universities, a staff of just four people can run about 1,000 classes and enroll more than 10,000 participants.

The bare-bones administration is a linking mechanism, not an educational provider. It does not counsel or advise; keep records;

maintain educational facilities; govern projects, teachers, or students; or seek linear organizational growth.

Here are some of the other administrative aspects that the free university model doesn't have:

janitors

building maintenance

guidance counselors

libraries, bookstores,
    record collections

school supplies

scholarships

extracurricular activities,
    sports teams

faculty senates

departments

deans and department heads

records

quality controls

curriculum development
    committees

Each one of these aspects carries a price with it. It has been reported that just recording one credit for a college student costs more than $23. That figure alone is more than the average cost of a free university class.

The free university class operation involves a good typewriter, a phone, an office, a small staff (one to five) and as many volunteers as possible. The outcome is noncredit classes that are offered inexpensively or for free, and low administration costs. This makes it possible for any community or any organization to set up a free university class program.

Although the steps may be simple, they must be executed well. Let's go forward to the basics.

Using Existing Facilities

Free universities benefit from maintaining organizational flexibility, and a great part of that flexibility lies in not becoming burdened by buildings. Instead, the free university program uses existing facilities. As course trends change, so do the facility requirements. Institutions often have been caught in the bind of building facilities to meet demands of a current popular subject, such as pottery, and then five years later trying to fill those facilities with students after the course popularity declines.

By renting or receiving free space in existing facilities, the free university remains both flexible in its space obligations and unrestricted by the necessary upkeep that buildings entail. Free universities have found space in public schools, churches, community centers, homes, offices, bank buildings, and libraries.

Because of its flexibility, the free university is not tied to any type of subject matter. Two years ago, when disco became a hot course item, free universities scrambled to rent, but not buy, ballroom space. The Indianapolis Free University, for instance, at one time had more than forty different sections of disco, accounting for thousands in its enrollments. But when that trend ended this year, the free university was not committed to its disco teachers or ballroom space. Because free universities are always "renting" rather than "buying"—whether it be space, teachers, or concepts— they are able to maintain their flexibility and change with the trends.

Creating Attractive Catalogs

A hallmark of the free university model is the attractive catalog. Catalogs have been the free university's main source of publicity, of image, and of information. To succeed, the free university has had to be successful with its catalogs.

The standard catalog not only lists the courses but also supplies a short description to create interest. Often that description is followed by a short biography, usually only one or two sentences, on the course leader. This is often used not only to establish the teacher's experience or skill level but also to establish that the teacher may also be a peer or fellow member of the community rather than an impersonal authority from afar. Here are some good course descriptions and biographies of the teachers:

Why Are There Mountains?

Why are there mountains, anyway? Why did the old earth go to all the trouble? Why doesn't the whole planet look like Kansas and Nebraska? We will examine the revelations of plate tectonics and explore the old and new theories of mountain formation. We will also take a kodachrome journey to the Himalayas. Depending on class wishes, a field trip may be scheduled.

Bob Michael is a freelance mining geologist. He has been captivated by mountains since childhood. He would not be caught dead in Nebraska. (Denver Free University, Winter 1980)

Political Advertising

The battlefield is the minds of American voters—and the ultimate weapon is television. With each election video politics has become more and more a prevailing force in American government.

Gary Yordan will present some examples of political advertising and the strategy and methods used in developing the ads. Yordan, who is a co-producer of TV-27's Accent show is also a member of Southwind Media, Inc., a firm specializing in political TV advertising. (Center for Participant Education, Winter 1980).

Both course descriptions deal with subjects currently popular (science and politics) and turn them into courses that make the reader want to take them. Both start out with entertaining or dramatic opening lines, and yet move deftly into a description that shows that the course is a serious and well-thought-out one. The biographies provide succinct qualifications, and with the course on mountains, a measure of devotee enthusiasm to convey the impression that this is not a professorial lecture situation.

The rest of the catalog usually includes a short description of what a free university is, conveying informality and enticing the reader to become a participant. Between the philosophy and folksy portrayal of the staff or organization of the free university is the distinct impression that "this is for you—dear reader."

Sometimes the free university will remind the reader that there are no prerequisites, no grades, and no credits. Some free university slogans:

"The Only Prerequisite Is Curiosity" (University for Man, Manhattan, Kansas)

"Consumer Sponsored Learning" (Open Education Exchange, Oakland, California)

"Learn Something New in 4 Weeks" (Toronto Skills Exchange, Toronto, Ontario)

"The Best Buys in Adult Education" (Indianapolis Free University, Indiana)

"Come Grow With Us—In Brooklyn" (Brooklyn Skills Exchange, New York)

The format of the free university catalog has varied throughout the years, from tiny catalogs slightly larger than an index card to huge posters. These days, however, two standard sizes have emerged as the most cost-efficient sizes for large press runs (10,000 to 100,000 copies). They are the newspaper size of 11 by 15 inches, folded over, and the 8½-by-11-inch magazine size, stapled in the center. Both are usually done in newsprint.

The crowning of the catalog is always the cover, which must be attractive to induce people to look beyond it. The centerpiece is a drawing or picture, usually large, but simple in design. Class photos, art work, and local community scenes are typical. They convey a sense of community, of creativity, and of beauty. It usually takes up more than half the cover. Surrounding the cover art work are a few words. There is the name of the free university, the name of the year and session, a slogan, a note that these are class offerings. Sometimes the word *free* is included so that people know they don't have to pay for the catalog.

The course catalog is the free university's best tool and marketing device. It has succeeded in reaching adults, and other organizations in adult learning are now using the same techniques.

Marketing the Catalog

The attractiveness of the free university catalog has usually been accompanied by a good distribution system. The marketing of the catalog is both extensive and inexpensive. Advertising people talk about "getting a position in the market." This means getting the jump and becoming identified with a particular advertising technique. Free universities print up to 100,000 catalogs each time and distribute them in businesses where people usually shop—grocery stores, drugstores, bookstores, liquor stores, record shops—anywhere where there is a counter with space. The distribution is free. Occasionally a free university will recognize its distribution patrons by printing a list of them or giving them a free ad in the catalog, but basically the system is free.

Counter space is limited and conceivably available to any good group with information free to the public. Free universities have gotten the jump on using this medium. By playing on its image as a community service and a low-cost operation, the free university has received the cooperation of local businesses.

For example, Communiversity in Kansas City has a well-heeled distribution system in a metropolitan area. It centers on two precious distribution routes—a large grocery chain with many stores around the city, and the public library, with eighteen branch libraries in town and the surrounding suburbs.

University for Man in Manhattan, Kansas, a town of only 50,000 people, has approximately 400 distribution points. After ten years, stores not only expect but also ask to distribute catalogs. "I've been waiting for these," said one clerk at the local Wal-Mart. Other store owners will call in when they run out of catalogs because customers ask for the catalog when they shop.

Some free universities supplement their staff at distribution time. One free university pays part-time people to distribute for a day. The Denver Free University offers reduced registration fees for people helping out. Communiversity in Kansas City uses scores of volunteers to distribute its catalogs.

In a media age, when educational institutions are competing for enrollments not only with each other but also with corporations that have huge and sophisticated advertising budgets and approaches, it is hard to gain the attention of the potential learner. The catalog distribution system, however, reaches a large audience, corners one advertising medium—the store counter—and is almost without cost.

Simplifying Registration

We used to say in college that if you could get through registration, you could get through the semester. Everyone looks back and winces at university registration. Students make a concentrated effort, and by the end of senior year make it through five class registrations, all at different locations on a huge university campus, in several hours. Such concentration is needed on campus; in the community it is simply a deterrent to enrolling participants.

Registration, like the other aspects of a successful noncredit learning program for the public, should be geared to the learner, not to the organization. Long lines should be cut down, and a variety of registration possibilities should be instituted to lure registrants, or at least make the process as painless as possible. These efforts, while never totally succeeding, will certainly greatly soothe the irritation of registration. In addition, your participants will recognize your efforts, and those lines won't be quite as unbearable.

Free universities have made registration simple. A typical registration form is about the size of an index card and is completed in triplicate: one copy for the learner, one for the teacher, one for the organization. The information on it is basic—name, address, phone, class, and class fee. Sometimes the free university does statistical data for its records. Although the data are helpful, the questions are kept to a minimum. "If we asked too many questions, our participants would just laugh and leave," says Dennis DuBé, former director of Community Free School in Boulder, Colorado. He says that such data as income and heritage not only are an invasion of privacy—at least in the participants' minds—but also are not very useful.

DuBé maintains that age, sex, and address are all that are needed for the organization to make accurate statements about its participants and to plan its publicity and targeting in the future.

A variety of registration techniques are used. Most free universities have in-person registration. Some start registration on Saturday so that laborers and others unable to get away during the week can make it to the first day of registration before the most popular classes fill up. But in-person registration involves lines, and a single location is usually inconvenient for people living in various communities.

The Learning Connection in Columbus, Ohio, registers its classes in four locations, including a Lutheran church, a hardware store, and an ice cream parlor. Other free universities pick a shopping center, a community center, or a public library as an alternative to the free university office for registration.

The participant fills out a simple registration form, gets a receipt, pays a fee if there is one, and is finished.

Other free universities supplement walk-in registrations. Some use phone registrations, which are especially helpful to the elderly, shut-ins, and people living far away. It also staves off disaster if your registration day happens to coincide with the heaviest snowfall of the year.

Another possibility is the mail-in form. Some free universities use this exclusively. The Denver Free University, however, found that staff time was greater for mail-in registrations than walk-ins because in-person participants filled out the forms in triplicate for themselves. But the mail-in form continues to be popular, and several free universities have added Mastercard and Visa payment plans to their mail-in registration.

The simple registration procedure provides all the data that the learner, teacher, and organization want. The learner knows when and where. The teacher knows how many are coming. The organization knows how many and a few vital statistics about the population that it is serving. Beyond that, record-keeping is minimal. The simple registration procedure is satisfactory to everyone. It eliminates lines, unnecessary questions, and hassles for learners. It causes no pain to the teacher who also likes to keep things simple. And it makes administration easy by reducing cost and time. Registration time is problem time already. By keeping it simple, the free university keeps those troubles to a minimum.

IMAGE

The second area in which free universities have achieved practical success is image. Image is not usually thought of as a practical aspect of the organization. In fact, it often evokes feelings of doubt or defensiveness among administrators. "What is our image?" is often a euphemism for "Who aren't we reaching," "What bad things are people thinking about us," and "Who hates us?"

Free universities are no less concerned about their image, but they have consciously or unconsciously set out to create an image that distinctly differs from that of other educational institutions, thus making free universities stand out in the public's mind.

Image is a tricky but important concept to project. That projection, or what you say your image is, must be followed up by an actual situation supporting that image.

Free universities project two images. Image I is an image for the individual learner; Image II is an image the free university has as a community organization.

Image I

Image is important to the individual learner. In fact, it may make the difference between a learner attending an educational organization, and ultimately, whether he or she actually is able to learn. Able to learn? How can a free university, which says that anybody can learn, say that someone may not be "able to learn"? The answer lies in a person's self-concept and self-image and in how one perceives the educational organization as relating to that self-image. Self-image may be the greatest barrier in adult learning today. People see themselves as too old, too uneducated, too slow, too clumsy, too confused, too immature, too ungraceful in a group, too uncoordinated, too poor, too unhealthy, too hopeless. The list of *too*'s could go on. The number of self-doubts in society today is large—in kind, quantity, depth, and importance.

The mother who has lived at home for years rearing children has self-doubts about working with or relating to other adults outside the home. While the population of "second-career women," as Malcolm Knowles has called them, is large, there is a whole segment of our population that failed in traditional schools or did sufficiently poorly to have negative recollections, sometimes very emotional ones, and reactions toward going "back" to any formal schoollike situation.

Anyone who has not taken a formal course in several years may experience such concerns, and legitimate concerns at that. The potential learner's perception of the educational organization is tied up not only in the institution's image but also, and more importantly, in the person's own concept of himself or herself and how that educational experience will improve or change the self-image.

The free university has worked hard at developing an image that attracts people from the general public. Generally speaking, the free university's image in any given community has the elements of informality, friendliness, independence, "groupness," and temporariness.

Informality. The foremost characteristic of a free university class is its informality, and free universities constantly publicize their courses as offering an informal and enjoyable atmosphere. Probably a majority of free university classes nationwide take place in instructors' homes, and this fact alone shifts the prospective learner's mental picture of the class from the traditional classroom to the living room.

Unlike classrooms, living rooms are not cold, hostile, formal, or colorless. They are inviting, warm, full of intrigue and curiosities. People like to visit other people's living rooms.

It is difficult to sit in the back or front row of a living room, difficult for the instructor to be an authority figure—difficult in fact to be anything but an equal in someone's living room.

The informality of the class attracts people who want to learn something but don't want to fail, people who want to learn something but don't want to be bored, people who want to learn something but don't want to be tested.

Of course not all people experience self-doubt when they want to take a class, but for those who are entering the formal learning sphere again, a pleasant reentry is favored over a crash landing.

Friendliness. The free university is also viewed as friendly. The staff is not so much administrators as people putting the program together. The teachers are not faculty. As a matter of fact, most of them are "just like me," and the other participants are apt to be fairly friendly as well.

Independence. The free university is also seen as an independent organization, even if it is associated with a larger organization. The free university does not attempt to enroll people in credit classes, persuade them to become members, or profess any particular viewpoint. The free university is usually seen as neutral turf. One way the free university has promoted its independent image is to select a name that conveys that spirit of independence. Free universities have also taken the naming of the organization as an opportunity to promote their image as attractive and interesting programs.

The emphasis on independence plays heavily into the potential learner's desire not to repeat educational mistakes of the past, to become involved in a group situation, and to participate in a new form of community.

"Groupness." The free university almost guarantees that each participant will meet a new friend or in some other way participate in a group. In surveys of free university participants, the desire to be with other people ranks second only to the desire to learn something.

The feeling of being a part of a group motivates people to attend the free university. It is a way to meet new people. Americans move on the average of once every five years (20 percent move every year), so free universities are a way for new people in town to meet others and for old-timers whose friends have all moved to restock the local friendship supply. A free university class is also a pleasant way to share an evening with a friend.

There is also the attractiveness of the group interaction. Although we demand our privacy, we also want to interact in a group. The group at once allows us our individuality and lets us share our experiences with others. In a group we can express our opinions, or listen to others; argue a point, or agree with the rest; learn from a peer, or teach what we know; explore people who are different from us, or find people who are similar. The group lets us do all those things not possible in other situations.

Temporariness. At the same time, the free university class is temporary. It may last one week or ten, but the participant does not become trapped into a long commitment. For people who may not always have Monday nights free, the free university class is ideal. In fact, its short commitment is a major selling point for the free university. The class does not require a large commitment of money, time, or energy. If the class stirs the interest, one can take the class again. Or, as has happened hundreds of times before, the teacher and participants may continue meeting after the class is formally over.

To the potential learner, the free university evokes a positive image. The free university does not claim to be a college education, and thus it sets itself no higher than any of its participants. The free university stresses the worth of the individual, not his or her deficiencies. The free university is an independent or neutral place. The free university promises a nonthreatening atmosphere —no tests, grades, pressure, or failure. It offers the chance to meet and enjoy other people, to be part of a group, and yet it lets its learners retain their ability to move on to other things.

Image II

Image II is the image the free university has with respect to the community or the area that it serves and is almost as important as its image to individual learners.

It is its image in the community that has provided the free university with the entrance into so many supportive efforts within the community. This image—as a local community organization, promoting community development and placing the community above the free university—has figured prominently in the free university's success.

It is because of this image that store owners allow free university catalogs to be placed on their crowded counters. It is because of this image that churches provide office space to the free university; that participants often "forget" to claim their refund on a cancelled class; that local foundations provide seed money to the free university, even though there are a multitude of educational institutions around; that radio stations air free university public service announcements so often.

Free universities carry the idea that they provide a sense of community, not just for the individual but for the geographic area as well.

Part of that sense of community is that the free university places the community rather than itself at the focal point. The free university says somehow that its classes are meant to promote the community, not the free university. The cover of the free university catalog is a good place to illustrate that priority. Although a formal institution of higher education may have an impressive picture of its administration building on its catalog cover, the free university will likely have a picture of a bridge, the waterfront docks, the downtown, or a park on its cover. That shift in concern —from one's own institution to the community that it is serving— is evident in the free university's demeanor.

A second picture is that of the free university integrating various elements within the community. The board of advisers represents various groups within the area—housewives, ministers, and businessmen—and reflects the feeling that the free university is for everyone.

There is concrete evidence of this concern for the community as well, because the free university actively promotes community development. Many times a community resident will wonder out loud about a particular local problem, and the free university will invite that person to do a class on the topic. Shortly thereafter, the class will evolve into a committee and then become an organization, and soon that class will have been turned into community action to better the neighborhood. Even in this time of alleged lack of concern for social issues, special projects continue to be spun off by free university classes and activities.

For example, in its eleven years of existence, the Community Free School in Boulder, Colorado, has started forty-one projects, including a drama theater, a food co-op, a medical clinic, an elementary school, and a healing arts institute.

In all, the free university has earned an image of placing the community above itself and of serving the community. This in turn has helped the free university, as people and groups in the community have gone out of their way to keep the free university alive and growing.

RESPONSIVENESS

The free university's primary response to meeting changing public interests has been through its courses. By creating contemporary courses, by publicizing intriguing courses, by offering a gamut of subjects to stay ahead of the trends, free universities have been able to respond to the interests of the general public.

In the next chapter we will explore how free universities respond to the changing public's interest in courses and subject trends, the third area where free universities have achieved practical success.

Chapter 11

Managing Courses

The free university has never had a captive audience. The early campus free university vied with grades, degrees, graduate school, and careers for student attention. Today the free university is contending with jobs, family obligations, television, sports, and sheer exhaustion at the end of a long day.

As other educational institutions offer noncredit classes to adults, they too will experience the same competing interests and obligations of the average adult.

Thus, the free university model has been built to go to the public, rather than presuming that the public would come to it. The free university has operated in a free enterprise situation, attempting to meet the public's desires and/or needs in courses, publicity, and orientation.

Here are some "how-to" tips that free universities have learned along the way as they have organized and promoted their courses to the public.

High-Publicity Courses

Courses—people sharing and learning—are at the heart of the free university. They are also at the heart of its publicity effort. Courses continually provide fresh news stories that can keep the free university in the limelight. There are always new courses, new teachers, and new ideas.

Not all of your courses are eligible for that elite category of classes slated for "high publicity." You want a big story with a bright headline and a photo on page three or the first page of the second section, after which you hope to receive a flood of phone calls and, of course, registrations. Most of your classes don't lend themselves to such attention, so you need to look for the high-publicity courses and promote them.

Courses should not be fabricated or constructed just for publicity, but once you get a course with publicity potential, you can make it attractive and let the media grab it.

There are two good ways to approach the media with your high-publicity courses. The first is to throw out several ideas to them and see which ones they are intrigued by. A general press release about your session can do this: "Some of the courses this semester at the Cleveland Free University are . . ." or "You can crash a party, fly high, or eat purple popcorn this semester at the Cleveland Free University. . . ."

A second approach is to call a specific person at a newspaper or a radio or television station with one class idea in mind. You can call the foods section editor of the paper about a Korean cooking class, or call a talk-show host about a psychic who will be teaching a course. There the approach is tactful: "We saw this course and thought it might make a good story," "I know you're always interested in good interviews, and I thought you might be interested. . . ." But don't tell the press what is good publicity. Allow them to make it their story.

Here are some top publicity-getters that gained extensive local or even national coverage:

CHEAP! Joan McCarthy of the Southeast Denver Free University taught a course on cheap living. It received so much attention and so many registrants that she followed it up with "Cheap Dating" and a seasonal "Cheap Christmas." Taught during a time of recession for many people, it was a current and practical course.

THE OTHER WOMAN. A course for women dating married men was offered by the Learning Connection in Columbus, Ohio, and taught by a professor writing a book on the subject.

IN PRAISE OF OLDER WOMEN.   The Class Factory in Houston offered this course for women dating younger men.

CRASHING EMBASSY PARTIES.   In social-minded Washington, D.C., where many residents constantly hear about embassy parties but rarely attend them, this course on how to get into one was a big public relations draw for Open University. When the Associated Press picked it up, it also received national publicity and a television appearance by the instructor.

HOT-AIR BALLOONING.   The color, grandeur, and glory of flying high over the city and countryside proved a visual delight for the media in Wichita, Kansas, who covered the course offered by the Wichita Free University.

LIVING OUT YOUR FANTASIES.   Radio talk-show hosts called in from all over the country when they found out that Cheryl Moffit was offering this course at the Denver Free University.

QUITTING YOUR JOB.   More and more people are quitting their jobs, a practice formerly unacceptable or regarded dubiously, and Open University in Washington, D.C., capitalized on this topic.

POPCORN.   Take a common household item like popcorn and do all sorts of strange and delicious things to it, and you've got a great publicity course, as the Southeast Denver Free University found out.

COMPUTERS FOR KIDS.   Be the first adult education program on your block to offer a course that is futuristic, practical, and for children, and you've got headlines and a couple of pictures to go with it, as the Community Free School in Boulder, Colorado, discovered with its popular "hands-on" class for children on operating and using computers.

HISTORY OF BOREDOM.   We all get bored, but Communiversity in Kansas City learned that boredom can redirect history and play an important part in the crime rate and other economic and social factors in society. Communiversity also learned that boredom wasn't necessarily boring to the media, who played it up more than any other course that session.

Determining what courses have high publicity potential is not always easy. Here are some characteristics of courses that get good publicity:

1. Slightly outrageous or offbeat. Something the average person hasn't done, but would like to, like "Living Out Your Fantasies."

2. Current and topical. People have usually tried to keep their jobs, not quit them; when more and more people did so in the mid-seventies it was a topical course. During a recession in the late seventies, a course on cheap living became a current item.

3. Strong visual aspects. While a picture may be worth a thousand words, there's nothing better for publicity than a picture *next to* a thousand words, and a colorful balloon in the sky or children operating computers capture the attention of both photographers and editors.

4. Extraordinary from the ordinary. Doing something extraordinary with something ordinary, like popcorn or boredom, generates publicity.

5. Broad appeal. While only a few citizens could or would take a course on mountain climbing, for instance, anyone could crash an embassy party, make popcorn, or live out his or her fantasies.

6. Teacher personalities. Interesting teachers with exciting or unusual lives often make a good story, even if their subject matter is rather mundane. Macrame is not an unusual course, but when a fifteen-year-old teaches it to elderly women, it's a story.

7. Legitimacy. While slightly outrageous and offbeat ideas are good publicity, they must also be legitimate ideas. There should be something there. Even if many people would not agree with women dating younger men, it is a legitimate point of view. The free university should sense that the course has solid educational value. Heliotrope in San Francisco offered a much publicized course on "Howling at the Moon." The resulting public impression of Heliotrope, however, was largely negative because howling at the moon did not seem to be a legitimate educational endeavor.

Another practical point to think about in publicizing a course is whether more people can register for it. Some high-publicity courses don't get any participants despite the publicity. The "History of Boredom" class drew widespread attention but no participants. "They were just too bored to register," said Communiversity director Rick Mareske. From a publicity point of view, the class need not draw a lot of participants for it to benefit the program as a whole. Communiversity's other 125 courses benefitted substantially from the publicity.

But some high-publicity courses will attract not only attention but also participants. The popcorn class drew so many inquiries that two more classes had to be set up. A good publicity class should be one that people can register for not only because the organization will welcome the additional registrations but also because there will be a lot of disappointed people if they can't register for it. A class limited to four learners, for instance, would bring more problems with publicity than people.

Classes are your best, but not your only, way to get publicity. Other more mundane activities can be turned into publicity as well. Notices of board meetings, annual reports, statistics, anniversaries, plans, and special projects all make for publicity.

Here are some activities and events related to various aspects of the free university that can be turned into publicity items:

Board of advisers or directors
    meetings
    new board members
    election of officers

Classes
    interviews with teachers
    parties or get-togethers for teachers
    trend courses
    most popular courses
    most unusual courses
    need for specific topics

Staff
    open houses
    new staff members
    staff promotions

Statistics
    enrollments
    numbers of classes
    annual report statistics

Others
    announcements of grants, foundation monies, donations,
        fundraisers
    anniversaries
    festivals or fairs that you sponsor
    special projects or conferences

A good free university also uses all the media available and then keeps a list or record of when it was last on a particular station or in the paper.

Publicity often takes a while to sink in. One free university staff person was at a bank when a teller told him, "Oh, I saw you on TV." The staffer couldn't remember it and then recalled that his television appearance had been more than a year earlier. Publicity also takes repetition. A person may not respond to your public service announcement on radio or your newspaper article but then suddenly call after seeing a poster. The cumulative impact of radio, newspaper, and poster combine to cause the person to act eventually.

The medium might determine what message you want to publicize because newspapers, radio, and television each look for stories that will best suit their own medium.

Free universities have had most publicity success with newspapers, probably because a newspaper has scores of feature stories a day, while radio or television can offer only a few. The newspaper is also the most versatile medium for free university classes.

For radio or television, the free university has to select its publicity courses based on the characteristics of each. Radio is a good medium for ideas, and radio will want to talk more about the course content than the course itself. Most radio stories will be interviews. Because radio is a more intimate medium, courses that reflect a problem, that are personal, or that have a story to tell are excellent for radio. A course on UFOs or on the problems that women face dating married men are good radio interviews.

Television is quite a different medium. It is an almost totally visual and image medium. Television stories and features are short, with few words, and must be easy to understand within a short time. There is the oft-told story of the television editor who asked his film crew what their story was about. "It's about two minutes," was the reply. While exploring the problems of dating younger men may not fit into a two-minute television segment, a course on hot-air ballooning is great television footage. Although chair-caning may be difficult to explain in a newspaper column or on radio, "how-to," practical, and craft courses are good stories for the television camera.

Downplaying Courses

Free universities don't want all their courses to get publicity and in fact would prefer that some of them not be highlighted. The diversity of free university courses means that some people will not like some of the courses, and the experimental, innovative nature of free university offerings also means that some courses will not be popular or regarded highly. But if they are legitimate courses, they deserve to be in the catalog. So while free universities have become adept at gaining publicity for their courses, they have also learned to downplay some of them.

Courses on child abuse, wine making, rape, homosexuality, and union organizing are all legitimate topics but, depending on the community, may not be popular ones. There are several ways to offer the courses without flaunting them.

1. Position the course strategically. As in a newspaper, the pages in the catalog that are read most often are the first and last pages. From looking at the first page in the catalog or brochure, the reader gets an impression about the types of courses offered, and certain courses will stand out and be remembered. A course on gay rights on the cover will gain certain attention, but the same description in the middle of the catalog will be more likely to be remembered only by those persons interested in taking the class. Another positioning tactic is to put a controversial course between two traditional or conservative ones, thus providing the impression that the free university presents all views, or that controversial ones are a minority compared to the traditional and "acceptable" courses.

2. Reword the title. In Wakeeney, a western Kansas town of 2,334, a woman wanted to offer a course on rape for the Trego Recreation Education Environment (TREE) program. But the

course title "Rape" would not only be disturbing to many towns-people but also discourage people from attending. So TREE co-director Miriam Miller and the teacher searched for a new title and came up with "Assault Against Women." Devoid of an explosive title but with its content intact, the course not only received no complaints but also garnered a good number of participants and was an important topic for the townspeople to understand.

3. "Legitimize" the course in some way. This can be done by scheduling it in a "respectable" location, such as a church. If the teacher is a respected authority or a professional, highlighting those credentials is possible. The Learning Connection's course on "The Other Woman" might have raised a few eyebrows, but with the instructor not only a professor but also an author on the topic, it appeared acceptable.

4. Make the course description less strident or activist. A course on boycotting Coors beer at University for Man in Manhattan created a stir that might have been avoided had the course description presented the issue in a more academic, more neutral, or less activist manner.

5. Present another side of an issue. This can be done either in the same course or in a course with a contrasting view. Some courses advocating a certain position have been restructured so that a panel representing other views is included, thus presenting a more objective view of the situation. Although some teachers may resent the watering down of their views, others may welcome the dialogue and see it as a way to draw more participants and a larger audience for their ideas.

Courses That Fail

Many courses in adult education programs fail to get enough registrations to make the class go. This is true as well for free universities. But free university leaders are less likely to look upon their course failure rate as negative.

One reason may be that course failures in free universities are not so costly as in other adult education enterprises where a teacher may be on contract, facilities rented, or equipment unused. Another reason is that free university directors view course failures as necessary counterparts to course successes.

If new trends are to be developed, and if free universities are to stay on top of new trends and discover successful classes, they must risk the chance that many other classes will also fail. Course failures also play a few other positive roles:

1. They are as much an indicator of trends and successful subject areas as are the classes with large enrollments. Cancelled classes tell the program administrator about what people like and don't like.

2. Cancelled classes may be successful classes in disguise. The timing may be off, and the class may succeed a year from now or even next session. Some unsuccessful classes are later offered again and, for some unknown reason, have excellent enrollments. Perhaps the original description was poor, or the title was not eye-catching enough. Perhaps the time, place, or other logistical matter created problems.

3. The course idea may be stimulating and useful in itself, even if the class doesn't go. The free university is a place not just for enrollments but for creative ideas, and even ideas that are not yet popular are important in the long run.

Trend Courses

One of the fascinating characteristics of adult learning in America is that learning tastes keep changing. While curricula in higher education remain basically the same or change slowly over the years, the pace in adult learning is much quicker. Adults are problem- and interest-centered, and those problems and interests keep changing. While in higher education, faculty and administration have the primary role either in changing curricula or in legitimizing new curricula, the adult education administrator has little control over what new courses will be offered or what directions adult learning will take. That impetus comes from individual learners and teachers, who collectively form trends and subtrends that adult education administrators can promote or try to ignore, but that they can rarely control.

While all adult education institutions are affected by trend courses, free universities are a barometer of those trends and are the first to reflect changes. Free universities have the most diverse offerings, and thus a trend in any area—crafts, arts, practical courses, ideas, social issues—will be reflected in free university offerings. In the free university, unlike most other adult education institutions, the initiative for new courses does not come from the administration but from teachers and learners. Thus, courses come from the general public, where trends are made and broken. Then, too, changes can be made in free university offerings overnight. There are no faculty committees to weigh the merits of a new course, no forces opposed to innovation, no obligations to facilities or other constraining factors. A new course can be added quickly or dropped quickly.

It has been only recently that free universities have been aware of the cycle of trend courses, even though the trends can now be traced back to the mid-sixties. We are just beginning to track the trend courses, to gain some understanding of them, and to become more alert in spotting them as they develop. Trend courses are basically a reflection of society's larger concerns at any moment, and they differ little from the trends in the general public's reading habits, avocations, and work concerns as a whole. There are really three sets of trends. First, there are larger trend areas such as interpersonal relations or the environment. Second, there are specific course trends. Disco has been the dominant course trend in the 1978–80 period, but there are others.

Third, there are subtrends. For example, within the Self courses from 1978 to 1980 some subtrends have been dance, holistic health, finance, time management, and appropriate technology. Specific courses within those trends have been courses like "Disco," "Buying a House," "Insulating Your Home," "Investments," "Massage," and "Self-Care."

At the 1979 national free university conference, several large independent free universities listed the winners—their most successful courses in terms of enrollment; the surprises—some courses that they didn't expect to do well but that did; and the bombs—courses that failed. Their list:

Winners

Disco	Disco Roller Skating	Computers
Music for the	Country Swing	Meeting People
Complete Idiot	Bartending	Karate
Ballet	Real Estate	Fencing
Bagels	Hypnosis	Psychic Phenomena
Jazz	Carpentry	Hot-Air Ballooning
Aerobic Dancing	Cooking	Reflexology
Social Singles	Living on a Budget	

Surprises	Bombs
Conversational Arabic	Christ Returns
Sanskrit	Sexology
Social Climbing	Disco
Balloon Sculptures	Pottery
Wind Surfing	Jewelry
Farsi	Religion
Chair-Caning	Human Potential
	Assertiveness
	Relating
	Meditation

Free universities have not tried to create or develop trends but to spot them, promote them, and ride the trend wave until it crashes. It is hoped that there will be another trend wave ready to ride. Interestingly, the free university's best strategy in spotting and benefitting from trends has been not to become absorbed by them or dependent upon them. Free universities have remained successful trend providers not because they provide the trend courses but because they provide other courses as well—the trend courses of the future.

Free universities have maintained their diversity in courses and have sought to develop and protect that diversity. They have looked for ways to extend that diversity—by offering classes for the elderly or trying to offer a few classes on social issues. Individual free universities have attempted to strengthen weak spots to keep that broad range of subject areas. By maintaining diversity, the free university's image as a provider of many kinds of courses is kept intact. Many other providers of adult education specialize or lean in one direction—toward courses in recreation, arts and crafts, fine arts, or academics. But there are several practical reasons why free universities seek to maintain the diversity in their course offerings.

1. The provider of adult education will never know when a trend is developing unless that organization has some courses in the trend area to watch for evidence.

2. Interests change, and it is unwise to write off any course category as belonging to the past. Classes in social issues were popular in the mid-sixties, for instance, and they will be popular again. It may be in five years, ten years, or fifty years, but that trend will come again.

3. The public will be less likely to perceive the organization as offering the trend course unless the organization has offered similar courses in the past. For example, if Middle Eastern studies (Arabic, Islam, Persian history, and so on) became popular, one would not be inclined to look for those kinds of courses at a city recreation department whose general image is one of offering recreation courses. If Middle Eastern studies became a trend, it would be reasonable to expect that city recreation departments would be left out of that trend offering.

By maintaining diversity, free universities are able to respond to each trend, especially when those trends are dissimilar. The recent trends of holistic health, appropriate technology, and dance, for instance, are different subjects. Yet they are all part of the overall interest in courses dealing with the self. By being able to offer courses in health, home insulation, and ballet all at once, the free university has been able to be a part of each one of those trend courses.

Spotting trend courses has not been a highly developed science. There are only a few general characteristics of trend courses. The most noticeable one is that trend courses have broad appeal. They cross all age, sex, income, and geographic lines. Yoga was a real trend course, as popular in rural areas as in the cities. And a course on "Yoga for Over Fifty" had as long a waiting list as yoga for younger people. Mountain climbing would be an unlikely candidate for a trend course. It is limited on the whole to robust people and, of course, can only be offered where there are mountains.

The only rule at this point in spotting trends as they develop is to observe. Best seller lists, newspaper and magazine articles, and store windows all point to current concerns of the general public. One theory is that the post–World War II generation is the generation that has and will continue to set societal trends, simply because of the great numbers of people in that age group. That certainly has been true for free universities.

Many free university leaders get their ideas for new classes and consequently new trends from looking at other free university catalogs. By observing new class titles, new subject headings, and the number of classes in a given subject area, one can pick up the trends and new courses being taught in other adult-learning programs.

Controversial Courses

Innovative, unusual, and unpopular courses sometimes become controversial courses, and controversy—and the attempt to avoid it—may lead to censoring particular courses. Since free universities believe that the educational implication of the First Amendment right to free speech is that anyone may teach any idea or topic that he or she wants, provided it is legal, they have sought ways in which to offer controversial topics with as little controversy as possible.

The controversial topics tend to be those that involve religion, politics, and morality. Here are some ways in which free universities are dealing with controversial courses:

1. Offering the opposite point of view. By encouraging classes that present the opposite point of view, the free university retains its neutrality and nonendorsement of any particular viewpoint. When a Christian fundamentalist called to object to a course on bartending, the free university director encouraged her to offer a course on temperance. "Will you teach a course expressing the other point of view?" she was asked. "It is important for people to hear what you have to say." Sometimes people will agree to teach, and sometimes they will not. When this woman declined, she was told, "I'm sorry that the community will miss your point of view." Thus, the responsibility for not offering the temperance perspective was put on the caller and not on the free university.

2. Seeking out favorable opinion. If there are courses that might offend a particular segment of the population, or if the image of the free university is not positive with a particular target audience, seeking out publicity with that group may prove worthwhile. One free university director deliberately sought an interview on a radio station catering to right-wing fundamentalist listeners. The half-hour interview ultimately proved constructive and beneficial to the organization.

3. Asking for outside support. One woman who worked for a four-year traditional university agreed to offer a free university course but was warned by university officials that she would lose her position if she did so. She eventually obtained a letter of assurance from a federal agency involved with her work, and she taught the class.

4. Relying on the Constitution. At times free universities have had to cite Supreme Court decisions and the First Amendment to the U.S. Constitution as justification for the freedom to teach a particular point of view. Although this approach is used infrequently and usually in formal public arenas, it is the basis on which free universities maintain their position on academic freedom.

Chapter 12

Learning and Teaching

LEARNING IN A FREE UNIVERSITY

When Allen Tough addressed the Eighth National Free University Conference in 1978, he began by saying, "I'm concerned with power and control. I guess the basic question around power and control is, 'Who has it? Who has the control, and who has the power?' "[1] Tough wasn't talking about politics, war, economics, or even education. He was talking about learning.

Learning—that innocent, mild, positive process that receives more approbation than motherhood and apple pie—is now involved in such harsh and divisive concepts as "power" and "control." It is part of a change that learners are going through, the results of which may have a subtle but enormous impact not only on learning but on other areas of life as well.

Tough is talking about the individual learner. Does the individual learner control his or her own learning? Does the power for deciding what, when, where, and how to learn rest with the individual or with some outside source? Tough sees a growing movement in society for individuals to control their own learning.

Susan Spragg, writing for the Denver Free University, notes,

People are taking charge of their own personal lives. They are taking back power and control. People are learning about their physical and spiritual well-being and taking back some of the power they had given over to the medical profession. Learners are deciding what and how they will learn instead of leaving that up to the educational institutions. People are taking assertiveness training and life planning so they can more effectively take charge of their present and future modes of living and people are getting together in groups and taking back in bits and pieces the power that they had relinquished to big government and giant corporations, and we hear talk of neighborhood government, appropriate technology and local self-reliance.[2]

While Spragg may be hinting at revolutions not yet realized, the implications for learner-centered education are already becoming clear. Spragg alluded to the self-care movement in health, which began with people learning about their own bodies—not teaching, doctoring, or administering. The self-care movement in medicine is essentially a learning movement. It stems from a belief that each of us is capable of learning more about his or her own body and that a more educated person will be a healthier person. By working with the medical establishment, advocates of the self-care concept may be able to improve health care in this country significantly by teaching people how to take care of themselves and when to go to a doctor.

The implications for individual control of learning that Tough speaks of could go far beyond noncredit classes in free universities. It could change our whole view of the world and our participation in it. Self-directed learning may easily lead to self-directed action and self-directed living, which would catalyze a whole new initiative in citizen action and participation. Robert Pirsig, in *Zen and the Art of Motorcycle Maintenance*, notes that there are some global events that change our whole perception of the world. He gives the example of the astronauts landing on the moon and Columbus discovering the New World, referring to the analogy that many commentators have made between the two. But Pirsig says that the moon landing did not change our view of the world but was only an extension of existing ways of thinking about it. Nothing in our individual lives has changed significantly because of that landing. Our attitudes, values, and behavior are still basically the same. Columbus's discovery of the New World, however, completely changed science, religion, politics, economics, attitudes, and values. So, too, may this new way of learning that Tough and others advocate affect the greater arena of living.

Not all the learning that people undertake will have such a direct impact on cosmic and intellectual change, but it is the process, not necessarily the content, that is important.

To a large extent, learning in a free university reflects this much larger notion and movement toward self-directed learning. Self-directed learning is based on the belief, supported by research, that learning is best accomplished when the learner takes responsibility for his or her own learning. That means that the learner decides when to learn, what to learn, and even how to learn. It rejects the notion that teachers or other outsiders know what is good for us. Education that is determined and enforced by external forces is neither positive nor growth-producing.

In much formal education, the impetus for and control of learning is determined by something or somebody other than the learner. It could be an institution, a teacher, or a legal requirement. Education is then provided to the learner, who is trained or taught. The learner becomes the recipient of this process and all too often a mere consumer rather than an active participant.

Self-directed learning begins with the learner. It sees the learner as the primary impetus for and initiator of the learning process. Teachers, classes, and other educational features are then put in a secondary light, as aids to the learning process rather than its central elements.

Before the early 1970s, self-directed learning had little prestige or recognition. This was due in large measure to misconceptions about how adults learn. Two assumptions were particularly misleading. One was that people basically were not capable of being self-directed learners, that people did not possess enough self-discipline to determine and then execute their own planned learning activities. Learning had to be forced, or at least encouraged, by others. Another assumption was that significant learning did not take place outside formal education—classes, tutoring, and so on. But in 1971, Allen Tough came out with his pioneering work on self-directed learning, which changed those notions and the way educators thought about adult learning. He discovered that people were doing a good deal of learning on their own—conscious, planned, and involved learning.

Says Tough,

In our study around 1971 we went and asked people to tell us about their efforts to learn. And what we find is that people are doing an enormous amount of learning. They're spending something like 500 hours a year, which is something like ten hours a week making efforts to learn. And most of that they're doing themselves—73% of it is self planned. The learner decides how to go about it, how to learn, each step of the way. The control, the power, the responsibility, stays in the hands of the learner. That's 73%, and that's what I see as the normal, natural way to learn. And when that doesn't work, then they'll go to some other ways to learn. It's not a solitary process. They get a lot of help from friends and neighbors and relatives and so on, but they do retain the control. They get advice and information and support, but they don't turn the control over to someone else.[3]

In 1975, Malcolm Knowles published *Self Directed Learning* and furthered the concept. Knowles says that the central concept behind self-directed learning is that one of the organic natural aspects of psychological maturation is moving from dependence to independence. The characteristics of self-directed learning, then, are those which support psychological maturation or independence. Knowles lists them as 1. a positive self-image, 2. nondefensiveness, 3. an ability to diagnose one's needs for learning, 4. planning skills, and 5. skills in evaluating what one has learned.[4]

Although free universities had postulated various beliefs and philosophies about learning, the process in a free university has never been studied nor have many practical hints been given to participants in free universities. The tenets of self-directed learning are restated here because they coincide with the thoughts on learning of most free university people. In terms of overall theory, practical pointers, and research, the work done on self-directed learning outlines the kind of learning that free universities promote.

Unlike most educational institutions, the free university does not make many assumptions about the kind of learner who participates. In the past few years, studies have been done on profiling the "average" lifelong learner. These studies have revealed the not-surprising characteristics of adult learners as mostly college-educated, young, white, middle-class, urban or suburban residents. Says noted educational researcher Patricia Cross, "Today's adult learners are disproportionately young, white, well-educated, employed in professional and technical occupations, and making good incomes."[5] While Cross distinguishes this profile both from "potential adult learners" and from adult learners as defined by Tough, the effect of such characterizations by higher education has been to limit the approach and scope of adult learning by more formal institutions. If adult educators believe that the average adult learner is a young white professional, then programs will be geared toward that population, reinforcing the stereotype and the statistics.

Too often these studies have led to programs that conform to the statistical stereotype rather than break it. By ignoring such statistical analyses, free universities have been able to reach adult learners not in that statistical profile. As a result, learners in free universities also come from low-income families, the elderly, small towns, and rural communities.

But the people who come to free universities are also under the same constraints as adult learners in other institutions. Perhaps free universities have succeeded somewhat in recognizing those constraints and tailoring their classes to overcome them. The three characteristics of the adult learner most commonly mentioned are these:

1. The adult learner has a time concern. There are several aspects to the time concern. Most obviously, adults tend to be working, and thus have less time for the evening and leisure activities. But on a more elementary level, adults see time in their lives as being limited, as compared with youth, who are more likely to see time as unlimited. Thus, adults want to learn something quickly and in a given time frame.

2. The adult learner is problem- or task-oriented. Learning as a child or youth tends to be subject-oriented. School children learn about social studies and English. But adults want answers to perplexing problems or issues that confront them, and their learning tends to be problem- or task-oriented. Adults undertake most of their learning not out of pure curiosity but from a desire to learn something useful that they can practice in life, or to help understand something important in their lives.

3. The adult learner is far more influenced by the physical surroundings of the learning situation than youth and children appear to be. Good lighting, comfortable seating, and well heated or

air-conditioned buildings all help to make the learner more comfortable—a precondition to good adult learning. Partly because free university classes tend to be in informal and comfortable settings, free universities have been able to respond to the need for enjoyable physical surroundings instead of subjecting adult learners to more rigid atmospheres that put learners ill at ease.

People come to free universities for a wide variety of reasons. They come not only to learn but also to meet new people, to socialize, to relieve boredom, to develop self-confidence, to become more self-actualized, to continue personal growth, to explore furthering their own formal education, to gain insights that might benefit them in the workplace, to explore new career areas, to create new projects, to solve personal problems, for self-expression, for enjoyment, for action. They do not come, on the whole, to advance their careers or to learn specific job skills.

Participants in a free university have internal motivations both for attending and for learning in the free university. There are no monetary rewards, no credits, no continuing education units, no points for career advancement, no recognition from family, boss, or friends.

Participants in a free university also have a few expectations. They expect courses to be introductory or basic in nature and that they will not need to have had any prerequisites before enrolling. If the subject matter is advanced, that will have been stated in the course descriptions. Learners expect there to be no homework and little outside activity in regard to the class. Learners assume that classes will meet once a week. Learners do not anticipate a great deal of reading to be involved. While learners want the topic to be adequately covered, they expect to focus on a specific skill or idea, not to cover a broad subject area or discipline.

In various ways, free universities have attempted to make the learner aware of his or her own responsibility in the learning process. Free universities demand learners to be active participants, not consumers of knowledge. Toward that end, free universities have tried to deal with the traditional attitudes and values many people still hold about learning. While the notions of self-directed learning are becoming more widely accepted, the majority of people in society know only the school as a model for learning. Most people know how to learn only by being taught. Free universities are not exempt from this problem. People know the skills of being taught; these have been learned in school, primarily for the purpose of passing the test, completing the course, and gaining the degree. These skills include not only a respect for authority but often a fear of it and a tendency not to challenge the authority of the teacher, a passive approach toward consuming information and facts, and a negative self-concept as "one who does not know."

Sue Rieger, in a UFM workshop at Manhattan, Kansas, listed three responsibilities of the learner in a free university:

1. Responsibility to oneself. Each participant has a responsibility to himself or herself to be a self-directed learner, to be an active participant, to develop some self-discipline and motivation, to attend regularly, to determine what he or she wants to know, to gain that knowledge, and to somehow evaluate how well he or she is doing.

2. Responsibility to the others in the class. The participant in a free university class has a responsibility to others in the class. Part of that responsibility is to be an active participant in the class, providing ideas, feedback, questions, and challenges both to the teacher and to other learners. Sharing in a class situation involves more than just one or two people and the teacher. We have all had classroom experiences in which only one or two students actively talk or provide answers for the teacher while the rest of the class is passive and silent. In a free university, all the participants have the responsibility of being involved in the class and providing attention and interest in what is going on.

3. Responsibility to the free university. The free university is merely the link between the teacher and the students. The free university depends on participants providing feedback to make it better. Not only are learners responsible for registering and attending, but they must help the free university improve as well. Unlike other administrative structures, free universities are not only responsive but also dependent upon student input. Free universities rely on their participants to tell the free university when a teacher is not teaching well or when there are complaints about the class and to make suggestions about how the class can be improved. The free university also needs to know how to improve its administration—its publicity, catalog, registration, facilities, and other services to the participants. Thus, the participant does have the responsibility to inform the free university about weaknesses.[6]

Learning in a free university is a different kind of experience. Learning is rarely standardized or routine, is sometimes uncertain, is sometimes disappointing, and sometimes an elation. Come expecting to share, to be involved, to enjoy, to depend on yourself for discipline and motivation. Learning in a free university has many of the traits of other adult learning—free universities are, after all, dealing with the same kind of people who attend other adult-learning institutions as well. But within that context, free universities are attempting to make self-directed learning a way of life, to actively involve learners as participants rather than as passive students, and to make learning a sharing experience.

TEACHING IN A FREE UNIVERSITY

From the free university perspective, a teacher is not a position but a role. It is a positive experience that we all can, and do, have. It would be impossible to say that children do not teach their younger siblings, that teenagers do not teach each other, that workers do not teach their fellow workers. Just as most adults are parents, adults are teachers. True, some adults will not be good teachers, but some adults are not good parents either. And as there are ways to assist adults in being good parents, so, too, are there ways to help people in becoming good teachers.

Teaching in a free university is distinctly different from teaching in any other situation. The assumptions, audience, atmosphere, and lack of constraints combine to make teaching in a free university an exciting, enjoyable, and yet demanding, experience.

People teach in free universities for many reasons, almost all of them from internal motivation. Unlike formal institutions, free universities offer few external rewards—money, prestige, career advancement—although these factors occasionally play a part.

We used to believe that there were few, if any, rewards for teaching adults, and that it was essentially an act of service or charity. Even today many people are recruited to be teachers from the perspective of helping others. A more appropriate approach is to give people the opportunity to teach, recognizing that teaching is a growing experience with many rewards for the teacher. As this author has written, in *Teaching Free,* "Most people volunteer to teach out of a healthy self-interest, not from a sense of responsibility to help others. Teaching, even for free, has many rewards."[7]

The internal rewards for teaching are many. It has long been recognized that by teaching a subject someone can brush up on the subject or gain a better understanding of the material. In the seventeenth century, Comenius observed, "The saying, 'He who teaches others teaches himself' is very true not only because constant repetition impresses a fact indelibly on the mind but because the process of teaching in itself gives a deeper insight into the subjects taught. . . ." Thus, the very act of teaching is a learning tool.

Another aspect of teaching to learn is that participants often bring additional insights or new information, and the teacher in a free university can learn from the students. This is made easier by the free university environment, which assumes that students know something and that the teacher doesn't know everything. Thus, the free university teacher does not have to pretend that he or she is the all-knowing authority on the topic and that learning from one's students is a threat to one's position or image. Free university teachers can be frank in their desire to learn from the students as well as to teach them.

Students also provide new ideas, perspectives, and questions. The Denver Free University teacher who wanted to teach because he was writing a book on becoming a landlord did not think that his class participants would have any important information to share about being a landlord, but that they would have questions he had not thought of and a curiosity and a perspective that might very well add to his presentation of the information in his book. In this respect, students in free universities are rarely passive learners; they ask questions, challenge ideas, and state their own opinions.

People do teach to help others, of course, and this is another reward for teaching—seeing people learn a skill, gain some knowledge, or develop more self-confidence in a given area.

Another important reason why people teach is self-expression—to articulate their thoughts. Sometimes those thoughts may be new or different, and free universities offer a way to test new ideas for inventors, researchers, and others to promote unusual views. But most people need self-expression even if their ideas or skills are acceptable or common.

Again, from *Teaching Free:*

We want to teach because we have a need to share knowledge. There are two reasons for this. First, we know more now. Every person has a wealth of information and skills to share with others. And secondly, there is a scarcity of ways to tutor or teach others. A few years ago we shared ideas through the family, church and other organizations. Today participation in these institutions is declining. While we know more, there are fewer avenues for expressing that knowledge.[8]

Historically, we know that people have always had ways in which to share their knowledge with their family, neighbors, and friends. One hundred years ago, there were relatively few colleges. Yet people learned, and they learned from each other. Fathers taught their sons a trade; mothers taught their daughters homemaking skills. Skilled laborers took on apprentices. Even fifty and twenty years ago there were plenty of opportunities to teach. Adults taught Sunday school, became scout leaders, and joined civic clubs, organizations, and associations. Community activities, like harvesting, barn raisings, and quilting bees, were also learning times. Civic activities, like local and national political organizations, were opportunities to develop leadership and to train others to be leaders.

Today, with participation in these institutions declining, the free university provides one way in which adults can share their ideas, and that release—that catharsis—is healthy.

Many people teach to meet new people. In small, medium, or large towns, it is stimulating to bring new people into one's life, and through teaching, a person has an opportunity to meet new people with similar interests.

Socializing as a whole is another reason why people engage in teaching. Teaching in a free university is an enjoyable experience that allows people to have a good time as well as to learn. Of particular interest to an increasing number of people is social interaction with people of all ages. Society has become peer-oriented, and those peers are almost always people in the same age bracket or with the same life-style. Yet, the interaction with older and younger people is stimulating, and free universities provide one way to meet and engage socially with people of all ages.

There are external rewards as well. Half the people who teach in a free university receive reimbursement for it. Teacher fees range from $100 to $200 per course—not a large sum, but certainly a welcome addition to one's income. There are teachers who make much more than that, and even some whose living is earned entirely by teaching in the free university.

Another reason why professionals and businessmen often offer a course is to gain new clients or customers. Although there are strict rules in free universities about peddling wares and soliciting in the class, the exposure of students to the teacher's business can lead to new customers. Stockbrokers customarily lead free university classes in part to promote awareness of stocks and in part to become acquainted with people who may use them as brokers. David Margolis of Denver Free University originally taught his course on financial independence on the tip of a customer who thought he could get more clients by teaching the course.

Some people use the opportunity to teach in a free university to advance their careers or to get needed experience in teaching or interacting with people or leading groups. Don Marchese at the Denver Free University taught astronomy for such a reason. He was interested in joining his corporation's training division. He had no previous teaching experience and was told that he would need some to enter that division. Teaching experience is also highly regarded on resumes and is good information for job interviews.

For independent artists and craftspersons, the free university not only offers a professionally rewarding and paying experience but also provides an atmosphere where the artist has the greatest artistic freedom available.

What is teaching in a free university like? Teaching in a free university is equal, independent, social, informal, enjoyable, and demanding.

Equal. Teaching in a free university is an experience in equality. The teacher has neither the privilege nor onus of being authoritarian, even though many authorities teach at free universities.

Independent. There is almost total independence for the teacher in a free university. There are no course outlines to have approved, no curriculum guidelines to follow, no textbooks to order, no attendance records to keep, no supervision, and no judgments of teaching technique. Once the class has been listed and people register, the responsibility for the class is up to the learners and the teacher. This gives the teacher a sense that the class is "his or hers," that imagination and creativity are welcome, and that there is freedom to instruct the class in the manner in which he or she chooses. This is especially true for many artists who have taught at free universities. "Free universities offer the most creative freedom," says David Knoll of Communiversity in Rochester, New York, "both for the learner and the teacher. Teachers enjoy the freedom. They aren't restricted in what they teach. It is a freeing experience."[9]

Social. There is much that is social about teaching in a free university. Some courses are very academic, taught in a classroom lecture-style with little social interaction. But the vast majority of classes involve relaxation and interaction. There are discussion classes in living rooms, with a pot of coffee brewing in the kitchen for the break. A few people start talking in a corner long past the end of the class, sometimes with the teacher, sometimes without. There are cooking classes in kitchens with students rubbing elbows in front of a hot stove and then sitting down together to enjoy the fruits (or vegetables or desserts) of their labor. In the summer of 1978, for example, a *Newsweek* reporter and a photographer came to University for Man in Manhattan to interview some classes and take pictures. At the Mexican cooking class, the reporter interviewed the teachers, a Mexican couple, while the photographer was busy snapping photos. When the reporter turned to go, she looked everywhere for the photographer, only to discover him seated at the table among the students, with a large plate of food, eating and talking with the other participants.

There are other classes that are almost purely social, such as hayrides, nature hikes, and other learning/social gatherings.

Informal. The social aspect of classes leads to another feature —informality. The learning style and the teaching style are usually informal. Sometimes informality means casualness, but not always. There are few notes taken, no attendance records, no tardy slips, few formal lectures, and no tests as a rule. But the informality has a specific educational function, which is to encourage learning. If adults are tense, unconfident, or too formal, they are less likely to learn. People often sit in a circle rather than in rows. Classes do not usually end exactly after fifty minutes. If the topic has been covered in less time, the class ends; if there is discussion, it may go on a little longer.

Enjoyable. If free university learning is informal, it is also enjoyable, even fun. There is not often a lot of pain in learning at a free university. Free universities have sometimes tried to deny that learning in a free university is fun, feeling that people might think that notion frivolous, or even not learning. But it is undeniable. Learning in a free university is most often a fun experience, not a difficult or painful one. While some things may best be learned in a more disciplined, painful way, there are a good many things that can best be learned in an enjoyable way. Again, enjoying the learning has some basic educational foundations. Georg Moncki, a native East German, who teaches conversational German for Communiversity in Kansas City, Missouri, does his class in a bar. Since many of us have had tense experiences learning a language in a classroom, Moncki sets his students at ease and lets them talk. Making the class enjoyable can also make it productive.

Demanding. Teaching in a free university is also demanding. There are probably more pressures on a free university teacher to hold a successful class than on teachers in formal institutions. This is because there is nothing to keep students from leaving. Students can walk out at any time, since they have committed little time, energy, and money to the class. If students are not learning or enjoying the class, they will leave. So there is some pressure on the free university teacher to make each and every class stimulating. Free university teachers must be prepared. They cannot spend too much time, and certainly not a whole class, talking about what students will learn ten weeks from now. The free university teacher must make his ideas plausible. It is not possible to say, "Because I told you so" or "Because I say so" in response to student questions. As organizer Bob Hagan notes, "Argumentation by authority is not possible in a free university."[10]

There are two things that can be said about the subject matter that people teach. First, it is more apt to be at a beginning or introductory level. There are few sequence courses in free universities. While some participants may be advanced in a given subject, most will be beginners. Thus the material is generally oriented toward the introductory level, at least at the start of the session. Secondly, although the material may be introductory, it is also more specific in nature than other educational courses. Broad subject categories are narrowed down to topics, so that teachers are teaching a topic and covering it well. There will be few courses on "History," for example, but there will be a course on "The Ancient Mayan," "The Beginnings of the Early Church," or "The

Russian Revolution." The narrow topics may seem to contradict the previous statement somewhat, for the fact that the topics are more specific also means that some of them are more "advanced." What is a free university class like? Beyond the generalities given, each one differs. Some are technical; some are basic. Some are ideas; some are social. Some are lectures; some are group discussions. Some are taught by professionals; some are taught by neighbors; some are taught by young people. What makes a free university special is that each class differs because the learning is up to the teacher and learners.

Teacher Recruitment

Teachers are recruited in many different ways. Many free university directors keep files on past, present, and potential teachers. New people are found by reading the pages of the daily newspaper or by subscribing to the host of organizational newsletters any town will have. Speaker files at the public library, volunteer files at the local voluntary action center, and Retired Senior Volunteer Program files at the local agency for aging are all sources. General recruiting announcements appear in the course catalog and in the teacher newsletter that a free university may put out. If the free university has a newsletter for its teachers, course topics for which people are needed can be listed. Present teachers can be encouraged to recruit other people. Classified ads, news notices, and public service announcements can be run in newspapers and on radio. For specific courses, the staff become educational detectives, using the Yellow Pages as a start to track down people who might know other people interested in teaching.

Teacher Orientation

Teacher orientation is a more difficult task in free universities than in formal education because of the diversity of people, class size, topics, and techniques. It is also more difficult because there are few data on what makes a class successful for adults. As we are just beginning to enter the era of lifelong learning, it is unclear what adults want and how teachers should teach. Denis Detzel, one of the founders of the Learning Exchange in Evanston, Illinois, says that "it isn't a question of what we think a good teacher is, but what the consumer or learner thinks."[11] What may be a good teacher to one person may not be a good teacher to another learner. Detzel cautions administrators against using the role model of the full-time professional teacher as the standard against which independent, part-time, and volunteer teachers should be measured and trained. At this stage, free universities must start with no assumptions or presuppositions about what a good teacher is, because lifelong learning is different from higher education.

Added to this relatively sparse knowledge about teaching adults is the fact that each free university class may be very different from every other class. There may be a hundred free university classes. While classes in a university are fairly standard—large lecture, small discussion, and so on—each free university class may require a different approach and technique. A nature hike will differ from a group discussion on current events. And a nature hike with five people will be different from a nature hike with twenty-five people. Given the various combinations of course topic, method, and class size, it is almost impossible to provide a standardized training program for teachers.

We are only beginning to find out what makes a class good, and because of the variations in class situations, teacher orientation is probably a better preparation than teacher training.

Although we should not assume that we know what a good teacher is, there are some things that we can share with potential teachers as an orientation. There are four basic topics that should be covered with prospective teachers—the educational philosophy, what to expect, logistics, and teaching techniques.

1. The educational philosophy of the organization. Teachers will want to know how the organization feels about the learning process, where responsibility for learning rests, and what "quality" learning is. Especially if the organization is a free university, teachers should be told how the organization differs from others in structure and philosophy of education.

2. What to expect. Most people have not taught adults before in a group setting, and most of us have the school as our model for education. Their free university class will be quite different from school, however, and teachers should be briefed on how their class might differ. The mix or types of people who might attend, their expectations, time restrictions, and other characteristics should all be explained.

3. Logistics. If there are problems about the class location, facilities, meeting time, length, or materials or supplies, they should be worked out.

4. Teaching techniques. There are some helpful hints and explanations of different kinds of teaching techniques and methods that can be passed on to prospective teachers. Depending on the type of class, prospective teachers may be interested in one or more teaching techniques that will enliven or stimulate the class. For the past forty years or so, various techniques for teaching adults have come into vogue. Some of those that have been popular at various times include the discussion method, audiovisual techniques, T-groups, and role playing. It is more common today to see each teacher use one or more techniques based on the needs of the class rather than any one currently popular mode.

There are several ways in which to orient new teachers. One is to publish a flyer or brochure stating your philosophy, rules, what to expect, and other helpful information. There are several pamphlets available on teaching adults, and a copy of one could be sent to new teachers. One of the better methods is to interview each teacher and cover the material in person with each prospective teacher. A third way is to hold a meeting, party, or other get-together for all your teachers. Although less than half your teachers are likely to attend any given meeting, it is a way to build support for the organization and to give teachers a chance to interact with each other.

With a philosophy like "Anybody can teach, anybody can learn," most free universities, in trying to actualize this goal, do not "select" teachers in the usual sense. But almost all free universities at one time or another have not allowed someone to teach a certain course, a decision sometimes based on the person and sometimes on the course content. On the other hand, although a few free universities have strict guidelines about who can teach, most free universities follow the practice of allowing anyone to teach. The free university practice of allowing almost anyone to teach is definitely different from traditional educational practice, in which teachers are selected and "certified" in some way by the administration. That certification may not be formal or on paper, but it does indicate approval and, to a greater or lesser extent, provides a guarantee from the organization to the learning public that the teacher is qualified.

Free universities provide no such guarantee or declaration that their teachers are qualified. Aside from the philosophical concept of consumer choice and learner responsibility, there are few practical ways in which teachers could be deemed qualified. College degrees are meaningless in most instances, as they do not indicate ability to teach a given subject, and because most subject matter in a free university does not fall neatly into a higher-education discipline. There are no degrees in toaster repair, for instance. Competency is a more accurate measurement of ability and can be employed in skills classes. But in many other kinds of idea classes, there are no standards. While a prospective teacher's ability to repair a toaster may be measured, there are few measurable standards for teaching a course on interpersonal relationships or creative writing. Finding a panel of qualified judges to measure quality and qualified prospective teachers employs a process inherently contrary to the free university's mode of operating, namely, freedom to teach and learn. Obviously the free university staff cannot judge teaching and performing ability in the thousand different categories of topics that a free university offers. Given the philosophical and practical impossibility of applying any successful measures of teaching or performance ability, free universities have resorted to honesty and several other measures. Almost all free universities use the following criteria in determining whether or not to allow people to teach: honesty, student complaints, mental and emotional stability, and duplication.

1. Honesty. This is probably the best protection for both the teacher and the free university. Teachers in a free university are required to be honest about their qualifications and experience and about their course description. If a teacher has only beginning knowledge of a subject, for example, he or she is asked to state that in the course description. Honesty in the course description provides the learner with the facts about the course, from which he or she can choose to take or not to take a course. A teacher who is found to be deceptive in the course description or classes is not allowed to teach again.

2. Student complaints. If the organization receives complaints about a teacher, the free university customarily pursues those complaints to determine their accuracy. Complaints about teachers are not common, so a number of them about any one teacher is usually sufficient to call the instructor's ability into question.

3. Mental and emotional stability. Although any particular viewpoint or idea can be expressed in a free university, in rare instances the holder of those views may not be mentally or emotionally stable. Although free universities do not, as a rule, formally state an opinion about a person's stability, if there is reason to believe that a prospective teacher is unstable, that person is dissuaded from teaching.

4. Duplication. Some free universities discourage people from teaching if the course topic is already adequately taught by other people. The rationale behind avoiding duplication is usually not to protect existing teachers but to avoid having too few people enroll in several courses on the same topic, thus resulting in several unsuccessful classes. By avoiding duplication in course offerings, enough students enroll in the classes to make them worthwhile.

In the teacher orientation and briefing, the free university staff can informally evaluate a prospective teacher's general competence, and the participant feedback mechanism inherent in free universities provides a system of evaluation for the free university teachers.

Teachers in free universities are subject to fairly heavy evaluative pressures, not from the administration but from the students. In traditional universities and colleges, faculty are not under such evaluation by the students. Faculty are protected by weak student evaluation forms and by a system of tenure which makes tenured faculty almost immune to corrective measures. Teachers in public schools and community colleges are in similar positions. Teachers in formal institutions of learning respond more to administrative interests than to student concerns.

Teachers in free universities are subject not to administrative evaluation but to the interests of the participants. Free universities have always been learner-centered. Students started the first free universities out of their concerns about their own learning. That tradition continues. Students evaluate their teachers in several ways.

The most severe and telling evaluation is whether participants drop out and/or take the class again. Participants have little time, money, or energy invested in the average free university class, and the easiest way to express dissatisfaction with a class is to drop out. Not all dropouts are expressing dissatisfaction with the class, of course, but an excessive number of people dropping the course is a good sign of dissatisfaction. Requests for refunds based on teacher inadequacy are another clear signal to the free university that the teacher is not satisfactory. Student complaints about an instructor bring a quick response from the free university administration eager to please the participants and maintain positive feelings about the free university.

This marketplace feedback system has been effective for free universities. Although there are both marketplace and more structured forms of evaluation taking place, there are not a lot of complaints about free university teachers. There is no evidence, and no reason to believe, that free university teachers, simply because they are drawn from the public at large, are any less qualified or able than other teachers. In fact, there is some evidence to the contrary. Respected adult educator Malcolm Knowles writes in his classic book *The Modern Practice of Adult Education,* "The best teachers are amateurs—at teaching."[12] Typically, there are more complaints about students than about teachers. Some teachers feel the students are not attentive enough, do not study, or are insufficiently self-disciplined. In this lawsuit-happy age when people get sued for just about anything, there has not been one lawsuit against a free university teacher or a free university for inadequate instruction.

Many free universities also conduct more structured evaluations from time to time. Usually these evaluations are not only of the teacher but also of the free university administration. They show that students are generally pleased with their teachers. The Denver Free University has instituted a consumer-oriented system of evaluative feedback. DFU distributes evaluations of teachers to its participants and then puts the evaluations in a large book, each under the name of the teacher. In this way, a new student who wants to find out what other students have thought of a particular instructor can read the evaluations of the teacher to help make a decision.

Not all student complaints lead to immediate axing of a free university teacher. Sometimes the problem is one that can be corrected. In one case at the Denver Free University, a dance instructor was dissatisfied with the students because of their appearance, demeanor, and attitude. Some came to the class chewing gum or wearing casual dress. Her attitude was conveyed to the participants, who began to complain about the teacher to the free university. Tracy Dunning, class coordinator, heard about the complaints and suggested to the teacher that she draw up a list of expectations before the first class so that participants would know what to expect. The teacher did so, stating her "class rules" humorously and inoffensively. The students, knowing her expectations in dress, attitude, and class behavior, were able to respond. The result was positive student evaluations of the teacher and a much happier teacher as well.

The thorniest problem with teaching and learning in a free university is common to all types of adult learning—self-discipline. It is also the one over which administrations have no control and only inadequate influence.

Just as motivation cannot be induced or created by another, self-discipline is an element that can only be encouraged, not structured or mandated. What passes for self-discipline—reading so many pages, taking a test, or consistently attending classes—has no relationship to self-discipline.

Free universities have not been concerned with self-discipline to this point, and perhaps they shouldn't be. Free universities have assumed that if participants are interested in a topic, and if the topic helps meet a need—most often a task or problem need—learning will take place.

This has been generally true for the past two decades. In the sixties, most free university participants and teachers were associated with a college or university and were therefore assumed to have a modicum of disciplined learning energy. In the seventies, participants learned in affective rather than cognitive patterns, focusing more on emotions and attitudes than on cognitive and thinking styles. The subject matter centered on persons as affective human beings and their avocational and leisure interests. Until now, interest and the need to solve a problem have probably been sufficient to create valuable learning situations for adults.

But the third decade of free university learning may see an interest in sustained cognitive thinking as a learning style. Career, individual survival, and community survival topics such as energy and nuclear power may dictate a more disciplined learning approach to conquering subject matter. Interest and the problem-need may not be sufficient for adult learning for these times. New ways of encouraging or highlighting the need for self-discipline may be required. This question, like all the other central questions dealing with teaching and learning in a free university, is common to all of lifelong learning, not to the free university structure alone.

We are becoming an increasingly technological society, and technology is becoming utilized more in education. The 1980s may be the decade in which learning by technology is in vogue. Computers, telephones, television, conference calls, correspondence, calculators, and video and tape recordings are all valuable instruments in learning. Free universities are at the completely opposite end of the spectrum as far as technology is concerned. Free universities are purely people. The teacher and the learners are the basic and essential unit in free universities. There is little technology in free universities. No home computers, no long-distance learning, even few audiovisuals. Will teachers in free universities, without technology, suffer as technological learning becomes more popular?

Teaching in a free university should remain as popular as ever, or even grow, as a result of technological advances in education. Even if there is a home computer in every household, there will still be a need for human interaction in a group setting. People need people, and the human warmth of the group learning situation cannot be replaced by technology. Perhaps because so much more learning will occur solely by technological means and without human interaction, there will be an increased interest in the teacher-participant learning situation. "I've got to get away from my computer," may be a common reason for people to come to free universities.

Some free universities may switch to technological forms of learning, but a major shift in that direction seems unlikely. The free university approach of "purely people" is more likely to be pursued in a different context.

Part IV
Where We're Headed

It is, in fact, nothing short of a miracle that the modern methods of instruction have not yet entirely strangled the holy curiosity of inquiry: for this delicate little plant, aside from stimulation, stands mainly in need of freedom; without this it goes to wrack and ruin without fail.

Albert Einstein

Chapter 13

Reaching New Populations

Despite the talk and clamor over lifelong learning's being available to any citizen, we know that most learning opportunities are offered to traditional learners—those who are predominantly well-educated, white, middle-class people with professional jobs. But if lifelong learning is to become a reality, it will have to be extended to all citizens and be reorganized and structured to meet the needs of the diverse populations in our society.

The free university model, because of its community orientation, flexibility, and low cost, may be able to effectively serve populations who have not had extensive learning opportunities offered to them before.

In this chapter we will look at four currently underserved populations—blue-collar workers, people in low-income and minority communities, rural residents, and the elderly. Free universities have already had success in reaching two of the groups, the elderly and the rural. The model shows potential for developing learning opportunities for workers and those in low-income and minority groups as well.

WORKERS

The American workforce is a population that has yet to be fully reached by educational organizations. The potential for providing learning opportunities at the workplace is great but has thus far not been explored in depth. Although there are thousands of training programs for workers, most of them are for job-related skills, and the area of personal or overall growth and learning has not been viewed as central to employee development.

Even though more adult learning goes on in business and industry than in any one other educational setting, there is an apparent need for more. A study of major collective bargaining agreements between management and labor showed that less than 20 percent of them contained training or retraining provisions.[1] Those opportunities that are available are not always used. A National Institute of Education report says,

> The formal school systems of the United States have made little serious effort to tap the extensive resources contained in educational opportunity programs provided unilaterally by American management or through collective bargaining agreements with American labor unions. . . . It is apparent that American workers are not able to take full advantage of seemingly readily accessible educational opportunity.[2]

Management in American business and industry offers a good deal of adult learning, but most of it is designed to help employees become better skilled in their present jobs or to train for another position within the organization. Unions have been only peripherally involved in offering education to their members. Writes Lawrence Rogin, "Very few unions take it seriously enough to invest sufficient funds for a meaningful program. The total number of unionists involved is only a fraction of the potential audience."[3]

The reason for labor's reluctance to become more involved with educational opportunities for its members is partly historical. In the past, unions have seen educational programs used to siphon off union leaders into management positions.

Labor union involvement in adult learning began as specialized and strongly ideological programs oriented toward the union. Residential labor colleges, such as the Bread Winners' College in New York City, were established around the turn of the century. Formal relationships between organized labor and institutions of higher education began in the 1920s, when Bryn Mawr College created a summer school for women workers in industry. Today there are approximately thirty university labor education centers around the country.

Adapting the free university model to the workplace would provide an educational program in which management and labor cooperate in offering learning opportunities to workers for their overall personal growth and development. It would be separate from any training or job-related education. There is one glaring statistic that draws the free university concept to the workplace: Men participate in adult learning far less frequently than women do. Men constitute only about a third of the participants in free university classes, and that figure is generally true for other adult learning organizations as well. So if male workers will not attend adult-learning organizations, the organizations may have to go to the male worker—which means going to the workplace. The workplace is an ideal setting as well, because workers are familiar with the surroundings and are more apt to feel physically and psychologically comfortable in the atmosphere.

Taking the free university model to the workplace could also be advantageous to business. In his work on developing human resources, Leonard Nadler distinguishes between employee training, education, and what he calls "employee development," the kind of personal growth and development that free universities offer. "Development is concerned with the future of the organization and the individual in directions which are not as clearly definable. The goals of employee development cannot be stated in specific behavioral terminology or specific terminal behaviors."[4] Nadler lists three reasons why business and industry should be interested in developing their employees:

1. Organization renewal. Employee development activities are designed to produce a viable and flexible workforce for the organization as it moves toward its future.

2. Worker input in decision-making. Employee development programs can meet the needs of workers for influence and movement within the organization.

3. Release of human potential. People usually have more in them than expected and can be more effective than they are.[5]

Concludes Nadler, "As individuals seek to grow on jobs, they need a legitimate and available mechanism for growth and development. If the organization does not provide it, they will either take their creativity and potential off the job or leave the job."[6]

The free university model, because it involves workers in designing, teaching, and sharing in their own learning program, has the potential for overcoming worker reluctance and can be a workable and cost-efficient mechanism for employee development within business and industry.

The free university can serve business and industry in several ways.[7]

1. Stimulate thinking. Employees who are thinking and growing will benefit the organization. Whether it be in the normal business day, when "self-directed learners" are going to be more responsive and quicker than others, or whether it is in formal training programs, when people with a learning life-style will learn more quickly and better than others, self-actualizing employees are beneficial, if not critical, to an organization's success.

2. Uncover talents. All companies have a wealth of untapped human skills and knowledge right inside their own organizations. Many of those talents may be unrelated to the job, but many others may be transferable. Free universities are a major way of uncovering these talents and of relating those talents to the work situation.

3. Get people together. Even small companies may not have as much communication going on as one may think. In a company where division lines are made by occupation and level of authority, a free university brings people together in a nonthreatening and nonauthoritarian situation. People can meet each other and get to know each other, and this communication has positive benefits for the job.

4. Reduce training costs. The free university represents the most cost-efficient way to learn. If the company can cut down on even some of its learning and training expenses or increase the benefits of those training and education experiences that it already pays for, it will get much more for its money.

5. Relate to other training. Although a good many classes and learning opportunities offered by the free university may not relate to the job, an increasing number will. Some of those areas include the following:

Preretirement concerns

Life management skills—time management and other work skills

Career preparation—job resumes, career counseling, and other topics

Practical and manual skills, some of which may relate to the job

Human relations and interpersonal skills—communication, writing, groups, and many others

Stress relaxation—yoga, biofeedback, and other techniques

New ideas, concepts, and other topics of interest to the company and the community

Personal finance skills—home budgeting, accounting, mortgages, credit-card buying, and others

Some sample topics that free universities currently offer and that might be of great interest to workers include these:

Health

Understanding Cancer
Holistic Health
Stage Fright
Creative Stress Management
Tai Chi Chuan
Slim Thinking
Fitness for You

Practical

Electrical Repairs
Toaster Repair
Plumbing Essentials
Motorcycle Maintenance
Auto Repair
Home Remodeling

Personal Finances

Prepare Your Own 1040
Buying a Home
Stock Market Strategy
Home Budgeting
Investments
Record Keeping

Life Management

Time Management
Law for the Layperson
Life Accreditation Workshop
Learning on Your Own
Life/Work Planning
Job Satisfaction
Resume Preparation

Preretirement Courses

Coping with Retirement
Financial Aspects of Retirement
Social Security and You
Retired Volunteers: Share Your Time
Spouse Workshop

Interpersonal Skills

Assertiveness Training
Communication Skills
Writing Reports and Memos

Community Issues

Downtown Redevelopment
Our Schools: How Can We Help?
United Way Seminar
(issues depend on each city)

Sports and Relaxation	Other
Beginning Yoga	Speed Reading
Biofeedback	Music Appreciation
Stress Relaxation	Poetry
Jogging	Creative Writing
Disco Dance	Spanish
Ballroom Dancing	French
Fly Tying	Cold Recipes
Preparing for Winter Camping	
Snowshoeing	
Cross-Country Skiing	

The workplace holds great potential for extending lifelong learning opportunities to workers, especially those with little formal education. Because of its flexibility and utilization of peer teaching and worker interaction, the free university can be an important program for workers.

LOW-INCOME AND MINORITY COMMUNITIES

One of the great challenges for education in the 1980s—and perhaps the true test of whether the idea of "lifelong learning" will mean greater educational opportunity or be merely another catchword for the traditional educational establishment—is to make learning opportunities available to people in low-income and minority communities.

An inexplicable discrepancy, verging on a shameful national failure, is the increasing gap between the adult educational haves and have-nots in the United States. Although the children of low-income and minority parents suffer a well-publicized lack of educational opportunity in formal schools, it is a little-realized embarrassment that adults from disadvantaged groups experience an even greater disparity between the learning opportunities serving their needs and those serving the mainly white, college-educated, and middle-class persons in this country.

The detrimental domino effect of this lack of opportunity to learn—from parent to child to adult to employment to survival skills—is enlarging the gap between a great many people and the knowledge and skills needed to live in a modern society.

The well-being of every segment of our population depends upon our ability to close that educational gap and to begin to equalize opportunity in learning. The imperative is even greater today than it was twenty years ago, when the situation was compelling enough.

The definitions vary. Some call them disadvantaged; others refer to them as minority, low-income, undereducated, uneducated, poor, unserved, illiterate, functionally illiterate, or functionally incompetent.

If the undereducated in low-income and minority communities have not had the opportunity to study, they have had the opportunity to be studied. The resulting statistics can be viewed from any number of different angles—income, formal educational level, competency, ethnic status. In their recently published book *Adult Illiteracy in the United States,* Hunter and Harman compile some of those statistics.[8]

If we look at formal school attainment, more than 56 million people, or 38 percent of the total population sixteen and older, have less than a high school education and are not enrolled in school. If we look at competency criteria, based on a person's ability to perform such survival skills as completing an employment form or figuring grocery bills, we find similar statistics. Almost 23 million Americans are said to lack the competencies necessary to function in society, and another 34 million can function but not proficiently —adding up again to 57 million Americans lacking functional competency in society.

Looking at income, of the more than 50 million adults who have less than a high school education, 75 percent earn less than $5,000 a year. Only 1 percent have incomes of $15,000 or more, compared with about 33 percent of all families in the country. The undereducated tend to be unemployed and on public assistance more often.

Looking at the ethnic and racial minorities in our country, we find similarly depressing statistics. The number of blacks and other minorities among the undereducated is disproportionately high. Among rural blacks, for example, 45 percent have not completed grade school, while the figure for the total population is about 15 percent. Only 40 percent of adult urban Native Americans have graduated from high school, and less than 25 percent of adult Native Americans living in rural areas have graduated.

Looking at the situation from any number of statistical view-points, the numbers seem to be about the same, suggesting that we are really looking at the same people. The interrelationship between income, education, and ethnic heritage is unmistakable. The poor tend to be undereducated, the undereducated are poor, minorities are poor and undereducated.

In any case, between 20 and 40 percent of our adult population is seriously disadvantaged, and the opportunities to eliminate that disadvantage via educational opportunity, skill, and knowledge attainment are few.

But the educationally poor in our society do not suffer only statistically—by income, formal education, or competency. They also are subject to a psychological poverty equally debilitating in its impact on overcoming educational and competency barriers.

In his excellent critique on the effect of institutions on modern society, Ivan Illich notes that the poor, in addition to coping with physical pollution and social polarization, suffer from psychological impotence. Nonmaterial needs, such as for learning or health, are transformed into commodities, and solutions are phrased in institutional language of treatments, services, delivery systems, or providers, rather than in terms of enabling individuals to do things for themselves. The result is the creation of more dependence, not less. Illich writes,

> Today in the United States the black and even the migrant can aspire to a level of professional treatment which would have been unthinkable two generations ago, and which seems grotesque to most people in the Third World. For instance, the U.S. poor can count on a truant officer to return their children to school until they reach seventeen, or a doctor to assign them to a hospital bed which costs sixty dollars a day—the equivalent of three months' income for a majority of the people in the world. But such care only makes them dependent on more treatment, and renders them increasingly incapable of organizing their own lives around their own experiences and resources within their own communities.[9]

State and federal programs to combat illiteracy and provide more educational opportunities for low-income and minority people have not been too effective. In its 1974 study on adult basic education programs, the National Advisory Council on Adult

Education notes, "At present, we use the rhetoric of an all-out war on illiteracy; but, in fact, we are just about holding our own. Few illiterates escape personal hardship in the job market and all of us pay for their inability to contribute to the nation's production of goods and services."[10]

This unencouraging statement comes as the federal government now spends more than $100 million a year to alleviate illiteracy and provide more learning opportunities for the undereducated. One of the reluctant conclusions that has to be drawn is that the formal schools have failed to respond to the needs of low-income and minority people. Most of the $100 million spent by the government in adult basic education funds goes to the formal school system—a school system that failed to respond to the undereducated while they were children and is now being given additional funds to fail once again. In citing a 1975 study, Hunter says that "most classes are taught in traditional elementary school teaching styles."[11] It is little wonder that undereducated adults, having failed once in a school system, are reluctant to try again or that they repeat the same disappointing process once they do enroll.

The situation in postsecondary formal education institutions is also disappointing. Although a good number of minorities may enroll in community colleges, their dropout rate is substantially higher than that for white students. Colleges and universities are also enrolling more minority students, but dropout rates there are high as well. The result is that the educational gap between the undereducated, the poor, and the minorities, and the white, middle-class, educated sector of our population is growing rather than lessening. And the educational ante is constantly being raised. A high school diploma was once a mark of educational attainment. Soon a college degree will experience the same deflation.

Continuing education divisions in our colleges and universities are concentrating on continuing professional development—providing learning for those who already have it, rather than for those with less education.

There is a growing recognition that organizations in the community outside the formal school system can provide learning opportunities that are both relevant and attractive to people in low-income and minority communities.

In their book, Hunter and Harman briefly and boldly signal the change needed:

Our principal conclusion can be briefly stated. A major shift in national education policy is needed to serve the educational needs of disadvantaged adults. Our principal overall recommendation flowing from that conclusion can also be briefly set forth. We recommend the establishment of new, pluralistic, community-based initiatives whose specific objective will be to serve the most disadvantaged hard-core poor, the bulk of whom never enroll in any existing program.

These community-based initiatives would focus on persons in the communities where they live. The initiatives would require the adults themselves to contribute to designing programs based on concrete learning needs growing out of specific issues affecting their lives in their communities.[12]

There are already some examples of community-based organizations providing positive learning opportunities for the undereducated. The Highlander Folk School in New Market, Tennessee, has been providing such learning opportunities for more than fifty years and has been influential in many positive social movements, such as the labor movement, civil rights movement, and coal miners' programs.[13] A number of groups forming a coalition called the Clearinghouse for Community Based Free Standing Educational Institutions have also been effective in providing relevant learning opportunities for their communities.

But these organizations are few. More community-based educational efforts need to be undertaken, and the free university concept and model are readily adaptable to the low-income and minority communities.

Educators have begun to realize the potential of the free university model. Nat Hentoff recently told a free university gathering, "What you're about in free universities is quite literally inexhaustible. It's about the only really alive development I know about that can cut across just about every conceivable dividing line in society."[14]

Malcolm Knowles, speaking at the Ninth National Free University/Learning Network Conference in Denver in October 1979, urged his audience, "I hope that you folks can give special consideration of spreading your sound concept of people sharing ideas with people who are undereducated. Here's where the free university concept could be the ultimate solution to this great need." [15] And Hunter adds, "It is certainly true that the basic philosophy of the free university movement is very close to the community development/non-formal education approaches that we advocate for the majority of the educationally disadvantaged adults."[16]

The free university model is relevant to low-income and minority communities both conceptually and organizationally. There are several reasons why the free university idea is appropriate to low-income and minority people:

1. It encourages self-confidence and self-empowerment, two essential attitudes for anyone to learn but particularly for the uneducated, who have few chances to gain confidence in themselves. With its informal atmosphere, no prerequisites or entrance procedures, and its lack of tests, grades, and pressures, the free university encourages people to learn. It also enhances self-confidence by encouraging participants to share what they know in the group setting, viewing the teacher and learners as equals in the learning process.

2. It develops human resources within the community. Too often, expertise and knowledge are not acknowledged in our poorer communities. Instead, people view that expertise as being provided by outsiders. But the free university taps the hidden wealth of human talent within the community. This not only creates a certain pride in being aware of its own skilled and knowledgeable people but also encourages others to learn or teach. If Mrs. Jones, a welfare mother, knows that Mr. Smith, an unemployed mechanic, taught a free university class, then maybe Mrs. Jones has something to offer as well.

3. It exemplifies peer-group learning. People learn from each other and enjoy learning from each other. If the teaching role models come from others within the community, the participants will be more likely to respond, and the teachers will be more likely to relate to the learners.

The free university model also fits in organizationally, with several requirements for community-based education:

1. Each program has a local identity. The program is located in the community, the board of directors or advisers comes from the local community, and even the name is chosen by the people in

the program. This identity and resulting image is essential in establishing community acceptance.

2. The free university can be run out of, or sponsored by, existing agencies and organizations within the community. The free university does not·need to be a separate organization that must gain the confidence of the people. It can be sponsored by already existing service organizations and complement their services. Churches, community centers, and other organizations already have earned the trust and respect of local people, and the free university is not a threat but a welcome addition to their programs.

3. Structurally, the free university is flexible. Classes can take place in homes, churches, community centers, businesses, or wherever attendance will be greatest. Classes can meet at night, on weekends, or during the day, depending on the time requirements of the population. Classes can last one day or ten weeks.

4. The free university is not expensive. The structure of the free university can be built around the need for low or nonexistent fees.

5. The free university runs on a small budget, and funding for the program does not have to be large for a community to have a free university.

Free universities always have been interested in reaching the low-income and minority populations in their areas. Various attempts have been made to include them. Special classes, projects, registration sites, and class locations have been held in low-income and minority communities. Free universities have sought out minority members to be on their boards of directors. Special efforts have been made in Denver, Indianapolis, Columbus, and Manhattan (Kansas), but with little success. Besides the Baltimore Free University and a few other exceptions, free universities, like other white, middle-class educational organizations, have not succeeded in reaching low-income and minority people.

What may be required is that free universities be set up within the low-income and minority communities and run by the local people, adapting the free university concept and model to that particular community. The result may be a new model for free universities—just as new models were required for large cities and rural communities. The new model may look very different from the others. "Classes" may be projects, tutoring may be involved, and other unpredicted changes may be made.

At the time of this writing, several community organizations are beginning to use the free university concept and model to develop a free university for their own low-income or minority communities. By starting with a clean slate, without any presuppositions or constraints, they may be able to construct a new free university model that will serve the undereducated. Given a certain level of support and resources, the task is possible. The dissemination of their results could be a significant effort in free university history to provide deserved learning opportunities for those to whom the opportunities are least available.

RURAL AND SMALL-TOWN AMERICA

Rural America is a new frontier. Previously forgotten, ignored, or consigned to the past, rural America is experiencing a renewal of growth and energy and an increase in attention to its unique way of life. There is no one rural America, of course. There is rich rural, poor rural, farming rural, nonfarming rural, white rural, black rural, Hispanic rural, older rural, and young rural. But the various kinds of people who live in rural America do share one common denominator—sparse population. That fact can be expressed demographically, in terms of numbers of people, or it can be expressed as a life-style, "small is beautiful." Because of its different demographics—of much space and few people, the opposite of city living—new approaches to the same kinds of questions have to be devised. That holds true for education as well.

For too long, rural America's social and civic institutions have been cut from the same pattern as those for urban areas. This is certainly true for education. Rural schools look just like urban schools. There are some differences, but basically they are alike. When rural high schools began to look less like urban high schools, the solution was to make the schools bigger. School consolidation eliminated the smaller schools and combined others, often locating a high school in the countryside midway between two or more small towns, rather than enhancing one or the other community with the distinction of having the school. When students graduate from high school, they usually leave the small town for several years. When they return in their mid-twenties, the young adults in rural America have few postsecondary educational experiences. Except for regular offerings through Cooperative Extension and more sporadic opportunities from a nearby community college, local public library, or possibly recreation commission, there is little intellectual or cultural stimulation in most small towns. Because there have been few community structures to tap their own resources, the small town has gained an undeserved reputation as a place where nothing happens, where people have little to do.

Free university organizers Jim Killacky and Tava Serpan write, "In America, progress has generally been viewed in economic terms under the heading that 'big is beautiful and small is backward.' Consequently, many people in rural communities feel they are the 'forgotten Americans.' "[17]

But rural America is also changing. The out-migration that has been occurring in many communities since the turn of the century has now stabilized or reversed itself. New people are moving to rural areas, some of whom have never lived in a small town before. The attitude toward small-town living is changing too. It is more upbeat now. With urban blight, pollution, traffic, and the high cost of living, there is a greater appreciation for the easier way of life in small towns. That style of living is becoming more attractive to people. The potential is also greater for community spirit and pride in the small town, for working together, sharing with one's neighbors, and working on community development.

There are, of course, many problem areas in rural American life: jobs, housing, medical services, and cultural and educational enrichment are a few. But it is becoming clear that to solve those problems, rural and small-town communities will need to devise answers relevant to the small town, not to urban America. In one area at least—that of education—there is a model that has been designed to work effectively in rural and small-town communities —the rural free university.

Studies indicate that good jobs and housing are not enough to keep people, especially young people, in the small town. There needs to be cultural and educational stimulation, especially for those with a college education or those who have been away to "the big city."

The rural free university model developed by University for Man in Manhattan, Kansas, is community-based, locally controlled, and cost-efficient. Perhaps most important, it uses local human resources in teaching, learning, and administration.

What the rural free university does is to promote not only learning and cultural activities in the small town but also a positive attitude about the town itself.

The term *free university* has not been used greatly in rural settings except as a generic term. Because most rural residents have not been to college, the word *university* is uncomfortable to them. And in conservative rural America, the term *free* also often has negative connotations. Thus, the term *community education* is more often used.

In its basic operation, of course, the rural free university is not new. The concept of neighbors sharing their ideas and skills is as old as our country. In most rural areas of the country, it has not been until relatively recently that formal education has replaced nonformal learning as the primary way to learn for most rural people. Through parents teaching children, workers training apprentices, ministers preaching, and community nurses teaching in barn raisings, quilting bees, and other community events, people have learned from each other. One hundred years ago the pioneers did not have colleges to attend; they taught each other. That concept is equally applicable to the small town today. There are some changes, of course. The advent of public television in rural areas has brought in outside educational programs. More rural residents are college educated. People overall possess more information, skills, and knowledge than they did before. Rural people now are more traveled than they have ever been before.

As one example, several years ago free university organizers went to Meade, Kansas (population 1,200). After the initial meeting, a steering committee volunteered and set a date for their next meeting. "Oh, I'll be in Russia that week," said one older woman, looking at her calendar. While the free university organizers were rather stunned, the local people were not surprised and just moved their meeting back one week.

As Killacky documented in his report on the first rural free university projects,

In nearly all cases in all of these projects leaders are from the community. This has had a profound effect, for it has created an enormous awareness of the boundless talents and resources that exist within the community when many folks thought there "was nothing to do except cruise Main on Friday nights"; it has created a sense that one need not be dependent on "outside experts" for every little thing, for by looking hard enough one can nearly always find such expertise right at one's own doorstep.

In these times when policy formulation, funding resources and related procedures have a distinct urban bias, programs such as these—not only for learning but for community and rural resource development and organization—can have a profound impact in terms of recognizing and responding to the untapped values which rural America provides for the nation as a whole.[18]

The typical small-town free university is run by a group of volunteers with a part-time paid coordinator if the town or county is large enough; it has a board of advisers composed of local civic and community leaders; the classes are free; funding is obtained at the local level; the program is controlled locally; teachers come from the community; a brochure of classes is printed two or three times a year. Sometimes the program is an independent organization; sometimes it is sponsored by an existing institution in the community, such as a recreation department, public library, or Cooperative Extension.

The usual free university model has several features that make it ideal for small-town and rural communities.

1. Local identity. Local identity is extremely important for small towns where having one's own public school or post office is a sign of community vitality. Each rural free university's community education program has a local identity. The program is run by local citizens, and the program's name reflects that community.

2. Local resources. The program extensively uses local people as volunteers, as learners, and most significantly, as teachers. The program unearths the variety and wealth of talent and skills possessed by local people. Some of those skills have lain dormant for years; others may not have been known even to people in the community. By leading a class, local people show themselves and others that the town has stimulating and interesting people, that there are exciting things to do in town. The classes sometimes lay the groundwork for further projects and community activities, thus providing a forum for community development.

3. Various and extensive offerings. The community education program can offer a wide range of course topics and provide a great number of courses at little or no cost. A small town of 3,000, for example, might be able to support three to five community college courses a year, with an average minimum number of twelve people paying $20 or so in fees. But a community education program can offer fifty or more such courses a year, providing a greater assortment and number of learning opportunities. Not bound by cost considerations, a free university class does not need a minimum number of participants. Thus, a class of even three people can be stimulating, enjoyable, and productive.

4. Variable budget. There is no minimum budget needed for the free university program. The minimum budget needed for any program is just $25 per year to print a brochure, an amount any community can raise. This means that any community can financially support a free university. Based on the size of the community, the budget of the free university can be adjusted so that the community can sustain the program with local resources. For a small community of fewer than 500, the program can easily be run by volunteers on a steering committee. The total yearly budget for this kind of program, which may involve more than 200 participants a year, may be only $100 to $200, almost all of it going for the printing of brochures. In a community or county of 1,000 to 2,000, the program may want to pay a part-time coordinator to coordinate the entire session. People to People in Dighton, Kansas, for example, has a steering committee and pays one member $500 to coordinate an entire session. In communities and counties of 5,000 to 10,000, there can be an office, telephone, and part-time coordinator, and the budget can still be reasonable enough to be sustained locally.

5. Local funding. Almost all of the rural free university programs are funded locally. This means that the local people are responsible for their own program and do not depend on federal legislation or outside support. This also means they are not subject to rules or guidelines from organizations outside their own community. There are a variety of ways to raise the money locally. Some programs attach themselves to existing institutions and receive support through their budgets. Others go straight to the county commissioners for direct funding. One has an annual flea market

to raise $300, its total budget for the year. Another seeks a variety of contributions from local clubs, municipalities, churches, and sources in the county. Several get United Way money.

6. Neutral and flexible structure. In most small towns, where people are used to their own social groupings in church, work, and other situations, the rural free university integrates people. Writes Killacky,

> The framework of a free university–community education project is in itself fairly neutral and very flexible. Participants can form groups immediately and on the basis of present-day needs and interests, and are not shackled by an organizational structure which is unable or unwilling to adapt to contemporary needs, interests and problems. Meetings can be one time or continue as long as they are needed by participants. Furthermore these groups transcend the traditional social divisions usually associated with participation in voluntary activities such as age, sex, race, socio-economic status and the farm/town schism. These are advantages over voluntary groups which devote more attention to structure than content, meet within certain preconceived times whether or not they are appropriate to the business at hand, and focus their program only on certain segments of the community.[19]

What is exciting about the rural free university model is not only that it has such potential but also that it has already been developed and is working successfully. Through the efforts of Sue Maes, Jim Killacky, and others, this model has been successfully tested and implemented and is now being expanded and disseminated not only throughout the Midwest but also across the country as a whole. The possibility that rural free universities can grow in numbers, people served, and influence is great.

The potential for extending the rural community education model to small towns across the country is virtually limitless. There are thousands of towns in this country with fewer than 8,000 people, and each town is capable of having its own free university. Maes, Killacky and their colleagues hope that hundreds of small-town free universities will blossom in rural America.

What this model can do for the millions of Americans living in rural America holds significant promise. As Killacky and Serpan note,

Drawing upon and developing the largely untapped reservoir of rural talents and skills is of enormous significance in restoring rural America to the place it so rightly deserves—that is as an important and crucial part of the whole society not only in economic, but educational, social and cultural terms as well.[20]

THE ELDERLY

In the mid-seventies a group of graduates, commenting on adult education and the aging American, wrote,

> Justice William O. Douglas spoke of a dilemma one encounters in an underdeveloped society. A swamp produces disease. For a few dollars, a plane can dust the area with DDT and people will live. But then, should one do so if one does not increase the means of life at the same?
>
> We have wiped out swamps in this land, and made it possible for people to live, for millions to survive past the age of sixty-five. Only we have done nothing for them. We have given them bare survival, but not the means of living honorable and satisfactory lives as valued members of our society.[21]

Although societal concern for the elderly has taken decades to develop, it now appears in the 1980s that the older American is at last seeing the swamp being filled in in terms of learning opportunities.

It has taken a long time for educators to realize two basic facts—that older Americans want to learn and that their requirements for learning differ slightly from younger people's.

The need to provide older citizens with learning opportunities has become demographically more evident each decade. In 1950 less than 15 percent of our population was over age sixty-five. By the year 2000 one third of the population will be over sixty-five. "The graying of the universe is a fact of life,"[22] says Maggie Kuhn of the Gray Panther Party, an advocacy organization for older citizens. In the year 2020, which Kuhn calls the year of perfect vision, the number of older people will be greater than the number of young. Even more startling is the percentage of people over age seventy-five, which will have increased from less than 5 percent to almost 15 percent of the population. Not only is the population growing older, but the old are growing older as well.

The concept of the elderly as constituting a separate group in society is relatively recent, but it has contributed to their isolation and lack of integration in services and education. It was only toward the middle of the twentieth century that the life span was prolonged so that it was not only allowable but also economically beneficial to have most citizens retire at age sixty-five, a luxury that previously was reserved for the few. The increasing dependence on Social Security also contributed to the delineation between old and young.

While studies as far back as the 1920s showed that older adults have a great capacity to learn, the old adage "You can't teach an old dog new tricks" remained conceptually intact until only a few years ago. Within the last ten years, however, the older adult's interest in lifelong learning has exploded. Whether this interest was sparked in the elderly themselves or was merely recognized by the rest of society is not clear. Hazel Gordon, herself a senior citizen on the staff of the Wichita Free University, believes that older people have always wanted to learn but that societal constraints didn't allow it. "Society didn't provide the learning opportunities," she says. "People said—'Social Security is going to be IT' and put older citizens on the shelf."[23]

Whatever the reason, senior citizens are starting to come down from the shelf, to show an increased interest in learning, and to receive more attention from adult educators than ever before. "Keep learning right up to rigor mortis,"[24] urges Kuhn.

But traditional education is not readily adaptable to the older citizen. The typical classroom is not a physically comfortable environment, and one of the most important things we know about senior learning is that the physical setting must be comfortable. Older people become colder more easily, and the room must be warm. Older people want comfortable chairs. The most outstanding inhibitor to learning for older people is not mental capacity but physical facilities. Vision deteriorates with age, and only 6 percent of workers over age sixty have normal sight. Hearing declines with age as well. Any learning situation for the older adult must consider these factors.

Traditional curricula are also not as adaptable to the elderly. Older people are more apt to be interested in subject matter that is of immediate or short-term usefulness. They are more likely to learn when working together with others. They are more responsive to a variety of educational stimulation techniques, such as films, games, and demonstrations. They also bring to the learning situation a lifetime of experience and wisdom, assets which normal curricula ordinarily do not consider.

Although all educational institutions can and ought to reach out to the older citizen, there are good reasons why the free university has succeded in involving them:

1. The free university is community based or oriented, thus existing in a surrounding familiar to the elderly. Says Bert Seidman, director of the AFL-CIO Department of Social Security,

Pluralism in social services is a part of the larger pluralism— ethnic, cultural, and religious—which the integration of services ignores. Unless social services are neighborhood based, they will be inaccessible. Unless they have ties to ethnic, cultural and religious institutions, they will be unacceptable. Traditional ties to family, neighborhood and organization will continue to be the most important social supports for disabled old people.[25]

Because the free university is responsive to these community ties, it is often more acceptable to the elderly.

2. Classes are nearby. Free university classes most often take place in the community, and the classes are nearby for many senior citizens. They also meet in familiar locations—homes, churches, community centers.

3. Cost. Free university classes cost little or nothing, and cost is an important priority in learning for older people.

4. Active participation. Free universities give the elderly not only a chance to participate but also a chance to become an active participant. The sharing of knowledge is welcome; demonstration, discussion, and disagreement are all encouraged. Because learners in the free university are seen as equals among themselves and with the teacher, the elderly are made to feel part of the group and esteemed for their wisdom and contributions.

In recent years, the elderly have participated in the free university with gusto. Many senior citizens are interested in the regular fare of free university learning, with its variety of courses appealing to all kinds of people. As we saw in Chapter 2, the senior citizens at the Baltimore Free University don't stick to the traditional senior citizen classes. In Baltimore at least, they are taking massage, swimming, Frisbee throwing, and cooking, among others.

At other free universities, special classes geared to the older citizen are set up. Some of them have been in Social Security, health, and other topics of interest to the aging. University for Man in Manhattan has had an aging series for years, offering a different topic of interest to older people each week.

In Wichita, Kansas, the Wichita Free University goes one step further and takes classes to the elderly. Hazel Gordon goes to retirement homes and nursing centers, talks to the residents, and then sets up classes in the centers. "If you remove the barriers, such as transportation, the elderly are eager to learn," she says. In Wichita, some of the big classes have been in the crafts, in social events like "Sing Along and the Good Old Days," and recreation such as bowling. Gordon says she has an eighty-year-old man in a wheelchair who takes the bowling class.

Gordon's classes, which are open to others, come under a section called "Sixty Plus" in the free university catalog. She also works with other agencies in providing services. The Red Cross Good Neighbor Nutrition Sites program helps with transportation to the classes, and the Retired Senior Volunteer Program (RSVP) cosponsors some classes.

Part of Gordon's mission to retirement centers and nursing homes is not to recruit students, but teachers. After getting residents' attention and curiosity, she asks not only for participants but for teachers as well. Perhaps more than any other educational organization, free universities have tapped the great wealth of teaching expertise that the senior citizen possesses.

"We have a throw-away society," says Gordon, "and we've been throwing people away as well." Most free university leaders agree. The rise in older free university people has been dramatic and noticeable in the last several years. Like their learning habits, their interest in teaching spans the subject range from crafts to social issues. At University for Man in Manhattan, for instance, an eighty-four-year-old man teaches creative writing. Another senior citizen, Lydia Quinlan, regularly offers a class in soap-making, a dying art that only older people know.

The potential for the older citizen to share his or her views and skills is unlimited. Teaching in a free university benefits not only the participants but the elderly as well, offering them constructive and important roles as teachers. Free universities are only beginning to discover the talents of the older citizen. In the arts, in crafts, history, practical skills, and social issues areas, the elderly have much to offer.

This opportunity has been especially valuable to people in rural and small-town communities. In smaller towns, there are fewer activities for senior citizens than in the large cities where senior citizen centers and special events are sponsored. In small towns, the elderly have a chance to preserve a sense of history, to promote the community, and to pass along to the young some useful skills.

Free universities have also conducted some special projects for the elderly. At University for Man in Manhattan, a solar greenhouse is being built to house programs for the handicapped and elderly. The elderly are involved in running the programs as well. Jose de la Torre, the local RSVP director, notes, "Energy for these kinds of programs used to come from the young. Now it is coming from the old."

But the involvement of free universities with the elderly hasn't stopped with special projects, teachers, and learners. In the last few years, several older people have joined the staffs of free universities, a development that is likely to grow and have a profound effect on the organization of free universities.

The mixing of younger and older people on the free university staff is bound to have several positive effects. New talents and perspectives will help the free university organization internally. Older staff members will be more likely to reach other special populations in the community. The presence of senior citizens will give the free university a different image in the community.

Older people may fit very well into the free university organization. The young and the old seem to have some things in common. They both have energy and enthusiasm, which leads to an exchange of new ideas and reinforcement of each other. They have a common concern for social change and meeting human needs. Another common characteristic is that they both experience lower than average incomes, which means that the free university will see more older people interested in staff positions. These similarities, plus a shared interest in lifelong learning, may make the young-old combination in free universities a dynamic one for the changing scene in learning.

Chapter 14

New Settings

During the sixties, almost all free universities were located on campus. In the early seventies, the independent free university developed as a separate incorporated entity. In the mid-seventies, community agencies began to sponsor free universities. In the last four years, an even wider array of community and educational organizations has begun to sponsor free university–type programs.

Because adult educators can adapt the free university model to their own educational setting, this chapter discusses three of the major settings in which the free university potential is being explored—libraries, Cooperative Extension, and the neighborhood free university—and several other areas where the free university model has been adapted, including small private colleges, recreation departments, YMCAs and YWCAs, college unions, churches, and community centers and organizations. In all these settings, one or more free universities are currently being sponsored, and it appears that the eighties will be a time when the free university model will be grafted onto existing institutions even more often.

LIBRARIES

One of the most exciting new settings for free universities could well be the public library, for the concept of a neutral open resource for adult learning is already mutually shared by libraries and free universities. Libraries, with a long tradition of service to the general public, are now at a crossroads regarding lifelong learning. Public libraries can either continue basically as warehouses of information, mainly written, for the general public to tap, or they can become aggressively involved in going beyond books to other types of information and services, reaching more people, and renewing their image as an educational force in the community. If libraries and their librarians choose the latter route, then free universities should gain a good deal of attention from librarians.

A report on the changing role of public libraries prepared for the 1979 White House conference on libraries says, "Gone are the days when the public library was simply the community's bookshelf. . . . Public libraries are changing from passive repositories to active purveyors of information and knowledge to all those who need it."[1]

The challenges that the public library faces today are quite different from those of the past and may require new responses. The White House report notes,

Today the public library is grappling with a whole new set of demands upon it—demands from students, from the increasing numbers of senior citizens, from adults seeking self-education, from people with reading disabilities, from the inmates of institutions, from people needing help with job information or career changes, from authors, journalists, and citizen activists.[2]

The revolution in our perception of learning that was brought on by Allen Tough's studies on independent adult learning has provided the public library both with new ammunition as to the value of the library and the function that it plays in adult learning and with disturbing facts that the library has not extended itself fully in that role. In 1977, Patrick Penland of the University of Pittsburgh released his nationwide survey of independent adult learning in America, which largely confirmed Tough's earlier results. But Penland also studied the libraries' role in independent adult learning. He found that "libraries are not generally perceived as a significant source of help by a majority of individual adult learners." Nearly 60 percent of Americans, he determined, "have never made use of a library to pursue a self-initiated learning project."[3] If public libraries are entering into a new mode of delivery, they have yet to convince a majority of the general public to use their services for adult learning.

Various libraries are involved in different kinds of adult learning services, but there is no rush to adopt any one type of service, nor is there any consensus about the library's role in adult learning. Fred Golden, in his paper on potential models of public library services for the adult learner, lists six components of adult learning that libraries have been and could be involved in: 1. literacy and adult basic education; 2. community education as in community schools; 3. educational brokering, learner's advisory services, or education information centers; 4. free universities; 5. learning networks; and 6. self-planned learning as indicated in Tough's research.[4]

Jacquelyn Thresher, former head of the Alternative Education Programs Section of the Public Library Association, writes,

> Libraries have always passively supported the education sector and have been resource centers for individual learners. Now public libraries are sponsoring free universities or learning networks, providing literacy and language tutoring, career and educational information and referral, career counseling, and in a few cases, are serving as advocates for adult learners. . . . Librarians and library administrators involved in developing new and innovative services to adult learners and other clientele with special needs are still a minority, but they are a growing and vocal one. . . . The public library as an institution is slowly moving into the mainstream of adult education, while many individual libraries, already in the middle of it, find it exciting and challenging.[5]

But there is a good deal of hesitancy overall on the part of librarians with regard to adult-learning services. In her article on brokering in libraries, for example, Thresher lists some of the problems facing more library involvement in adult learning:

1. Some administrators consider all but information and referral components as "tangential frills."

2. Spiraling library costs, reduced budgets, and inadequate staffing do not encourage new programs in libraries.

3. Many administrators are comfortable with the library's passive, supportive role.

4. Most librarians are trained to work more with books and other resources than with clients and people.[6]

Thus, the involvement of public libraries in all adult learning, not just in free universities, does not look like a sweeping inevitability in the near future. Yet there are enticing reasons why free universities can be and are being sponsored by public libraries.

The first public library to sponsor a free university was the New Orleans Public Library. Former Free University of New Orleans (FUNO) director Meredith McElroy describes FUNO's adoption by the library:

> Like most free universities, FUNO got its start on a college campus—Tulane University, under the auspices of the student union, in 1969. Overloaded with work, no money, and discouraged by limitations in scope, Jason Patterson, the coordinator, approached a receptive person in the New Orleans Public Library—the head of the community relations office, Ann Gallmeyer, one of those rare birds who believes that most anything is possible and furthermore believes in change.
>
> The transition, which later became total sponsorship, was easy once the decision was made. The only difficulty was in making adequate clarification of the basic and essential tenet of free universities, that is, freedom for instructors and students without screening of methods and/or content. Besides being philosophically important, this stance turns out to be a real time-saver.[7]

Because of the library support, FUNO grew to become a stable and well-managed free university, now more than ten years old. The free university is coordinated by a paid library staff person, expenses are kept to brochure printing, and a small fee has been charged since 1979 to pay for those expenses.

In 1978, Betty Cattrell, librarian for Haysville, Kansas, population 8,000, thought that a community education program, free university–style, would provide more publicity, visibility, and patrons for her newly established library. She was right. Soon after, the Education Connection was begun, and enrollments approached 300 in the first year alone. In Iola, Kansas, population 6,493, librarian Elaine Brown started Communiversity with the help of a volunteer committee. Both free universities are examples of a thriving adult-learning program for the small-town public library.

There are several reasons why free universities view sponsorship by the public library as positive:

1. The educational philosophy of the public library is essentially the same as that of the free university—that learning resources should be made available to all, with little or no censorship as to content; that the responsibility for learning rests with the individual; and that the role of the institution is to be a linkage mechanism, not a provider or guarantor, of the educational resources. In the past, libraries have been concerned with physical resources—books, films, video, art—while free universities have linked human resources—people with skills and knowledge to learners. The bridge from material to human resources is an easy one to cross.

2. The library offers its services for free or at very little cost. Free universities and public libraries both believe in low-cost or free services to the adult general public, and free universities sponsored by libraries maintain that low-cost feature.

3. The physical and staff resources for sponsoring a free university are all present in the library. The library has space for an office, and sometimes even for classes; it has a phone answered on a regular basis; it has staff to coordinate the free university; it has learning aids—books, films, and so on; it has a readily available publicity mechanism through branch libraries, regular library patrons, and other library publications and media.

4. The library is seen as community based and neutral. Says McElroy,

Public libraries are neutral institutions—sometimes boring, sometimes staid, sometimes just too quiet, but neutral. They don't have the same built-in class barriers and elitism as universities. There are a host of people, poor people, minorities, who use the public library with great regularity and who support it with a political fervor, who would not set foot on a campus even for free classes because the university is the symbol of the rich. . . .[8]

In small towns, the library may be the only educational institution serving the adult population in the community. In small or large towns, the public library is a community-based institution charged with serving all the general public. In addition, the public library generally has the esteem and support of the community and its civic leaders, providing a solid base of support.

There are several reasons why public libraries should want to sponsor a free university:

1. It fits perfectly with the mission of the public library. No other adult education service matches the purposes, goals, and philosophy of the public library as does the free university concept of matching resources and learners.

2. The free university is not a departure from the library's service mission but an extension of it. Classes can be offered at no cost, just as book loans are.

3. The free university will reach a great many more people for the public library. The "population served" statistics for the library —important in its mission, and important in continued funding— will increase dramatically. Many of these people may never have used the library's service before. The public libraries on the whole appeal largely to the schooled middle class. The free university program can reach beyond this traditionally served audience and bring in new kinds of people to the public library.

4. Unlike other new programs, the free university is not a drain on the financial resources of the library, but an asset. Free universities can be funded in various ways through the library. If the library has a policy that allows charging for certain services, a small registration fee of $1 to $5 can make the free university program self-sustaining. This has been done at the New Orleans Public Library. By adding a free university–community education component to the library services, new sources of funding open up to the library. Federal resources outside the regular library funding agencies would become available.

The major stumbling block to acceptance of the free university idea seems to rest in the attitudes of local librarians, some of whom are eager to involve the library as an active advocate of adult learning, and some of whom express reservations about such an involvement, and about free universities as well. Library consultant Barbara Conroy outlines some of those hesitancies:

The majority of librarians are a traditional breed, particularly in the administrative levels, and their view of free universities is that they are offbeat and strident and enthusiastic. I'm sure some are a bit alarmed that there is not more careful definition of what free universities are (and are not).

Libraries are bureaucracy-based, tradition-bound, and the advantage of flexible organizational delivery of services dependent on decentralized precepts is not comfortable for many librarians. A possible point of relationship is on the value of the exchange of information through such a base, but the production and control end of the free universities will be difficult for many to understand and endorse. Yet this structure is essential for free universities to maintain. If free universities change to meet the library's priorities, they will lose the essence they have.

The word Network is another possible problem. Librarians are familiar with, and generally accepting of, networks which are hardware-based and exchange information (like the interlibrary loan connection) to serve their clientele. For the most part, however, they have not seen the real relationship to people networks. Nor do they see that networking with hardware is just as political as is networking with people. So, they feel that people networking is generally a corruption of the clean hardware networking exchange of information.

Libraries, with some exceptions, are unwilling to take on the advocacy role. That has blocked the more ready adoption of information and referral centers, for instance. Librarians are taught to be objective, balanced (and distant), and free universities usually don't relate that way with that value.[9]

Despite the reality of these perceptions on the part of some or many librarians, the free university model will spread via public libraries. The congruence of philosophy, the need for the public library to reach more people, and the cost effectiveness, popularity, and large participation associated with a free university, all are attractive. Although the free university may not become a standard component of every library, it can be expected that many libraries will adopt such programs in the future.

COOPERATIVE EXTENSION

The Cooperative Extension Service, often referred to as Agricultural Extension, offers another setting in which free universities can be sponsored. Extension's presence in just about every county in the nation and its interesting mix of professional and lay initiative provide a compatible structure from which to develop a countywide free university.

Cooperative Extension Service was created by the federal government out of the Smith-Lever Act of 1914 and is shared by three levels of government—county, state, and federal. Working with land grant universities, Cooperative Extension at the state level provides special expertise in many areas of agriculture and family living, such as community development and various agricultural specialties. But the basic unit of Extension is at the county level, where county offices are usually staffed by an agriculture agent who assists farmers and others in outdoor activities, a 4-H agent who works with the 4-H clubs for youth, and a home economist who assists homemakers and has recently become more involved in family life as a whole.

Cooperative Extension offers a wide range of educational activities to the general public, including workshops, public meetings, pamphlets and how-to literature, individual assistance and consultation, and clubs. Extension has been called the world's largest publicly supported, informal adult education and development organization, and America's first and only national system of adult education.[10]

There are several reasons why a free university can thrive in the Cooperative Extension setting. Extension educational programs are noncredit, informal, and open to the general public. The free university format of informal learning fits in comfortably with the way Cooperative Extension has been providing learning opportunities for half a century. Extension programs are offered at little or no cost, and free universities offer learning for the most reasonable cost to the learner. Cooperative Extension reaches out to the general public.

There are also several reasons why Cooperative Extension should be interested in the free university model.

1. It increases the population served by Extension. Because most programs are free, Extension's programs, and eventually budgets, are measured in terms of the numbers of people served by Extension.

2. A free university can reach new audiences and give the local Extension office a new image. Adding a new program to an orga-

nization is always an opportunity to reach previously unserved groups, and a free university program can be geared to reach new populations, such as the urban dweller, the elderly, the minority community, or the handicapped.

3. The free university is another format in which to present existing Extension programs and educational offerings. In many free universities, the local county agents offer classes and other programs through the free university. There is even greater potential for this if the free university is sponsored by Extension.

4. The budget needed to operate a free university out of Extension is not prohibitive. The greatest expenditure for a free university is for staff, and if the free university coordinator is an Extension agent, then some time will need to be allocated, but no extra staff will be needed. Since Extension has an excellent record in using volunteers and free universities are effective with volunteer energy, additional human resources can be tapped from volunteers in the community.

Cooperative Extension county organizations offer two ways in which free universities may be sponsored, one using professional initiative and the other using lay initiative.

In Kinsley, Kansas, county seat of Edwards County (population 4,581), a free university is run from the Extension home economist's office, providing an example of professional initiative. There the Community Free School was started largely through the efforts of home economist Carol Young, who serves as the program's coordinator.

The Extension office serves as the Free School's office. Materials are duplicated there; registration and meetings are held there. Young works with a volunteer committee of nine people, and they provide most of the class ideas and the energy to make them happen.

Founded in 1978, the Free School offers approximately thirty classes a year. The program is unusual in that it does not have a catalog. Instead, it has access to the front page of the county's two newspapers, and thus each new class is given prominent publicity in the Free School's weekly column. The nine-person committee meets and talks about new class ideas and requests. Standard class forms are duplicated and passed out to each steering committee member, who takes from one to three of the class ideas and agrees to find a teacher and a location and to return with the class description at the next meeting. With the number of personal contacts increased ninefold, and the amount of work distributed among the entire committee, it does not take a great deal of effort to develop a lot of classes for the community. The Kinsley Community Free School continues to hold its volunteer committee together after three years of operation. Young reports that no new volunteers have been needed on the committee because no one has dropped out yet. Even when that does occur, new people can be asked to serve on the committee, providing new class ideas and other personal contacts in the community for class leaders.

Using the professional home economist as coordinator, the Kinsley Community Free School maintains the continuity that a paid staff person can provide. By working with a volunteer steering committee, the local Extension office can add a new program and yet minimize the time that the professional staff person needs to devote to it.

While a free university using professional initiative is thriving in the wheat fields of Kansas, a free university using lay initiative is being developed in the hills of Kentucky, where the Kentucky Cooperative Extension Service has hired Arlene Gibeau, a state leader in homemakers clubs, to set up the free university style of community education programs.

There the Kentucky homemakers developed the idea of Sharing Our Selves (S.O.S.) Learning Networks. When state Extension specialist Sam Quick found out about University for Man's free university model for community education, he realized the similarity. The result was a working relationship between UFM and the Kentucky Cooperative Extension to start free universities in Kentucky.

Gibeau doesn't see much difference in the UFM free university model and the original purpose of homemakers clubs. In the early 1900s, Cooperative Extension was founded to provide learning opportunities to the public. Before local agents were established in every county, Extension provided demonstration trains to travel through rural areas, bringing visual materials and demonstrations on food preservation, sewing, and consumer education to isolated people. The first Extension agents were often circuit riders, going from county to county.

During this time, the home demonstration clubs were set up for rural women, and there wasn't always a professional agent there to assist them. Homemakers would be instructed in various leader lessons by home economics agents, and they would take the lessons back home to share with other women. The lessons were geared toward survival skills. "They weren't making macaroni lamp shades as some people think we're doing," says Arlene. Those survival skills included food preparation and crafts, which were considered essential creative efforts for people. Although some homemakers clubs may have lost that orientation toward survival, Gibeau sees a new need for homemakers clubs—that of family and community survival. She also sees free universities as helping homemakers clubs achieve this goal of working toward family and community survival.

"Not everyone is a joiner these days," she says. "In a free university you don't have to join, and free universities don't have to sell a philosophy, just offer what people want. If homemakers are what we say we are, then we will not be completely successful unless we reach all people, or appeal to everyone, including men."

Free universities can help homemakers clubs reach out to the general public and involve people who would not join a homemakers club.

Gibeau sees a different free university model developing in Cooperative Extension in Kentucky. Using the leadership skills developed by women in homemakers clubs, she sees the free university being implemented by the lay initiative in homemakers clubs, working with the professionals in Cooperative Extension and involving all types of community groups.

Cooperative Extension is a likely setting in which free universities can be fostered. Extension reaches every county in the country, has a tradition of free informal adult learning for the general public, and has the involvement of both professionals and volunteers. Using either the professional initiative, with the local agent as program coordinator, or the lay initiative, with volunteers and lay leaders as program coordinators, Cooperative Extension can be an exciting center for free university learning.

THE NEIGHBORHOOD FREE UNIVERSITY

The local neighborhood has been an important element in the growth of free universities. Most big-city free universities grew out of a particular geographic community before establishing a more metropolitan appeal. But in recent years the metropolitan free university, with enrollments of more than 10,000 a year, has begun to feel the impersonality and bureaucracy of the large educational institution.

The Denver Free University is one such free university. It grew out of the Capitol Hill area of Denver, where most of its participants came from, and gained a more metropolitan base, with 15 percent of its participants coming from the suburbs and less than 30 percent coming from the Capitol Hill area, where previously a majority of participants lived. But the greater metropolitan draw was not necessarily spread equally among the neighborhoods and suburbs of Denver. So while DFU had become more metropolitan in nature, it definitely drew registrants from some neighborhoods more than others. This uneven feature in DFU's ability to reach the total Denver population was one reason why DFU developed the concept of the neighborhood, or branch, free university.

Another reason was internal. By 1976, DFU had grown very large. That largeness was a problem. Bureaucracy had begun to set in. Increased size meant increased staff and more costs. In the fall of 1977, for instance, the number of courses offered jumped from 250 to 350.

Susan Spragg, a staff member who had joined DFU several months before, suggested that a branch or neighborhood free university be created by DFU to siphon off some of the growth in DFU. Susan ran an article in the DFU catalog, "Will Success Spoil DFU?" and a meeting brought out some interested people who would offer a course on starting a free university in the southeastern area of Denver. Out of the class, several people decided to make it happen. They presented a plan and budget to the DFU board of directors, who approved the Southeast Denver Free University (SEDFU) as part of the DFU corporation, with course terms to be offered at different times than DFU's classes and a separate staff and office.

At the same time, there was concern that a rival free university might be created, making competition for DFU, taking away registrations, and debilitating the original organization.

Volunteer efforts by Cheryl Moffitt and Joan McCarthy put together the first term in June of 1978, after which McCarthy was hired half time as coordinator. While legally part of DFU, SEDFU became institutionally and financially separate. The Washington Park Community Center lent it office space for the first few months, and stores donated space for registration and some classes. The *Denver Post* and other local media picked up on the new free university, and public service announcements on twenty radio stations brought in the first teachers.

Now in its third year, SEDFU registers more than 2,000 participants a year, has two part-time paid staff, and has some statistics behind it with which to chart future growth.

SEDFU's success as a neighborhood free university has prompted DFU to look to other neighborhoods to start more branch free universities. Interested people in the northwestern part of Denver began meeting to start another neighborhood free university, and the Northwest Denver Free University started in the summer of 1980.

SEDFU's young presence has created new enthusiasm and support for the free university. Residents donate items to SEDFU, and many participants decline to collect refunds on cancelled courses, preferring the extra money to go to the new free university. "People will do anything for SEDFU," says DFU staffer Mary Ann Van Buskirk. "The aura of energy around it is just incredible." She says SEDFU has helped to decentralize the free university concept and bring it back to the community. Despite earlier misgivings about competition and rivalry, SEDFU's participants have not detracted from DFU's enrollments. In fact, DFU continues to increase in registrations.

DFU's initial exploration of a neighborhood free university holds a good deal of promise for free universities in other large cities, some of which feel they are growing too large and others where the metropolitan area is just too big for any one free university to serve.

There are few other adult education models working on an independent neighborhood basis. Large educational providers, like community colleges, have branches or neighborhood classes but not independent entities. And neighborhood adult-learning centers are usually small and not replicated in other areas of the city.

The creation of neighborhood free universities has promise for extending lifelong learning to many segments of the population. With independent, decentralized organizations, each one can respond to the particular characteristics of the community. Each one can have its own identity, name, board of advisers, staff, office, and catalog. The courses can be geared to the people in that neighborhood.

Another impetus for the neighborhood free university is travel. In early 1980, free universities began to notice that the gasoline crunch had started to affect their classes. Some teachers in big-city free universities requested that their class locations be moved even three or four miles so that they would be closer to their likely participants. The cost of automobile travel, along with a reticence by many in the city to travel at night, is another consideration for adult-learning programs.

The neighborhood free university can retain that sense of community, personal attention, and lack of bureaucracy and rigid structure that is becoming difficult for the metropolitan wide adult education program to hold on to.

OTHER SETTINGS

There are also a good number of other institutional settings in which free universities can operate. Some of these are briefly discussed below.

Small Private Colleges

Small private colleges have found the learning scene in higher education moving away from eighteen- to twenty-two-year-olds toward adult learning. They are hard pressed to compete with larger public universities in the areas of continuing education, off-campus courses, and noncredit courses.

A free university is practical for a small private college because it does not require a lot of staff or administrative time, huge expenditures, or risk. Although the free university probably will not benefit the small college financially to any great extent, the free university will give the college a wider sphere of involvement in the surrounding community and a positive community image. This could be important for many small colleges that experience a definite town-gown divisiveness. Furthermore, a new direction for private colleges in small towns may be short-term community development projects, in which the college faculty assists in research, project design, or training. If that is the case, then the free university can provide the framework in which to develop strong college-community ties and clear the way for the small college to participate in projects which may benefit it financially.

In rural areas, many small colleges garner the bulk of their student enrollments from the surrounding territory. Thus, increased recognition and support from parents as participants in the free university may help in bringing their children to the college in the future.

Some small colleges are sponsoring free universities. At Bethany College in Lindsborg, Kansas, a free university program called The Other Term was offered once a year in January for Bethany students. In the fall of 1980 it will become a year-round program and involve the community as well. In South Dakota, several small colleges in a consortium, the Colleges of MidAmerica, have hired a person part time to work with University for Man in Manhattan to set up free universities, both in the towns where the colleges are located and in smaller surrounding communities.

Recreation Departments

Recreation departments are ideal locations for free universities. Recreation departments are already involved in leisure-time learning and recreation, and the jump to a full-fledged offering of courses in all areas is not a big one.

For a recreation department to initiate a free university program, it need only expand its existing offerings of leisure and recreation to include academic, social, and interpersonal topic areas as well.

The major barrier to adopting the free university model is not so much a programmatic one as a conceptual one. Some recreators are not comfortable with an expanded definition of leisure to include social and intellectual topics, and many recreators may not feel comfortable with the free university philosophy that anyone may offer a course on any topic.

In Abilene, Kansas, a town of 8,000, the recreation department took on the free university–community education program. It offers about twenty-five community education classes each session, which are open to the public at no charge. They are listed alongside the traditional recreation activities, which do carry a fee.

YMCAs and YWCAs.

Y's are also "natural" places for a free university to be spawned, though only two free universities in the country currently are sponsored by the Y. Y's have a tradition of offering classes, and unlike many other organizations, they are not limited by tradition or charter to certain subject areas. Many Y's offer noncredit classes already, so the programmatic aspect of the free university is not new. What the free university would bring to the Y is a greater involvement in the community and a greater flexibility in programming.

In a time when fewer Americans are joiners of organizations, a community-oriented program of classes will create more interest in the organization.

Communiversity in Champaign, Illinois, is sponsored by the YMCA and is a self-sufficient program financially. It not only brings a few dollars to the parent organization but also brings people who would not otherwise have heard about the Y programming.

College Unions

Free university programming is still popular on college campuses. Through college unions, the free university can be offered to both college students and the community at large. The free university program is attractive to college unions because of its simple administration, involving only one program director and the possibility of getting students as volunteers or assistants in operating the program. Many college unions currently operate free university–type programs. The largest is the Wisconsin Union Mini-Course Program at the University of Wisconsin in Madison. The program enrolls more than 8,000 participants a year and uses a computer for registrations and record-keeping.

Churches

In areas where other educational organizations have not filled the need, churches or church-related organizations may be instrumental in initiating or even sponsoring a free university program. In the 1960s, campus ministries helped start numerous free universities, including the Tucson Free University in Arizona and the Free University at North Texas State University in Denton. Today, Praxis Project in Tulsa, Oklahoma, and the Baltimore Free University are run from the campus ministry office.

Almost 10 percent of courses in free universities are related to religion, philosophy, ethics, and moral issues. The free university is an excellent way for ministers or other church leaders to offer their talents and ideas to the wider community outside church congregations.

In Westmoreland, Kansas, a town of 1,100 people, the United Methodist Church initiated the Westy Community Education Program. By opening up the advisory board and the teaching and leadership positions to members of other churches, the program was able to receive widespread community support. If free universities are to be run from church-related organizations, they must be open to the entire community, and some actions, such as inviting civic leaders to be on the advisory board, need to be taken to ensure understanding of the program as a community-wide activity.

Community Centers and Organizations

Community centers and community organizations already have a strong community base and neighborhood orientation. A free university program can become a popular and important program for a community center. Free university classes lead into other community projects that the center may want to promote. The course catalog is also an excellent way for the center to promote its other activities.

Communiversity in Rochester, New York, is sponsored by the Genessee Co-op, a community-center organization that also has vocational service centers, a printing co-op, and several other projects. Communiversity offers about 100 courses a session and emphasizes the arts, with almost 50 percent of classes in fine arts and crafts areas.

Community centers may be the best way to offer learning opportunities to unserved populations, such as low-income, minority, elderly, handicapped, and young people. Because of their "in" with these groups, community organizations are ideal places in which to sponsor free university classes for unreached populations. Its flexibility, low cost, and community orientation all make the free university an attractive program with potential for the community organization or community center.

Chapter 15

Lifelong Learning
in the 1980s

For almost three years now, the eighties have been proclaimed the decade of lifelong learning. Almost without exception, educators have approved of the increased adult-learning activities of this new era and the potential benefits which increased adult learning can bring to society as a whole. But there the consensus ends. Educators differ as to what the concept of lifelong learning means and what kinds of educational activities should and should not occur. Rather than making predictions about the future of adult learning, it would be more useful here to set up a paradigm for understanding the different directions into which lifelong learning will be drawn in the coming years. At this point it does not seem clear that adult learning in America is moving swiftly and unalterably on any one bearing.

TWO VIEWS OF THE FUTURE

Two separate surveys taken in the last half of 1979 reflect the divergency in opinion about the future of adult education. One was formal, extensive, and tallied; the other, spontaneous, informal, and unscientific. Yet they both illustrate well a given perception of the future as "the way it's supposed to be."

The first survey was taken by the College Board; it asked more than 600 people in formal adult learning institutions about their goals for lifelong learning.[1] Their overall response was extremely supportive toward future expansion of lifelong learning. But the educators were interested in some goals more than others.

Goals concerned with functional illiteracy and general education were given a high priority. Work-related goals consistently ranked higher than goals related to leisure, cultural enrichment, and personal growth. The exception to this was work-related goals for women, which were considered as lower priorities than traditional family goals. Affirmative action also was downplayed in favor of equal opportunity in education and employment, and the lowest priorities were for special interests of minorities, the military, and religious organizations.

Some interesting tendencies relating to lifelong learning emerged in the survey. Individual needs and aspirations in lifelong learning were subordinate to available jobs and institutional standards and admissions. The traditional educators did not think that educational information and counseling should take place through agencies other than schools and colleges. They did think that cooperation among different educational providers was important, as was civic education to enable Americans to function in a democratic society. Although the traditional educators approved of using more volunteers, they opposed using adult volunteers in learning situations such as teaching.

They gave high marks to the areas of the disabled, senior citizens, employment, professionals, and liberal education. Their priorities were low for leisure learning, financing lifelong learning, minorities, and religious values.

This was a detailed and comprehensive goals survey of educators in traditional educational institutions—community colleges, universities, schools, and so on. The respondents were largely white males. Only 15 percent of the respondents were women, and just 2 percent were minorities.

The other survey was considerably less scientific, took less than half an hour, and was quite informal. It was a survey of free university leaders at the 1979 national conference, and was initiated by Malcolm Knowles, who asked each person to write down his or her goals for lifelong learning in the 1980s.[2] Their responses are listed below.

Education will become more practical, more relevant.

Participant-funded neighborhood education centers will evolve.

The use of educational vouchers will be good at any educational institution.

Lifelong learning will attract a mixture of all age groups.

Assessment centers will assist the self-directed learner.

There will be more self-supporting learning institutes than publicly funded university-affiliated organizations.

Educational empires will dissolve into community networks.

Compulsory education will be restructured.

Teachers will become more of facilitators.

Unserved populations will have more resources as educational outreach grows.

The working class will be reached more often.

A less punitive attitude in education will prevail.

There will be federal subsidies in lifelong learning.

A system of credits for educating children will extend beyond schools.

More acceptance of free university classes in other institutions for credit will occur.

A greater use of educational television and other technology will reach people in isolated areas.

More control of learning will be based on individual choices.

The less-formally educated will have more motivation to learn.

There will be more interest in ideas than in skills.

The concept of self-directed learning will be introduced at the very start of one's "schooling."

Although the answers are not directly comparable to the survey of traditional educators, a distinctly different direction can be discerned. The free university leaders were interested in financing lifelong learning, in community-based institutions, in self-directed learning, in ideas and learner-oriented content rather than work-related or formal education requirements.

The two different views are useful in constructing a paradigm for lifelong learning in the 1980s. There are two opposite directions in which lifelong learning is simultaneously moving in the 1980s. One is toward institution-based learning, and the other is toward community-based learning.

Institution-based learning involves the formal traditional educational providers, like schools, colleges, and universities. It is provider-oriented rather than learner-oriented. There is a tendency toward centralization of education. The learning process is usually one-way, with an emphasis on pedagogy.

Community-based learning takes place in a host of lesser institutions, such as churches, Y's, community centers, and, of course, free universities. It is learner-centered rather than provider-centered. It is decentralized and local in orientation. The learning process is usually two-way, with learners serving as teachers and having input into the learning process. Self-directed learning and andragogy are promoted.

But the issues in lifelong learning do not have so much to do with institutions as with learning content and process. Each issue may be settled in a different manner, lending momentum to one or both of the directions.

MAJOR ISSUES IN LIFELONG LEARNING

The Learning Process

The proponents of andragogy, or learner-oriented education, have not yet won the day over pedagogy, or teacher-oriented education, despite the widespread writing, advocacy, and approval of the concepts of self-directed learning. In actual practice, pedagogy is still the favorite, meaning that learning participants are more likely to be involved in skill training and in receiving information rather than sharing it, and that the teacher is still the dispenser of knowledge and the focal point of the learning process. More active modes of learning are gaining attention, but they are best achieved through participatory learning with idea rather than skills content, and personal and group needs rather than economic, career, or societal purposes for education.

Mandatory Continuing Education

The mandating by law of classroom education for a growing number of Americans has been a tendency since the early seventies. For traditional educators, it means a captive audience of adults and certain income and credits. For some learners and nontraditional educators, it means forced learning that is nonproductive, sterile, and measured by meaningless hours in the classroom rather than by competency. Although an increasing number of adult educators are coming out in favor of voluntary learning, there is enough concern over professional competency and regulation that the mandatory continuing education issue has not yet been settled.

Who Is to Be Educated?

Another issue in adult learning concerns who is to be educated. The obvious answer is "Everyone," but limits on time, energy, and orientation do not allow such all-encompassing inclusions. Professional education is winning out in many areas, which means that professional workers in primarily well-paying positions are receiving continuing education while blue-collar workers and others in less-skilled areas are not getting so much attention. The advantage of offering professional education is, of course, money. Educational opportunities for professionals such as lawyers, doctors, nurses, social workers, teachers, and others far outweigh the learning opportunities for factory workers, gas-station attendants, and waitresses. Whether or not this trend should be sustained, and at what cost to government and taxpayers, has not yet been determined.

Financing Lifelong Learning

How the government structures its financing of lifelong learning will have a great deal to do with determining who learns what and how. While it appears that governmental support for lifelong learning will not constitute the major way in which adults pay for their learning, the portion of adult-learning courses paid for by the government increased from 10 percent in 1969 to almost 20 percent in 1978. Expanding government support to include part-time college students as well as full-time college students seems likely. Yet any kind of voucher system that would include nonformal educational organizations is not a possibility.

Academic Content vs. Personal Growth

Whether adults seek out learning that promotes their own interests and needs or learning that is in some way related to an academic or work-related goal will help determine the range of topics

offered in adult learning. The standard educational curricula have
included literacy training, high school diploma content, disciplines,
and work-related courses. In recent years the content of adult
learning has exploded outside those boundaries to include personal
growth, interpersonal relations, societal issues, arts, crafts, environment, practical and home skills, and just about any other
area imaginable. Whether the learning content in the eighties will
follow the changing personal interests of learners or the more
traditional societal goals of formal education and careers remains
to be seen.

Technology

The increasing use of technology in education has almost been
taken for granted. How will that technology be used? Technology
could proceed along the lines of one-way consumer-oriented learning, such as television. Or it could be used to create more two-way
active modes of learning, such as video, cable television, and home
computers. Whether or not learners will have a voice in determining the content of course materials—and how much they will share
their own ideas and knowledge—is still a question.

How each one of these issues in lifelong learning is settled will
affect one direction or the other in adult learning for the eighties.
Self-directed learning is more suitable to community-based learning, though traditional education could be adapted to it. Mandatory continuing education would certainly benefit the coffers of
institution-based learning and limit the time that learners would
have for community-based learning. An orientation toward serving
professionals would benefit institution-based learning. Reaching
diverse population groups might favor the greater flexibility of
community-based learning. Governmental support for part-time
college students will benefit institution-based learning, while
other methods of government support for lifelong learning could
promote the community-based sector. An emphasis on academic
and career content areas will benefit institution-based learning,
while personal growth and a wider range of subject area interests
will promote community-based learning. One-way technology
can be profitably used by institution-based providers, while two-
way and low-cost technology could be used by community-based
providers.

The issues are interrelated, but they are still separate issues, and each could be decided with different outcomes.

PROSPECTS

The end result of all the issues in lifelong learning and the directions they support will not destroy either institution-based learning or community-based learning. It will be a question of balance, of emphasis, of opportunity.

It is our contention here that both must be maintained, but that community-based learning must be considerably strengthened. In a society where there is a strong tendency toward centralization, community-based learning will have to be strengthened to be preserved. This need not occur at the expense of institution-based learning, but it certainly will mean that institution-based learning will not dominate the adult-learning scene.

Some respected educators have raised the question of preserving nonformal learning as well.

Norman Kurland, director of the Study of Adult Education for the State Department of Education in New York, writes,

> Much of the learning activity of adults takes place outside of the formal structure of education. Libraries, museums, the media, churches, employers, and community agencies of all kinds are significant providers of learning opportunities. One of the great strengths of existing arrangements is the wide diversity of options that are available. . . .
>
> A lifelong learning strategy must certainly build upon this existing provision and foster its continued expansion. It would be a disaster of major proportions if in our desire to expand learning opportunities, steps were taken that had the effect of diminishing the role of the private, informal structures. There is no way that the diversity, responsiveness to changing needs, and vitality of this "system" could be replaced by a formal, largely public system.[3]

In speaking on the topic of lifelong learning in the 1980s, Allen Tough said,

> The future I see for lifelong learning in America and Canada is an even wider array of resources and opportunities to choose from. The worst thing that could happen would be to have a

single, centralized system run by the government or the school system or university or any other single agency. The hallmark of adult learning is the diversity . . . so I'm all for the pluralism, the diversity, and the worst thing would be any kind of centralization as we've rather stupidly done with children's education.[4]

If there is a favorable attitude toward maintaining the community-based learning sector, there is also a paucity of ideas about accomplishing or strengthening it. There is no strong national advocate for nonformal and community-based adult education organizations. There is little communication among different kinds of community-based organizations, and there is no federal policy regarding the community-based sector in adult learning. Some of the suggestions for strengthening the community-based sector have included an assembly of educational leaders from various organizations, an institute for the study and promotion of nonformal adult learning, and federal initiatives not in direct funding but in research, development, and dissemination of community-based adult education.

With tightening economic conditions, pressures for enlarging one's "market" in adult learning, and a race toward innovation in content, process, and clientele, the tugs and pulls between lifelong learning that is essentially institution-based and that which is more community-based will continue through the decade. There are few good reasons for lifelong learning not to be a win-win situation for both sectors. There is no reason that we cannot expect both sectors to be strengthened and begin to reach the 75 percent of our population that has not yet participated in adult education.[5]

Free universities obviously have a stake in the strengthening of the community-based sector, of which they are a part. The overall promotion or decline of community-based learning will affect the future of free universities, for it will determine the climate in which adults learn and the kind of learning and teaching that will predominate. Just how free universities will fare in the eighties is the subject of the next chapter.

Chapter 16

The Future of
Free Universities

Just where will free universities be headed in the 1980s? To get
some specific answers, let's go back and visit some free universities
and talk with their coordinators.

Baltimore Free University

Judy Reilly, coordinator of the Baltimore Free University, thinks
the future is bright for her free university. She doesn't measure
that assessment in quantitative terms, however. She does not fore-
see a large increase in the numbers of participants, budgets, salaries, or staff. Instead, Judy hopes that BFU will continue to promote the joy of learning, the spirit of inquiry, and the sense of
sharing.

Although her volunteer teachers occasionally are drawn away
to paying positions, she doesn't see BFU changing its policy on
volunteer teachers. Even though the university administration at
Johns Hopkins has not always been totally supportive, she is hop-
ing for more involvement from students and faculty on campus.
Finally, she also hopes to continue to broaden BFU's participation
base, to serve the elderly, blacks, and lower-income residents in
the surrounding neighborhoods.

Denver Free University

Where will the Denver Free University be ten years from now? DFU is currently highly visible and a target for other adult education providers in the area. "Don't wait until the Denver Free University puts out their class catalog. Ours start now," reads one rival advertisement. But DFUers are not too concerned about the so-called competition. "I'm not worried about it," says financial coordinator Mary Ann Van Buskirk. What Van Buskirk is concerned about is planning for the future.

"We've done very well for ten years," she says. "But we're on the shirttails of a phenomenon that happened in the sixties. We lucked out in the seventies with a sixties mentality. If we plant our feet in cement, the world will pass us by. We're a business, not a funky freebie. There is a demand, and we supply a brokerage for ideas and energy."

Van Buskirk puts forth four directions for DFU to move in in the eighties:

1. Focusing on special populations. DFU sees a need to go to people, to reach the elderly by going to nursing homes, to go to those living in condominiums and ask what their needs are.

2. Becoming an information exchange. Many people have individual needs that can't be met in a group, such as learning to ride a bike. A one-on-one tutoring situation would fill a need. Van Buskirk sees a "wide open market" for some kind of learning network to link individuals.

3. Counseling. Whether it be for a career, for further formal education, or for life, Van Buskirk sees that DFU could offer a real service by developing a counseling component.

4. Establishing branch or neighborhood free universities. Three considerations favor DFU's moving in the direction of branch or neighborhood free universities. One is the time it takes to travel in the large city. Another is the energy crunch and the potential for gas to become more of a precious commodity. Thirdly, many people fear traveling at night in a large city. All these considerations, plus the advantages of smaller neighborhood-based free university programs, lead DFU into branch or neighborhood free universities.

Along with her projections, Van Buskirk also has a few challenges on her list of items to be dealt with in the eighties. DFU has grown steadily and, at 17,000 participants a year, is becoming big-time. How does an organization handle such growth? DFU is contemplating buying a computer, and problems can accompany a new technological entry into the office, especially one so costly. DFU is also thinking about buying a building. The move into larger or more permanent facilities weighs heavily on the long-term planner's mind. DFU also is concerned about the personal contact it has maintained over the years which is associated with free university learning. Keeping that personal contact while growing will be a tough assignment.

In all, DFU wants to continue to lead the adult education crowd, to explore new directions in learning, and to keep its informal and personal style of education. "We want to stay one step ahead," says Van Buskirk. "We want to be different, yet butter our bread."

University for Man

For Sue Maes of the University for Man in Manhattan, Kansas, the future of that free university revolves around three goals— reaching new populations, developing sound management, and effecting change. UFM already has reached a sizable portion of the local community, enrolling 12,000 a year in a town and campus of 50,000. A greater challenge for UFM is to reach the unserved populations, such as the handicapped and the elderly. Outside the local community, Maes sees her outreach staff continuing to expand its technical assistance program in helping small-town and rural free universities to develop. "Developing small-town free universities is still one of the best places to work, and I'd like to see it developed to its highest potential," she says.

Developing a sound management system without becoming overly institutionalized is a second goal. Until now, UFM has operated in a fairly democratic manner, opting for maximum individual freedom and sharing of responsibilities, such as telephone hours and cleaning chores. "There's a challenge in the alternative management system," Maes says. "How thick can our policy manual become? There are certain values we've been able to hold on to, and I'd like to maintain them."

Maes has seen other organizations become traditional in their management procedures and is concerned that UFM could easily fall into the same old pattern. But while others warn that the free university is becoming too "institutionalized," Maes does not view that word in the same negative sense. "We're becoming institutionalized in the sense that we now have compensatory time for our staff; we have a janitor and a secretary. But there's a spirit and a fight that says we're here to create change. The Audubon Society is institutionalized in a sense, and I see UFM fitting into that kind of category—established, yet working for change."

The third area that Maes sees as challenging for UFM is change and policy-making. This challenge is perhaps why Maes has stayed with UFM for ten years, the longest term of any free university director in the country. "I still get intrigued by the problems we encounter," she says. "This is one way to fund me to be a change agent. The town here is small enough to see some results and know you are affecting people. UFM lets me work on environmental issues, in aging, on small towns." Future issues for UFM include the water table—a concern for Kansas wheat farmers—and nuclear power, she indicates. But Maes sees UFM's potential for greater impact than it now wields. She would like to see UFM's community-education model influence other educational systems, like public libraries. She sees that UFM has a long way to go both locally and nationally in determining policy. There are still some courses that are viewed as threatening to community leaders, such as discussions on union organizing or consumer boycotts. In the future, Maes would like free university programs to be less threatening to people in positions of influence. Locally, she would like public officials to ask UFM to participate as policy-makers at some point, determining or at least influencing community issues. That holds true for UFM as a national leader in education as well. "How do national agencies take seriously what the free university is about?" Maes asks. "We affect people. Free universities are at the heart of where people are learning. They need to know that."

CHALLENGES TO FREE UNIVERSITIES

Although there is no question that free universities will be around in ten years, and probably grow as well, there are a few formidable challenges that each individual free university will have to undertake to maintain both its educational vitality and organizational stability. Those areas seem to be staff, management, and other educational programs.

Staff

Free universities cannot easily replace their top leaders. If an executive from an established educational institution leaves, the institution can advertise and find a well-trained, usually experienced, replacement. The fate of that institution is not tied to its leadership, because that leadership can be replaced. Free universities, on the other hand, depend almost totally on the personal leadership of their executive directors or top staff. This situation lends itself to personally rewarding and creative work for free university staff, contributing greatly to the free universities' overall strength and ingenuity. But it has serious detrimental effects on organizational stability.

Free universities, like many other nonprofit organizations, are not able to pay their staffs even average salaries. For the last few years, the average full-time salary probably has been in the $8,000-to-$10,000 range. Individuals have been able to support themselves at that level, but only barely, and supporting a family is out of the question. The result is that free universities suffer from what free university leader Dennis DuBé calls "transient personnel." Few people stay longer than two to three years in a free university.

Staff do not leave, on the whole, because they are dissatisfied with the free university but because of personal necessity. Many leave to take jobs with more money. Others leave to embark on careers in established institutions with more respect, recognition, influence, and responsibility. Others leave because of a common mental condition called "burnout." With few external rewards, free university staffs have to call on inner resources for job satisfaction. Those inner resources can hold out for only so long.

Some staff people are quite dedicated to the free university and work long hours at it. But a person can become worn out mentally and emotionally from working too diligently. Some free universities have tried to cope with the problem of staff burnout by instituting benefits that do not cost the organization, such as keeping shorter office hours during the day or offering a four-day work week or more vacation time.

The quick turnover in staff presents several problems for the free university. An immediate effect is organizational instability. When people leave, there is a void in leadership. The resulting reorganization takes time, energy, and sometimes power struggles just to keep the free university intact, taking away precious capabilities for expansion, long-term planning, and other necessities for sustaining an organization over the long haul.

New staff have to be trained, and that training often comes on the job rather than from a couple of books and a one-week training session. Most new staff come to the free university with no previous training in operating noncredit programs. So there is an entire new training process each time a staff member leaves. New staff people cannot pick up from past mistakes or gain a historical perspective on the organization very readily, thus perpetuating inexperience. While a free university can be ten years old, its staff may have been there only a year and a half at the longest.

Then, too, turnover in staff means that long-term development plans cannot be conceptualized, begun, and implemented systematically. Free universities lack the experienced veteran who has seen the organization's failures and successes over a five-year period and who can plan and develop new approaches to engineer program stability and organizational self-sufficiency. This lack of expertise, experience, and farsighted planning is perhaps the most negative factor of all.

Free universities have attempted to cope with staff turnover, but they have met with only sporadic success. There are no standard training manuals or workshops, no widespread fringe-benefits programs to deal with burnout, or part-time consulting structures to tap the experience and expertise of former free university directors.

Yet there continue to be eager, if inexperienced, hands ready to fill existing free university positions. When the executive position of a large free university recently became vacant, more than fifteen people applied, including three former free university directors. But if free universities in the eighties are going to climb all the mountains they hope to, an answer to the problem of staff turnover that has reasonably widespread applicability will have to be found.

Management

Free universities have only begun to recognize the value of sound management principles, and it remains to be explored how free universities can best apply principles to their own organizations. There are numerous areas in management in which free universities are weak:

new staff training

accurate file
maintenance

development of office
procedures

standardization of catalog
production

course evaluation

statistics development

decision-making

time management

effective group or staff
management

financial accounting

market studies

long-term planning

crisis management

utilization of outside
consultants and expertise

working with boards of
directors and advisers

If sound management can be instituted in free universities, then other problems, such as pressures from other educational organizations and even staff turnover, can be dealt with. Sound management can also help solve another one of the free university's basic challenges—money.

Free universities usually receive income from one of three sources: registration fees, affiliated institutions, or local community funds. Most free universities depend on only one of the three. If the economy or social conditions affect that source, the free university is at the financial mercy of those conditions.

Even registration fees, the apparent answer to financial independence, do not cover the cost of operating a successful free university. "You can't charge what a class is worth," says DuBé. "The universities found out that a long time ago. You can make a lot of money, but not enough." Free universities dependent on grants, income from a parent institution, or local monies, like United Way or local revenue sharing, are even more susceptible to rises and falls in financial fortune.

DuBé feels that the answer lies in diversifying, in becoming a "real business," as he says. If the free university can develop auxiliary enterprises to generate additional money, then a variety of sources of income can balance any decline in one or another source. To do that, DuBé says that free universities need economic advice and a development program.

Other Adult Education Programs

Pressures from other adult education organizations constitute another challenge, especially to large free universities that have garnered a good deal of the participant market. Two advantages that other adult education organizations have are their constant ability to co-opt any new techniques or methods instituted by free universities and the tax base that public institutions have, lowering their costs to learners.

Bart Brodsky of the Open Education Exchange in Oakland, California, writes,

> In an attempt to recapture students, adult schools are co-opting our format like never before. Adult schools have the advantage of lower fees, free class space, and tax assistance. We can operate more cheaply overall, with smaller classes, and we can be more responsive to new trends. But it's no piece of cake, and the future for the 80s is far from certain![1]

For free universities that charge fees, competing with tax-assisted organizations is difficult. For all free universities, the certainty that new courses, good teachers, brochure format, and other techniques will be adopted by other educational organizations puts pressures on the free university to remain on the creative edge at all times.

The challenge for free universities will be in part to maintain their constituency, but equally as important, to stay ahead of the game and reach new constituencies and develop programs that advance and keep them on the creative edge of adult learning. It does not seem plausible that free universities can ever break out of the pressures from other adult education organizations. The "competitive" spirit seems too ingrained in our formal educational institutions. That is unfortunate, because competition today is defined not so much in terms of competing for a definable market but in terms of "I want what you have." There is no competition for extending education to factory workers, for instance, and certainly not to minorities. But as soon as an institution can reach those population groups, then others will want to reach them as well. It seems that as long as other educational organizations want what free universities have, pressure from other organizations will not let up.

PROMISING AREAS

But if there are challenges facing free universities in the eighties, there are also promising areas. It would be hard to guess, and impossible to forecast, where free universities will go in the coming decade. No one in 1970 could have foreseen the changes and growth that free universities would undergo in the seventies. But at this time, there are several areas of endeavor which show great promise, and in which free universities may well become more involved.

More Free Universities

The number of free universities, approximately 200 at present, is only a fraction of the number that could be started in the United States. The independent fee-charging free university has thrived in larger cities, and its potential has not been exhausted. Such a free university probably could sustain itself in any of the 200 larger metropolitan areas of the country, and only about 40 of them currently have free universities. In addition, the largest metropolitan areas—New York, Chicago, and Los Angeles—could sustain between five and ten free universities. The city of Houston already has four large free universities.

The exploration of free universities by other institutions has just begun. If other agencies, or even just one other educational system, adopt the free university model on any scale, there could be a proliferation of free universities in medium-sized towns across the country.

The other area wide open to free universities is the rural free university. No other educational institution has developed a program or model that serves small communities in such an extensive and comprehensive fashion, using local residents and gaining community support and pride. There are currently thirty free universities in small and rural communities in Kansas, the state that created the model. The potential in Kansas alone is four times that. Nationwide, more than a thousand small-town free universities could be started in towns with no other source of postsecondary education. America needs education that is low-cost and locally oriented, and the free university fulfills these requirements.

New Populations and New Approaches

Free universities' success in reaching new populations has already been documented, but the potential for reaching people in a wide age range is exciting. Free universities began with the age group of twenty- to thirty-year-olds, who are now twenty-five to thirty-five, the generation of the sixties. This generation has been a trend-setter in many areas of American life and will probably continue to be so in the future. The sixties group is the bread and butter of the free university participation rolls. From that age group, the free university in the past few years has extended to older age groups. We have mentioned the elderly, but free universities have also begun serving people in their forties and fifties as well. Acceptable now to the adult public, free universities are increasing their participation among adults aged forty to sixty. "You don't look twice when you see one in a free university class anymore," says DuBé. "They're not the majority of participants, by any means, but they are common in free university courses."

The generation that DuBé points to as crucial is not the sixties generation, not the mature adults aged forty to sixty or the elderly, but the young. "Free universities have made insignificant penetration with the young," says DuBé. When the gap in services becomes large enough, and when the age difference between the young and the sixties generation widens even further, some kind of participatory organization, as yet undefined, will emerge to serve that generation, DuBé predicts. Just as the Boy Scouts were popular in the fifties, and free universities were popular with the young in the late sixties, so another service organization will emerge to fill the needs of the new younger generation. "Will free universities be flexible enough to take advantage of that gap?" DuBé asks. Whether they are could be critical to the free university's ability to maintain its position as the current educational fad among young adults.

Other free universities, especially campus-based ones, continue to enroll large numbers of eighteen- to twenty-two-year-olds, thus filling that gap in part. Whether the younger generation will graduate from campus free universities to community and independent free universities remains to be seen. But if so, free universities in the eighties could extend their participatory age range from only one generation to include people from twenty to eighty, a significant change and a positive prospect.

Learning Networks

Learning networks have been mentioned only occasionally throughout this book because a comprehensive and complete treatment of the topic could not be dealt with here. But learning networks are sisters to free universities—identical in philosophy and similar in structure and format.

Instead of offering classes, learning networks are telephone referral services linking people who want to learn with people who are willing to teach them. The list of all teachers is kept on card files, and the learning arrangements, including place, time, fee, and length, are between the learner and teacher.

The largest learning network in the country is also the oldest, the Learning Exchange in Evanston, Illinois. It has more than 3,000 subjects from Spanish to lion-taming indexed on its card files. Approximately 10,000 people a year learn a new topic through the Learning Exchange.

The Learning Exchange was started by Robert Lewis and Denis Detzel after visiting Ivan Illich's center in Mexico in 1971. The learning network model stems from Illich's concept of "learning webs," neutral two-way mechanisms in which anyone can have access and input into the educational mechanism. The Learning Exchange also has helped foster other learning networks around the country, and at any given time, approximately thirty of them exist. Most of them are independent organizations, and a handful are sponsored through public libraries.

Learning networks appeal to a complex society in which learning needs are varied and group meetings are too cumbersome, inconvenient, or lacking in individual attention. By centralizing a system of human teaching resources, a learning network can offer all 3,000 of its teachers at any one time, including several teachers in the same subject area. Through a learning network, the learner can choose from among several different teachers and can choose based on the teacher's qualifications, orientation, location, time, or cost.

Learning networks have a promising future in and of themselves, but they also provide free universities with a new direction in meeting learning needs. Free universities can establish a learning network within their own organization and, in addition to offering classes, can provide a linking service to individuals which will complement and expand the free university's services to the community.

Learning networks offer instant gratification as well. There are no waiting periods until the next registration or semester starts. If printing costs, paper shortages, or catalog costs become prohibitive, the low cost of operating a telephone service is another attraction to the learning network.

There may be millions of adults whose primary learning needs can be satisfied by meeting with a teacher once over coffee or during a Sunday afternoon, who need only a piece of information or a reference to a good book. There are probably thousands who would like to link up with people of similar interests, for chess games, to talk about international affairs, or to collaborate on amateur research projects.

With its existing setup, adding a learning network to the free university is a relatively easy process. There are some problems with learning networks, of course, such as the need for continual publicity and the need to collect fees to pay for the service. Yet, for a well-developed free university looking for a new direction in adult learning, the learning network has a great deal to offer.

Community Development

Free universities have always been involved in community betterment, most often by seeing projects evolve from free university classes, and then seeing them spin off into independent projects or organizations within the community. In this way, the free university maintains its sleek administration and singular purpose of providing classes to the public, while at the same time fostering community growth in a direct and conscious manner. As we have seen, several free universities have spawned many community projects.

A possible new direction for free universities is a greater integration of education with community development, with free universities becoming engaged in sponsoring and operating programs related to, but not central to, the educational class-offering process.

In Indianapolis, the Indianapolis Free University sponsors a writers' collective. In Monterey, California, University for Man sponsors a program of arts for the children in the public schools. In Rochester, New York, Communiversity is linked with a printers' co-op, photography studio, and potters' guild.

In Manhattan, Kansas, University for Man has set a major new direction for itself in appropriate technology. It has an appropriate-technology staff of four people. UFM conducted insulation and energy conservation demonstrations, built solar collecting devices, and in the summer of 1980 completed work on a $50,000 solar greenhouse, the result of a Department of Energy grant. UFM has committed itself both to the concept of appropriate technology and to its own program of demonstrations, research, workshops, and construction.

The advantages of becoming involved in related projects in community development are several. The projects give the free university an additional opportunity to serve the community and to be seen as a positive social agency contributing to the benefit of the community. For large free universities, community development projects allow the free university to expand and to be innovative without building up uncontrollable numbers of classes. If free universities do indeed have to diversify their funding base, special projects—whether supported by grants, local fundraisers, fees, or memberships—provide a way in which to achieve this diversification. Special projects also bring a new perspective to the classes in the free university. Many more arts classes are offered at Communiversity in Rochester, New York, as a result of the art projects associated with the free university. At UFM, a whole new section of skills classes related to energy conservation and appropriate technology has resulted from the new appropriate-technology program.

There are perils in this new direction as well. Advocacy projects attached to the free university may lessen the neutral image that free universities have been able to maintain in terms of specific issues. Projects also may slant the course offerings too far in one area, leaving the free university without other valuable course offerings to provide that critical balance which has been so popular with the public. Long-term programs such as appropriate technology require maintenance and long-term support commitment.

Free universities have become so successful on their shoestring budgets in part because they have not latched on to long-term financial commitments in terms of space, buildings, or programs. By committing themselves so directly and inextricably, free universities may in the future have some costs that they are unable to maintain. One free university had such an experience when it bought a computer. At first a sound idea, the computer eventually cost the free university thousands of dollars before it was able to sell it.

With careful planning and a commitment to long-term maintenance, community development projects may be an exciting new endeavor for free universities in the eighties.

A BALANCE SHEET ON THE FUTURE

With a look at both the problems and promises facing free universities and the bright spots on the horizon, we can try to summarize both the positive and negative aspects of the future of free universities.

Free universities in the eighties will provide a counterbalance to education via technology. Although technology will be used more in adult learning, it will assume its place alongside other adult learning methods, and free universities do not seem to be threatened by its expansion.

There are some questions about the fate of the volunteer teacher. Will the no-cost free university survive in difficult economic times, thus preserving the volunteer status of some teachers in free universities? As course catalogs expand, will the average person be left out of the free university teaching ranks simply because so many professional people will be teaching and taking up the limited catalog space?

Large free universities seem to be able to survive, and even to stay ahead of the adult-learning game. They will need to reach new populations and remain flexible in their programming and ability to change. Rural free universities have a clear field before them and appear to have a great future. Medium-sized and small free universities can grow larger, cease, or maintain their size if they have a clear sense of purpose. Smaller free universities with no large clientele will need some distinction, some uniqueness associated with their organizations, for them to have a rationale for continued existence. Planning will be essential to all free universities, whether to keep a large free university creative or to add or keep a firm sense of mission for the smaller organization.

All free universities will have to be concerned about academic freedom and the core philosophy of allowing any citizen the right to share any idea or skill that he or she wishes to. The pressures for so-called quality control and competition for the market will increasingly put into question the central free university philosophy. The free university's ability to withstand such pressures will be tested.

If lifelong learning is to be financed by the participants themselves, free universities offer an attractive alternative to high-cost education. The National Center for Education Statistics study of adult education participation in 1978 indicates that 57 percent of adult-learning courses were paid for by the participant, the same percentage as in 1969.[2] But the percentage of courses paid for by public funding rose from 10 to almost 20 percent in the last ten years. If participants continue to pay for a majority of adult-learning courses, then free universities will retain their cost-effectiveness and appeal to many adults.

Management, planning, and organization will be the keys to the future of individual free universities in the eighties. All questions of survival or growth depend on some hard thinking and wise deliberations.

The central organizational issue for the free university will be its degree of institutionalization and establishment of structure. Until the past few years, free universities have not had the choice to become established. But with their level of participation, growing expertise in funding and management, and larger financial coffers, free universities will find it difficult but necessary to walk a tightrope between becoming overly established and being underorganized.

Free universities will want to pay more comfortable salaries to their staffs and yet remain independent of outside funders. They will want to become sound business managers and yet retain their creativity and experimentation in courses and programs. They will want to be accepted by civic leaders and yet offer nontraditional courses that challenge the status quo.

To become either overly established or too loosely structured will be fatal. If free universities are overly established, they will lose their missionary zeal for academic freedom, their creativity, and their zest. If free universities are too loosely structured, they will be unable to enact the kinds of management and planning needed to survive in a time of tight economics. Some would claim that free universities cannot have it both ways, that there is no tightrope to walk. "An impossibility," they would argue. And yet free universities have always been ready to do the impossible.

Chapter 17
Education for Community

The success of the free university, and indeed other adult-learning organizations like it, may well be tied not only to its educational philosophy, current popularity, or pragmatic success but also to its ultimate function in society.

In this respect, the history of adult education in the United States may shed some light on understanding the public's intrigue with the free university idea. Traditionally, adult learning has been secondary to some greater purpose. Today, with adults interested in learning that relates to a problem or an immediate task, learning also depends on a larger personal goal. For most adults, most of the time, education in and of itself is not a goal. Education must lead to something. The adult-learning organization must play some larger role in society as well, in order to be interesting and useful to a large number of people over a span of time.

To be viable, adult-learning organizations will have to play an important role in society. For the free university, that function is providing a sense of community. The quest for community is a continual one for people in any given society, and over a period of time the institutions or forces that fulfill that need vary and are replaced. The concept of community is more often felt than

279

thought about or verbalized. The community we are talking about is not a geographic community, though it often includes some boundaries, especially in small towns or neighborhoods. It is much more personal than that. Sociologist Robert Nisbet says,

> Community is founded on man conceived in his wholeness rather than in one or another of the roles, taken separately, that he may hold in a social order. It draws its psychological strength from levels of motivation deeper than those of mere volition or interest, and it achieves its fulfillment in a submergence of individual will that is not possible in unions of mere convenience or rational assent. Community is a fusion of feeling and thought, of tradition and commitment, of membership and volition.[1]

It is characterized by a high degree of personal intimacy, emotional depth, moral commitment, social cohesion, and continuity in time.

There are different ways to achieve a sense of community, and various institutions over time have provided for it. There is the community of heritage, provided by the family, the clan, and ethnic groups. There is the community of geography, supplied by the neighborhood association or small town. There is the community of membership, fulfilled by clubs and associations. The community of ideas is another, fulfilled by the church, political parties, and others. And there is the community of work, met by the employer, business, or labor unions.

All these kinds of organizations have fulfilled the need for community at one time or another, and many still do so to some extent today. Yet there are obvious shortcomings in many current community-filling organizations. America is less a nation of joiners today than it was thirty years ago, and clubs and associations are not so well attended as before. Political parties are experiencing a decline in membership, and church membership has also dropped in the past decade. The woes of the family and clan are often reported, union participation is dropping, and there is no widespread sense of loyalty to one's employer or business.

While society in the last thirty years has become more individualistic, personal, and isolated, there is still a need for community. The calls for some kind of unity continue, one of the most recent being Christopher Lasch's analysis in *The Culture of Narcissism:*

The contemporary American may have failed, like his predecessors, to establish any sort of common life, but the integrating tendencies of modern industrial society have at the same time undermined his "isolation." Having surrendered most of his technical skills to the corporation, he can no longer provide for his material needs. As the family loses not only its productive functions but many of its reproductive functions as well, men and women no longer manage even to raise their children without the help of certified experts. The atrophy of older traditions of self-help has eroded everyday competence in one area after another, and has made the individual dependent on the state, the corporation, and other bureaucracies.[2]

While not denying the necessary role of other institutions and structures in society in contributing to our national sense of community, perhaps there is another kind of community that free universities have a role in fulfilling—the community of individuals. Seemingly a contradiction, the community of individuals is an opportunity for people to grow and interact for their own personal well-being and development. It is a community in which the level of information and commitment is determined by each person and in which a sense of groupness, of wholeness, and of community evolves from creating an environment that encourages personal growth.

It could be the "pursuit of happiness" rooted in the American psyche and in our Declaration of Independence.

Free universities have always treated the notion of community with sanctity, and they believe that they contribute to that sense of community. In large towns and rural ones, the notion of community comes through. In 1971, the Denver Free University said,

We have created a community, a "free university" that will enable you to know and to act on your capabilities as a human being. Our ultimate aim is the flowering of human beings so that we can share ourselves with others because we are wholly integrated and firmly founded in our innermost selves.[3]

In speaking about free universities in Kansas, rural organizers Jim Killacky and Tava Serpan note,

With the demise of small towns and family farms, we are also witnessing the breakdown of many long held human values—

such as caring about our neighbors, giving a hand in hard times, etc. Their extinction marks the deterioration of a quality of life not only to the lifeblood of a state like Kansas, but the entire nation. Our free university–community education programs speak directly to the matter of keeping small towns and rural areas alive and active. The potential for a genuine sense of community, missing from many of these places and around the country for years, can be realized through community education.[4]

The kinds of community that free universities provide are probably unlike those obtained through other structures in society, past or present. There can be a very temporary kind of experience, ranging from a one-night gathering to a ten-week friendship with the others in the free university class. But there can also be a continued involvement. Many people take four or five courses, and others are free university regulars, providing a great continuity in time. The commitment can be slight, or it can be great. There are no memberships, no large dues or fees, no ideals to embrace. Yet some participants become deeply involved in the free university idea, and for the thousands of people who teach in free universities, the commitment is much greater.

Taking a class, meeting people, or becoming involved in a project may not seem like a satisfying way to gain a sense of community, but in a time of disaffection and disaffiliation, it is difficult for people to find institutions and structures in which to believe. The free university, not only through a weekly learning experience but also through its concepts of learning and sharing, and through its image as an organization serving the larger community and its creative and innovative approach to educational and social change, does provide people with something in which to believe. Free universities have been able to create a sense of community, a structure in which education leads to community.

Free universities have blazed a new trail in adult learning, one that sees learning as enjoyable, informal, and contributing to the betterment of the community. Along the way, they have picked up methods and techniques—tried, proven, and then verbalized— that have contributed not only to the practical success of free universities but also to the formation of a new model in lifelong learning, applicable in other adult-learning settings and institutions as well. Already, the free university movement, from 1964 to 1980, has been significant and intriguing enough to be added to the history of adult education in this country as a unique response to adult-learning needs in the twentieth century. But the promise of the free university model is even greater for the future than for the past. New methods and ideas continue to be developed in free universities, to be implemented and passed on to other educational providers as well. There are new populations to be served, new settings in which adult learning can be promoted, and new ways in which education can promote community betterment.

Free universities have discovered that learning can be joyful; that sharing one's skills, ideas, and knowledge with others is a positive and necessary experience for all people, not just a select few. They have uncovered a huge vein of human talent and expertise in our society, and they have found that the kinds of ideas and skills that people have to offer are as unlimited as the universe, changing and expanding every day. Rooted in our American heritage of First Amendment rights and academic freedom, free universities have gone beyond mere talk to link learning to positive community and social change.

In the coming decade, as in past ones, the free university model will have much to offer those who want to be lifelong learners. For those who are curious, for those whose natural state is a perpetual sense of wonder, for those who want to rediscover that million-year state of life-wisdom in their blood, the free university has something exciting to offer.

Notes

Chapter 1 Anyone Can Teach—Anyone Can Learn

1. Patricia McCormack, "Free University Idea Catches Fire," United Press International Wire Service, June 1976.

2. Learning networks are "sister" organizations to free universities, sharing the same educational philosophy but differing in structure. A learning network is a telephone referral service that links those who want to teach or share an interest or skill with those who want to learn that skill. The learning network maintains a file-card bank of topics and teachers, and anyone may list one or more topics with the learning network. When people call requesting a teacher on a particular topic, all the names of teachers filed under that topic are given to the caller. The learner and teacher make all arrangements, including time and place of meeting, length of contact, and fees. Learning through a learning network is usually on a one-to-one basis rather than in a group setting as in free universities, though the learning network does assist individuals in setting up groups as well.

The oldest learning network in the country, the Learning Exchange in Evanston, Illinois, is also the largest, listing more than 3,000 topics and receiving 30,000 calls a year. There are usually about thirty learning networks in the country operating at any one time. This book does not attempt to discuss thoroughly the concept and operation of learning networks, leaving that for another more comprehensive treatment.

However, learning networks are occasionally referred to in this work, and they are discussed as a future potential development for free universities in Chapter 16, "The Future of Free Universities."

The best work on learning networks to date is a book by Robert Lewis and Diane Kinishi, *The Learning Exchange* (1977), available from The Learning Exchange, P.O. Box 920, Evanston, IL 60204.

3. Richard E. Peterson, *Lifelong Learning in America: A Sourcebook for Planners*, (San Francisco: Jossey-Bass, 1979), pp. 48–49.

4. Rolf M. Wulfsberg, Foreword to *Free Universities and Learning Referral Centers 1978*, Robert Calvert Jr. and William A. Draves, National Center for Education Statistics (Washington, D.C., 1979), p. iii.

5. Scott Kraft, "Do It Yourself Learning Comes of Age," Associated Press Wire Service, 24 September 1978.

6. Gil Sewall, with Donna M. Foote, "Free Schools Are Alive and Well," *Newsweek*, 9 July 1979, p. 74.

7. Charles Bunting, commenting in a panel presentation, "Lifelong Learning in the 1980s," Eighth National Free University Conference, Kansas City, Missouri, 21 October 1978.

8. Gordon C. Godbey, "Freeing the University," *Continuum*, National University Extension Association, December 1978.

Chapter 2   A Visit to Three Free Universities

1. Cheryl Moffitt, "Denver Free University Celebrates Tenth Year," Denver Free University catalog, Fall 1979, p. 2.
2. Patricia Calhoun, "Credits and Debits," *Westword,* 7 September 1979, pp. 7–8, 10.
3. Judith Freeman, "Baltimore Free University," *Harry,* 22 January 1971, p. 14.
4. Elise T. Chisolm, "Modern Science for the Rest of Us," *Baltimore Evening Sun,* 9 February 1978.
5. Nancy Cornblath, "Expanding and Evolving, The Free University Prepares to Enter Its Seventh Year in Baltimore," *Baltimore Jewish Times.*
6. Scott Kraft, "Do It Yourself Learning Comes of Age," Associated Press Wire Service, 24 September 1978.
7. *Kansas Report on Community Education,* "Humanities from the Middle of Nowhere" (Manhattan, Kansas: University for Man, August 1978), p. 2.
8. *Clay Center* (Kansas) *Dispatch,* 1 May 1979.

Chapter 3   A Look at the Data—And the People

1. "Them vs. Us," *The Berkeley* (California) *Tribe,* 11 December 1969.
2. One of the myths about free universities is that they are only temporary and are doomed to an early death. Although many free universities fold in less than ten years, almost fifty testify to some longevity, especially when one considers that the free university movement is only fifteen years old.

EC–Davis is currently a large, thriving free university sponsored by the university and run by students, as it has been since its beginning. It has sponsored a large and successful Whole Earth Festival for years. EC–UCLA has been a stable medium-sized free university and is now undergoing a period of reevaluation about its program, according to other free universities in the area. SEARCH is one of the two free universities in the country that offers credit courses and has medium-sized enrollments. It is part of the University of Oregon.

The other nine older free universities in the country, all started before 1969, are Experimental College–Northridge, California; Free University, University of Kansas, Lawrence, Kansas; and Freespace Alternative University, New York City (all started in 1967); and Experimental College–Sacramento, California; University for Man, Manhattan, Kansas; Wichita Free University, Wichita, Kansas; Free University, Lexington, Kentucky; Baltimore Free University, Baltimore, Maryland; and Experimental College, Seattle, Washington (all started in 1968). With the exception of Freespace Alternative University, they are all associated with a college or university, as were most of the early free universities in the 1960s.

3. Joseph K. Rippetoe, "Non Credit Courses and Adult Learning Needs: An Exploratory Study" (summary of a presentation at the Fifth Annual Conference on Open Learning and Nontraditional Study, Kansas City, Missouri, 19–21 October 1978).

The population of learners surveyed was the total population of learners registered for UFM courses during the fall of 1976. The sample consisted of 491 responses, with a return rate of approximately 18 percent.

4. Ibid.

5. Ibid. The Flint Hills Free School in Council Grove, Kansas, population 2,403, which Rippetoe surveyed in 1976, had an average of forty-eight participants with an age range from nine to seventy-six. Of the participants, 85 percent were women; 15 percent, men.

The Tri-County Community Education Program in Herington, Kansas, population 3,165, gave Rippetoe similar results. There, 90 of the 197 surveys were returned. Participants ranged in age from thirteen to seventy-six, with an average age of forty-three. Women comprised 76 percent of participants; men, 24 percent.

The reasons for participation in community education for all the programs was also surveyed by Rippetoe, with the results shown in the table below.

Reasons for Taking the Course	Percent of Respondents Checking Reasons			
	University for Man, Manhattan, Kansas	Neosho River Free School, Council Grove, Kansas	Flint Hills Free School, Council Grove, Kansas	Tri-County Community Education, Herington, Kansas
A. To gain knowledge or skill which satisfies personal curiosity or interests	91	85	77	80
B. To gain knowledge or skill which has, or may have, some vocational application	32	26	38	48
C. To have an opportunity to meet other people	28	28	23	43
D. To overcome boredom; to try to make life more interesting or full	28	25	16	28
E. To share interests or concerns with others; to develop friendships	27	23	41	41
F. To become more informed on some community problem or social issue	14	11	18	14

Chapter 3   A Look at the Data—And the People *(continued)*

6. Letter from Esther Gray, Manhattan, Kansas, to Sue Maes, August 1979.
7. Gil Sewall, with Donna M. Foote, "Free Schools Are Alive and Well," *Newsweek*, 9 July 1979, p. 74.

Chapter 4   Courses Unlimited

1. Red Rohe, "The Free School Explosion: Meeting People's Needs in the Educational Marketplace," *Well-Being*, No. 36 (Spring 1979), p. 28.
2. Robert Calvert Jr. and William A. Draves, *Free Universities and Learning Referral Centers 1978*, National Center for Education Statistics (Washington, D.C., 1979), p. 20.
3. Patricia McCormack, "Anyone Can Teach Free University Courses," United Press International Wire Service, 18 June 1977.

Chapter 5   Free Universities on Campus: The Sixties

1. I. Bruce Hamilton, *Postsecondary Planning for the Nontraditional Learner: The Third Century*, (Princeton, New Jersey: Educational Testing Service, 1976), p. 31.
2. A. A. Liveright offers this matrix to compare the involvement of government in adult education as compared to elementary and secondary education:

Elementary & Secondary Education	Adult Education
Controlled by state and local agencies	Large federal and private interest
Few but large organizations	Small and multiple organizations
Traditional approaches to legislation	Bold innovations common
Programs largely in office of education	Programs scattered throughout government

3. Myles Horton, as a college student in the late 1920s, was organizing vacation Bible schools around Ozone, Tennessee, when he got an idea about how and why people learn. The result was Highlander Folk School, started in 1932. Highlander educated adults to participate in the three most convulsive social movements in the South—the labor organizing drives of the thirties, the civil rights movement of the fifties, and the Appalachian poverty program of the sixties. See also Note 13 in Chapter 13, "Reaching New Populations."
4. Jane Lichtman, *Bring Your Own Bag: A Report on Free Universities*, (Washington, D.C.: American Association for Higher Education, 1973), pp. 9–10.
5. Ibid., p. 10.
6. Ibid., p. 13.
7. Staughton Lynd, "The Freedom Schools: Concept and Organization," *Freedomways*, April 1965, from Lichtman, *Bring Your Own Bag*, p. 14.
8. Paul Lauter and Florence Howe, *The Conspiracy of the Young*, (Cleveland, Ohio: World Publishing Company, 1970), p. 50.

9. "The Port Huron Statement," *The New Student Left,* eds. Mitchell Cohen and Dennis Hale (Boston: Beacon Press, 1966), pp. 9–16. Other relevant passages:

Beneath the reassuring tones of the politicians, beneath the common opinion that America will "muddle through," beneath the stagnation of those who have closed their minds to the future, is the pervading feeling that there simply are no alternatives, that our times have witnessed the exhaustion not only of Utopias, but of any new departures as well.

Feeling the press of complexity upon the emptiness of life, people are fearful of the thought that at any moment things might thrust out of control. They fear change itself, since change might smash whatever invisible framework seems to hold back chaos for them now. For most Americans, all crusades are suspect, threatening.

The fact that each individual sees apathy in his fellows perpetuates the common reluctance to organize for changes. The dominant institutions are entrenched enough to swiftly dissipate or entirely repel the energies of protest and reform, thus limiting human expectancies. Then too, we are a materially improved society and by our own improvements we seem to have weakened the case for change.

10. Ibid. Other relevant passages:

The significance of these scattered movements lies not in their success or failure in gaining objectives—at least not yet. Nor does the significance lie in the intellectual "competence" or "maturity" of the students involved— as some pedantic elders allege. The significance is in the fact that the students are breaking the crust of apathy and overcoming the inner alienation—facts that remain the defining characteristics of American college life.

11. Ibid. Other relevant passages:

We regard men as infinitely precious and possessed of unfulfilled capacities for reason, freedom and love. In affirming these principles we are aware of countering perhaps the dominant conceptions of man in the twentieth century, that he is a thing to be manipulated, and that he is inherently incapable of directing his own affairs. We oppose the depersonalization that reduces human beings to the status of things.

If anything, the brutalities of the twentieth century teach that means and ends are intimately related, that vague appeals to "posterity" cannot justify the mutilations of the present. We oppose, too, the doctrine of human incompetence, because it rests essentially on the modern fact that men have been "competently" manipulated into incompetence. We see little reason why men cannot meet with increasing skill the complexities and responsibilities of their situation, if society is organized not for minority participation but for majority participation in decision-making.

12. Michael Rossman, "Breakthrough at Berkeley," *The Center* 1, No. 4 (May 1968), p. 42.

13. Robert G. Greenway, "Free U's and the Strange Revolution," *New Schools Exchange.*

14. H. Junker, "Free University: Academy for Mavericks," *The Nation,* 16 August 1965, pp. 78–80.

Chapter 5   Free Universities on Campus: The Sixties *(continued)*
15. Free University of Berkeley catalog, Fall 1966.
16. Free University of Berkeley catalog, 1970.
17. "Manifesto," Midpeninsula Free University catalog, Fall 1967.
18. Dennis R. DuBé, "The Natural State of Man is Ecstatic Wonder," Community Free School (Boulder) catalog, June 1979, p. 33.
19. Lichtman, *Bring Your Own Bag*, p. 7.
20. William Barlow and Peter Shapiro, *An End to Silence*, (New York: Pegasus, 1971), p. 75.
21. Ibid., p. 77.
22. Ibid., p. 79.
23. Ibid., p. 78.
24. Ibid., p. 84.
25. Ibid.
26. Lauter and Howe, *Conspiracy of the Young*, p. 90.
27. R. Vaughan, "It's a Groovy Thing to Do," *Life*, 20 May 1966, pp. 119–120.
28. El Paso (Texas) Free University catalog, 1971.
29. H. Junker, "Free University," p. 80.
30. R. Vaughan, "Groovy Thing," p. 119.
31. "Universities, Free Style," *Newsweek*, 10 January 1966, pp. 59–60.
32. David Macleod, Department of History, Central Michigan University, letter to the author, 15 October 1979.
33. "The Coming of the Crocus: A Haggadah of Eros," Martin Buber College, Oakland, California, 4 April 1966, pp. 13–14.
34. El Paso (Texas) Free University catalog, 1971.
35. Phillip Semas, "Free Universities: Many Still Thriving," *The Chronicle of Higher Education*, 22 November 1976, p. 4.
36. Letter to the author, anonymity requested.
37. Fred M. Hechinger, "No Grades, No Exams—And Now, No Schools," *New York Times*, 22 August 1971, Sec. IV, p. 9.

Chapter 6   Free Universities in the Community: The Seventies
1. Catalogs from Experimental College–Northridge, California, 1974–1976.
2. Patti Pruett, speaking at the Great Lakes Regional Free University Conference, DeKalb, Illinois, 12 March 1977.
3. Donn Vickers, speaking at the Midwest Regional Free University Conference, Emporia, Kansas, March 25–26, 1977.
4. Dennis DuBé, "Free U Born in Boulder," Community Free School (Boulder) catalog, July 1979, p. 1.
5. Bart Brodsky, "The Exchange: A Community of Teachers and Students," Open Education Exchange (Oakland) catalog, January–February 1975, p. 7.
6. David Cudhea, "California's 'Free' Universities," *Change* 6, No. 7, (September 1974), pp. 19–20.
7. "Alternative Education in America Part III," National Public Radio, Options in Education, Program No. 54, 22 November 1976, p. 7 of transcript.
8. Lona Jean Turner, "DuBé and N.P.R.," *National Free University News*, No. 16 (February 1977), p. 8.
9. Ibid.

Chapter 7   The Rural Story

1. Calvin Trillin, "U.S. Journal: Manhattan and Atchison, The Maes Family," *The New Yorker*, 21 June 1971, p. 93.
2. Sue Maes, interview with the author, 29 January 1980, Manhattan, Kansas.
3. University for Man (Manhattan, Kansas) catalog, Spring 1980, p. 2.
4. Barb Nelson, testifying before the House Education Committee of the Kansas state legislature, Topeka, Kansas, 25 February 1979.

Chapter 8   The Philosophy

1. Jane Lichtman, *Bring Your Own Bag: A Report on Free Universities*, (Washington, D.C.: American Association for Higher Education, 1973), p. 2.
2. Michael Rossman, *On Learning and Social Change* (New York: Vintage Books, 1972), p 105.
3. Adult educator John Ohliger has written extensively on the concept of mandatory continuing education, or requiring by law that adults must spend time in the classroom. These laws are most often made in connection with retaining one's occupational license but have also extended into other areas, such as for welfare recipients. Mandatory continuing education, mandated by law and carried out as classroom activities within a traditional university, is philosophically in direct opposition to the kind of voluntary and informal learning that free universities promote. For a discussion of the issue see, for example, David Lisman and John Ohliger, "Must We All Go Back to School?" *The Progressive* 42, No. 10 (October 1978), pp. 35–37.
4. Robert G. Greenway, "Free U's and the Strange Revolution," *New Schools Exchange*.
5. John McKnight, "Learning Networks in the Next Five to Ten Years," The Learning Exchange Project Directors Workshop, Evanston, Illinois, April 5–6, 1979.
6. Lori Andrews, "Legal Issues in Teaching Self Care" (Manhattan, Kansas: Free University Network, May 1979), pp. 2–3.
7. "Alternative Education in America Part III," National Public Radio, Options in Education, Program No. 54, 22 November 1976, pp. 8–9 of transcript.
8. Robert Pirsig, *Zen and the Art of Motorcycle Maintenance*, (New York: Morrow, 1974), pp. 175, 178.
9. Richard Kostelanetz, "The Prevalence of Paul Goodman," *New York Times Magazine*, 3 April 1966, p. 98.
10. Lyra Srinivasan, *Perspectives on Nonformal Adult Learning*, World Education, New York City, March 1977, p. 8.

Chapter 9   How to Start a Free University

1. Greg Marsello, "How to Start a Free University" (Manhattan, Kansas: Free University Network, 1977), p. 23.
2. Ibid., p. 12.

Chapter 10   Keys to Success

1. *Webster's New World Dictionary of the American Language*, (Cleveland and New York: World, 1955).

Chapter 12   Learning and Teaching

1. Allen Tough, commenting in a panel presentation, "Lifelong Learning in the 1980s," Eighth National Free University Conference, Kansas City, Missouri, 21 October 1978.
2. Susan Spragg, as quoted by Allen Tough, above.
3. Tough, "Lifelong Learning."
4. Malcolm Knowles, "Self Directed Learning Workshop," Ninth National Free University/Learning Network Conference, Denver, Colorado, 26 October 1979.
5. K. Patricia Cross, "The Adult Learner," *The Adult Learner: Current Issues in Higher Education,* (Washington, D.C.: American Association for Higher Education, 1978), p. 4.
6. Sue Rieger, commenting at a University for Man workshop, Manhattan, Kansas, 12 December 1979.
7. Bill Draves, *Teaching Free: An Introduction to Adult Learning for Volunteer and Part Time Teachers* (Manhattan, Kansas: Free University Network, 1976), p. 3.
8. Ibid.
9. "Free U's and the Arts," Free University News 5, No. 10 (November 1979), p. 4.
10. Bob Hagan, commenting at a University for Man workshop, Manhattan, Kansas, 12 December 1979.
11. Denis Detzel, in personal conversation with the author.
12. Malcolm Knowles, *The Modern Practice of Adult Education,* (New York: Association Press, 1970), p. 162.

Chapter 13   Reaching New Populations

1. Herbert A. Levine, "Paid Educational Leave," National Institute of Education Papers in Education and Work, No. 6 (Washington, D.C., 1977), p. 29.
2. Ibid.
3. Lawrence Rogin, "Labor Unions," *Handbook of Adult Education,* (New York: Macmillan, 1970), pp. 301–311.
4. Leonard Nadler, *Developing Human Resources,* (Houston: Gulf Publishing Company, 1970), p. 88.
5. Ibid., pp. 89–95.
6. Ibid., p. 96.
7. Parts of this section are reprinted by permission from "Developing Internal Learning Networks," by Bill Draves, from The SourceKit, Learning Concepts, Austin, Texas, 1980. For a more detailed discussion of the mechanics of setting up a free university in the workplace, see this article.
8. Carman St. J. Hunter and David Harman, *Adult Illiteracy in the United States* (New York: McGraw-Hill, 1979), pp. 65–70.
9. Ivan Illich, *Deschooling Society,* (New York: Harper & Row, 1970), p. 4.
10. *A Target Population in Adult Education,* National Advisory Council on Adult Education (Washington, D.C.: Government Printing Office, 1974), p. 156.
11. Hunter and Harman, *Adult Illiteracy,* p. 68.

12. Ibid., pp. 104–105.

13. For a fascinating account of the history of the Highlander Folk Center see Frank Adams, *Unearthing Seeds of Fire: The Idea of Highlander,* (Winston-Salem: John F. Blair, 1975).

14. Nat Hentoff, commenting in a panel presentation, "Lifelong Learning in the 1980s," Eighth National Free University Conference, Kansas City, Missouri, 21 October 1978.

15. Malcolm Knowles, "Adult Learning: The Last Fifteen Years, The Next Fifteen," Ninth National Free University/Learning Network Conference, Denver, Colorado, 26 October 1979.

16. Carman St. J. Hunter, letter to the author, 19 October 1979.

17. Jim Killacky and Tava Serpan, "Beyond the Little Red Schoolhouse: Community Based Free University Education" (paper prepared for delivery at the Second National Institute on Social Work in Rural Areas, Madison, Wisconsin, July 1977), p. 7.

18. Jim Killacky, "Free University Movement Rolling in Rural Kansas," *Catholic Rural Life* 28, No. 3, (March 1979), pp. 6–8.

19. Jim Killacky, "Kansas: Going Beyond the Little Red Schoolhouse," *Journal of Alternative Human Services* 4, No. 2, (Summer 1978), pp. 30–31.

20. Jim Killacky and Tava Serpan, "Little Red Schoolhouse," p. 7.

21. Zelma Littlejohn et al., "Adult Education and the Aging American" (unpublished paper, George Washington University, Washington, D.C., Fall 1974), p. 1.

22. Pam Good, "Wrinkled Gray Panther Will 'Go Down Swinging,'" *Kansas State Collegian,* 6 December 1979, p. 1.

23. "Free U's and the Elderly: Learning, Teaching, Even Staffing," *The Learning Connection* 1, No. 1 (Winter 1980), p. 4.

24. Pam Good, "Gray Panther," p. 1.

25. Bert Seidman and Lyndon Drew, "The Injustices of Aging," reprinted from *AFL-CIO American Federationist,* July 1978, p. 4.

Chapter 14   New Settings

1. "Continuing Education Services: How Public Libraries Can Expand Educational Horizons for All Americans," National Citizens Emergency Committee to Save Our Public Libraries, New York Public Library, 1979, p. 1.

2. Ibid.

3. Ibid., pp. 7–8.

4. Fred M. Golden, "Connections: A Guide to Potential Models of Public Library Services for the Adult Learner" (unpublished paper, Detroit: Wayne State University, 1979).

5. Jacquelyn Thresher, "Public Libraries Are Natural Homes for Brokering Services, but Are Librarians 'Natural' Brokers?" *Bulletin,* National Center for Educational Brokering, *Bulletin* 4, No. 5 (August/September 1979), p. 2.

6. Ibid.

7. Meredith McElroy, *Libraries, Free Universities, and Learning Networks* (Manhattan, Kansas: Free University Network, 1980), pp. 4–5.

8. Meredith McElroy, letter to the author, 30 June 1977.

Chapter 14   New Settings *(continued)*

9. Barbara Conroy, letter to the author, 10 November 1979.
10. Edgar Boone, "The Cooperative Extension Service," *Handbook of Adult Education* (New York: Macmillan, 1970), p. 265.

Chapter 15   Lifelong Learning in the 1980s

1. Robert Glover, "Future Needs and Goals for Adult Learning 1980–2000," Future Directions for a Learning Society, (New York: College Board, November 1979), pp. ii–11.
2. "Next 15 Years Predicted," *Free University News* 5, No. 11 (December 1979), p. 4.
3. Norman D. Kurland, "A National Strategy for Lifelong Learning," *Phi Delta Kappan* 59, No. 6, (February 1978), p. 388.
4. Allen Tough, commenting in a panel presentation, "Lifelong Learning in the 1980s," Eighth National Free University Conference, Kansas City, Missouri, 21 October 1978.
5. Tables from "Participation in Adult Education, 1978," National Center for Education Statistics, (Washington, D.C., February 1980), p. 6.

Chapter 16   The Future of Free Universities

1. Bart Brodsky, letter to the Free University Network, January 1980.
2. Tables from "Participation in Adult Education, 1978," National Center for Education Statistics, (Washington, D.C., February 1980), p. 6.

Chapter 17   Education for Community

1. Robert A. Nisbet, *The Sociological Tradition*, (New York: Basic Books, 1966), pp. 47–48.
2. Christopher Lasch, *The Culture of Narcissism*, (New York: W.W. Norton, 1978), pp. 9–10.
3. "Denver Free University," *Chinook*, 26 November 1971, p. 4.
4. Jim Killacky and Tava Serpan, "Beyond the Little Red Schoolhouse: Community Based Free University Education" (paper prepared for delivery at the Second National Institute on Social Work in Rural Areas, Madison, Wisconsin, July 1977), p. 7.

Resources for Further Investigation

Organizations

1. The Free University Network, 1221 Thurston, Manhattan, Kansas 66502. Phone: (913) 532–5866. The national association for free universities and learning networks, the Free University Network (the Network) assists free universities, other adult educators, teachers, learners, and the general public. Its major activities include publishing, research, publicity, regional workshops in the spring, an annual fall national conference, responding to inquiries, and providing technical assistance via phone or mail. The Network acts as a coordinating agent for the free university movement, publishing a list of available consultants for specific areas of expertise. A membership organization, the Network nevertheless opens its activities to others as well. An important function of the Network is to help people and organizations start free universities.

2. University for Man, 1221 Thurston, Manhattan, Kansas 66502. Phone: (913) 532–5866. A large free university, UFM has pioneered and developed the rural free university model. It has started twenty-five rural free universities in Kansas and is now working in five other states to help start small-town free universities. Activities include publications, workshops, and in-person technical assistance. UFM staff members are available for consulting or assistance in developing small-town and rural free universities nationwide.

3. The Learning Exchange, P.O. Box 920, Evanston, Illinois 60204. The Learning Exchange receives requests from people all over the country on joining, participating in, or starting a learning network. It distributes a book, *The Learning Exchange*, by Robert Lewis and Diane Kinishi, and promotes the concept and operations of learning networks on a national basis.

Publications

The following publications on free universities are available from the Free University Network. A current listing of all publications is also available.

The Learning Connection. A quarterly newsletter for learners, teachers, and adult educators. News, information, how-to articles, trends, and ideas are included in each issue. $8 a year for individuals and libraries; $12 a year for institutions.

Free U. Manual, University for Man, Manhattan, Kansas. A 422-page resource book with practical approaches to the operation, maintenance, and development of free universities and community-education programs. Sixteen chapters on such topics as catalogs, publicity, teachers, staff, and finances. $50.

1980 National Directory. The directory lists more than 180 free universities and learning networks across the country, including address, phone, and organizational characteristics. 20 pp. $2.

How to Start a Free University, Greg Marsello. A concise guide to setting up and maintaining a free university. Includes information about budgets, publicity, advisory boards, etc. 24 pp. $3.

Teaching Free, Bill Draves. An introduction to adult learning for volunteer and part-time teachers, 18 pp. $2; $1 each for ten or more.

Research and Resources. The complete bibliography of the free university movement from 1964 to 1979. Contains lists of articles, periodicals, books, films, ERIC listings, catalogs, *Free U. News* index, and unpublished papers. $2.

Rural and Small Town Community Education Manual, University for Man. How to start a free university–style community-education program in a small town. Contains sections on getting started, advisory boards, operations, and long-term planning. $20.

Libraries, Free Universities, and Learning Networks, Meredith McElroy. A look at five case studies in which public libraries sponsored free university or learning network activities. Includes a "how-to" section for librarians on getting started. $2.

Films

Grassroots Education. A 16mm film, produced by University for Man, Manhattan, Kansas, 1977. Directed and filmed by Dennis Lofgren.

University for Man's 16mm account of its establishment of community-education programs in rural areas in Kansas is a great way to introduce your community to the free university model of education. The film stimulates discussion and answers many questions that are frequently asked concerning what a free university can do for a community. The twenty-minute film is available upon two weeks written notice. (Please suggest an alternative date for showing the film.) Available from the Free University Network. $45.

Appendix

National Directory
of Free Universities
and Learning Networks

Alabama

University Program Council Classes
Foy Union
Auburn University
Auburn, AL   36830
(205) 826–4244

Free University
Box 1247, SGA
University of Alabama
Huntsville, AL   35807
(205) 895–6428

Ferguson Center
P.O. Box CO
University of Alabama Station
Tuscaloosa, AL   35486
(205) 348–6114

Arizona

Tucson Free University
1041 E. Sixth St.
Tucson, AZ   85719
(602) 622–0170

Know-How Exchange
1639 N. 43rd Place
Phoenix, AZ   85008
(602) 275–2139

Arkansas

Russellville Learning Center
116 S. Glenwood
Russellville, AR   72801
(501) 968–6633

Open University
University of Arkansas–Little Rock
c/o Student Government
33rd and University
Little Rock, AR   72204
(501) 569–3210

California

UCLA Experimental College
409 Kerchoff Hall
308 Westwood Plaza
Los Angeles, CA   90024
(213) 825–2727

Experimental College
California State University–
   Northridge
18111 Nordhoff St.
Northridge, CA   91330
(213) 885–2172

Feminist Free University
908 F St.
San Diego, CA   92101
(714) 233–8984

Experimental College
University of California–Irvine
ASUCI
Irvine, CA   92717
(714) 833–5547

The Learning Network
838 Wilbur Ave.
San Diego, CA   92109
(714) 272–1435

University for Man
Monterey Peninsula College
980 Fremont
Monterey, CA   93940
(408) 649–1150 x283

Lavender U
3816A 19th St.
San Francisco, CA   94114
(415) 771–1450

LETS
3145 Octavia, #5
San Francisco, CA   94123

Orpheus
1119 Geary Blvd.
San Francisco, CA   94109
(415) 474–3775

Communiversity
P.O. Box 42093
San Francisco, CA   94142

The Gorilla Grotto
775 Frederick
San Francisco, CA   94117
(415) 731–9735

The Learning Exchange
324 Senter Rd.
San Jose, CA   95111
(408) 629–1552

Experimental College
Y.E.S.
Humboldt State University
Arcata, CA   95521
(707) 826–3340

Experimental College
6 Lower Freeborn
University of California–Davis
Davis, CA   95616
(916) 752–2568

Experimental College ASI
California State University
6000 J St.
Sacramento, CA   95819
(916) 454–6784

Open Education Exchange
6526 Telegraph Ave.
Oakland, CA   94609
(415) 655–6791

All of Us Learning Exchange
22787 Foothill Blvd.
Hayward, CA   94541
(415) 881–1753

The Learning Exchange
1403 28th St.
Sacramento, CA   95816
(916) 452–3919

Smorgasbord
Apt. S., Yosemite Hall
Cal-Poly
San Luis Obispo, CA   93407
(805) 546–4601

Colorado

Denver Open Network
762 Lafayette
Denver, CO   80218
(303) 832–9764

Denver Free University
Box 18455
Denver, CO   80218
(303) 832–6688

Community Free School
P.O. Box 1724
Boulder, CO   80306
(303) 447–8733

Winter Park Forum
P.O. Box 233
Winter Park, CO   80482
(303) 726–5405

Experiential Learning
Lory Student Center
Colorado State University
Fort Collins, CO   80523
(303) 491–7226

University of Northern
Colorado Open University
c/o University Center ASUNC Office
Greeley, CO 80639
(303) 351–4807

Colorado Springs Free U
16 S. 25th St.
Colorado Springs, CO 80934
(303) 633–3331

Animas Free School
Rt. 1, Box 3
Hesperus, CO 81326
(303) 385–4542

Southeast Denver Free U
615 E. Jewell Ave.
Denver, CO 80210
(303) 777–9305

Parker Community Center
P.O. Box 327
Parker, CO 80134
(303) 841–3827

Wingspan Free University
Box 1022
Paonia, CO 81428
(303) 527–3365

Office of Student Activities
University of Southern Colorado
2200 N. Bonforte Blvd.
Pueblo, CO 81001
(303) 549–2151

Shining Mountains Center
400 Broadway
Pueblo, CO 81004
(303) 543–7919

Delaware

Diversity
Student Center, Room 252
Academy St.
University of Delaware
Newark, DE 19711
(302) 738–1203

INFO
Wilcastle Center
2800 Pennsylvania Ave.
University of Delaware
Wilmington, DE 19806
(302) 571–8100

District of Columbia

Open University of
Washington, D.C.
3333 Connecticut Ave., N.W.
Washington, DC 20008
(202) 966–9606

Free University
The Catholic University
Box 203, Cardinal Station
Washington, DC 20064
(202) 635–5770

The Advisory and Learning
Exchange
1101 15th St., N.W.
Suite 1170
Washington, DC 20005
(202) 331–1707

Florida

Center for Participant Education
251 University Union
Florida State University
Tallahassee, FL 32306
(904) 644–6577

Common Learning Network
c/o Student Government Center
156E
University of South Florida
Tampa, FL 33620
(813) 974–2408

People Index
Leon County Public Library
1940 N. Monroe
Tallahassee, FL 32303
(904) 487–2665

Orange Fact Tree
2316 DePauw
Orlando, FL   32804

University of Miami
Student Activities
P.O. Box 248146
Miami, FL   33124
(305) 284–5646

Georgia

OPTIONS
Program Area
Georgia Institute of Technology
Atlanta, GA   30332
(404) 894–2805

Atlanta Network
P.O. Box 14432
Atlanta, GA   30324
(404) 876–8888

Illinois

The DeKalb Learning Exchange
138 S. Second St.
DeKalb, IL   60115
(815) 758–5418

College of DuPage
Alternative Learning
22nd and Lambert Road
Glen Ellyn, IL   60137
(312) 858–2800 x2147–8

The Learning Exchange
P.O. Box 920
Evanston, IL   60204
(312) 273–3385

Experimental College
Box 79, Knox College
Galesburg, IL   61401
(309) 343–0112 x303

Communiversity
Office of Academic Services
Western Illinois University
Macomb, IL   61455
(309) 298–1728

Communiversity
University of Illinois YMCA
1001 S. Wright St.
Champaign, IL   61820
(217) 344–1351

Full Circle Resource Exchange
1131 S. Grand Ave., E.
Springfield, IL   62703
(217) 525–0044

Free School
Student Center, Third Floor
Southern Illinois University
Carbondale, IL   62901
(618) 536–3393

Discovery Center
2930 N. Lincoln Ave.
Chicago, IL   60657
(312) 348–8120

Mini-U
Continuing Education
5500 N. Saint Louis
Chicago, IL   60625

Triton College Program Board
2000 Fifth Ave.
River Grove, IL   60171
(312) 456–0300 x499

Indiana

Indianapolis Free University
526 E. 52nd St.
Indianapolis, IN   46205
(317) 357–6430 or 357–7854

Fort Wayne Learning Exchange
1120 Crescent Ave.
Fort Wayne, IN   46805
(219) 422–2233

Monroe County Information
   Exchange
Monroe County Public Library
303 E. Kirkwood Ave.
Bloomington, IN   47401
(812) 339–2271

Iowa

Creative Alternatives
827 Broad St.
Grinnell, IA   50112

New College
Drake University
Olmsted Center
26th and University
Des Moines, IA   50311
(515) 271–3711

Link
P.O. Box 1666
Iowa City, IA   52240
(319) 353–5465

Health Link
Rt. 1, Box 162A
Toledo, IA   52342
(515) 484–4509

Kansas

Free University
Student Union Activities
University of Kansas
Lawrence, KS   66045
(913) 864–3477

University for Man
1221 Thurston
Manhattan, KS   66502
(913) 532–5866

Olsburg Rural Education
   Opportunities
Box 126
Olsburg, KS   66520
(913) 468–3627

Free University
Student Union, Office 5
Pittsburg State University
Pittsburg, KS   66762
(316) 231–7000 x249

Neosho River Free School
501 Merchant
Emporia, KS   66801
(316) 343–6555

Wichita Free University
Box 56, Wichita State University
Wichita, KS   67208
(316) 689–3464

Community Education Project
Abilene Recreation Commission,
   City Building
Abilene, KS   67410
(913) 263–7266

Clay County Community Education
   Program
Box 387, 1401 Third
Clay Center, KS   67432
(913) 632–3422

Tri-County Community Education
   Project
c/o City Library
102 South Broadway
Herington, KS   67449
(913) 258–3268

The Other Term
Philblad Memorial Union
Bethany College
Lindsborg, KS   67456
(913) 227–3311

Norton County Community
   Education Association
408 N. Norton
Norton, KS   67654
(913) 877–5344

Phillips County Community
   Education Program
County Courthouse
Phillipsburg, KS   67661
(913) 543–2182

Rooks County Community Education
    Program
c/o Chamber of Commerce
Stockton, KS   67669
(913) 425–6162

Trego Recreation Education and
    Environment
325 S. Third
Wakeeney, KS   67672
(913) 743–6673

Decatur County Community
    Education
107 E. Ash
Oberlin, KS   67749
(913) 475–3553

People to People
Box 113
Dighton, KS   67839
(316) 397–2413

Westy Community Education
    Program
Box 157
Westmoreland, KS   66549
(913) 457–3676

Courtland Community Education
    Program
Box 182
Courtland, KS   66393
(913) 374–4418

Burlington Community Education
    Program
P.O. Box 402
219 N. Third
Burlington, KS   66839
(316) 364–8776

Community Resource Program of
    Bonner Springs
205 E. Second St., P.O. Box 38
Bonner Springs, KS   66012
(913) 422–1020

The Education Connection
230 E. Grand
Haysville, KS   67060
(316) 524–5242

Little House Free University
6917 W. 76th St., Room 104
Overland Park, KS   66204
(913) 381–5599

Iola Communiversity
218 E. Madison
Iola, KS   66749
(316) 365–3262

Paolans United
Swan River Museum on the Square
Box 368
Paola, KS   66071
(913) 294–3312

Penn House
1035 Pennsylvania St.
Lawrence, KS   66044
(913) 842–0440

Summerfield Community Education
    Program
Box 127
Summerfield, KS   66541
(913) 244–6561

Anderson County Recreation &
    Education Program (ACRE)
Rt. 2
Garnett, KS   66032
(913) 488–3479

Flint Hills Community Education
c/o Flint Hills Regional Council
Strong City, KS   66869
(316) 273–8503

Southeast of Saline
USD #306, Rt. 1
Gypsum, KS   67448
(913) 536–4657

Community Free School
Extension Home Economist
Edwards County Courthouse
Kinsley, KS   67547
(316) 659–3241

New Lane University
Lecompton, KS   66050
(913) 843–7122

Marysville Free U
706 N. 12th
Marysville, KS   66508
(913) 562–5431

Pawnee Rock Free U
Pawnee Rock, KS   67567
(316) 982–4323

Free University
Kansas Wesleyan Student Senate
Santa Fe at Claflin
Salina, KS   67401
(913) 827–5541 x220, 223

Blue Valley Community Education
Box 95
Stanley, KS   66223
(913) 681–2866

Kaw Valley Free U
611 Spruce
Wamego, KS   66547
(913) 456–7340

Stone Prairie Life Center
Rt. 1
Marion, KS   66861
(913) 382–2057

Kentucky

Louisville Free University
Student Center, Room 2
University of Louisville
Louisville, KY   40208
(502) 588–6695

Free University
Student Association Office
Powell Building
Eastern Kentucky University
Richmond, KY   40475
(606) 622–3696

Free University
Student Center, Room 203
University of Kentucky
Lexington, KY   40506
(606) 258–8867

Free University
Box 3094
University Station
Murray, KY   42071
(502) 767–4588

Free Media
188 Woodland Avenue
Lexington, KY   40502
(606) 253–2624

Louisiana

Free University of New Orleans
New Orleans Public Library
219 Loyola Ave.
New Orleans, LA   70140
(504) 586–4927

Gumbo U
USL Box 42611
University of Southwestern Louisiana
Lafayette, LA   70504
(318) 233–3850

LSU Union Leisure Classes
P.O. Box BU, University Station
Baton Rouge, LA   70893
(504) 388–5118

Education Treatment Council
Lake Charles, LA   70601
(318) 433–1062

Maine

New Age Community Center
97 Danforth St.
Portland, ME   04101
(207) 773–5703

Mid-Coast Community College
  Services
University of Maine–Augusta
2 Maple St.
Rockland, ME   04841
(207) 596–6979

Maryland

Free University of Maryland
P.O. Box 294
Beltsville, MD   20705
(301) 937–8259

AUM Study Center
4801 Yellow Wood Ave.
Baltimore, MD   21209
(301) 664–6959

Baltimore Free University
c/o Chaplain's Office
Johns Hopkins University
34th and Charles
Baltimore, MD   21218
(301) 338–8188

The Baltimore School
P.O. Box 4833
Baltimore, MD   21211
(301) 366–6800

Charles County Community College
P.O. Box 910
Mitchell Rd.
LaPlata, MD   20646
(301) 934–2251 x240

Massachusetts

The Learning Connection
122 North St.
Pittsfield, MA   01201
(413) 442–6596

Lowell Cooperative Learning Center
10 Kirk St.
Lowell, MA   01852
(617) 458–7812

Boston Community School
107 South St.
Boston, MA   02111
(617) 542–5352

Boston University Free School
c/o George Sherman Union Building
725 Commonwealth Ave.
Boston University
Boston, MA   02215
(617) 353–3641

Free University of the Fenway
68 Saint Stephen St.
Boston, MA   02115
(617) 247–1919

The Hillel School
233 Bay State Rd.
Boston, MA   02115
(617) 266–3880

The Learning & Skills Exchange
Campus Free College
14 Beacon St.
Boston, MA   02108
(617) 742–3060

Free University
Boston College Undergraduate
  Government
Boston College
Chestnut Hill, MA   02167
(617) 969–0100

Boston Area Interest File
32 Summitt Ave.
Somerville, MA   02143
(617) 666–8341

Michigan

Artworlds Institute of Creative Arts
213 S. Main St.
Ann Arbor, MI   48104
(313) 994-8400

Flint Freedom School/Learning
  Exchange
5005 Lapeer Rd.
Burton, MI   48509
(313) 742-1232

Parallel
Britton Hall-Valley I
Western Michigan University
Kalamazoo, MI   49007
(616) 383-1994

Free University
Northern Michigan University
Student Activities Office, Box 58
Marquette, MI   49855
(906) 227-2440

Minnesota

Hackensack Open University
Rt. 1
Hackensack, MN   56452
(218) 675-6303

Technical College Student Activities
University of Minnesota-Waseca
Waseca, MN   56093
(507) 835-1000

Coffman Union Mini-Course Program
220 Coffman Union
300 Washington Ave., S.E.
Minneapolis, MN   55455
(612) 373-7603

The Metropolitan Connection
1222 Fourth St., S.E.
Minneapolis, MN   55414
(612) 379-7777

Free University
Room 113, Library Building
University of Minnesota-Duluth
Duluth, MN   55805

Missouri

Free University-Saint Louis
2922 McNair Ave.
Saint Louis, MO   63118

Cheap U
Southwest Missouri State University
Campus Union
Springfield, MO   65802
(417) 836-5885

Communiversity
University of Missouri-Kansas City
5100 Rockhill Rd.
Kansas City, MO   64110
(816) 276-1448

Communiversity
107 Gentry
University of Missouri
Columbia, MO   65201
(314) 882-2635

Montana

Community University
Student Union Building
Room 259
Montana State University
Bozeman, MT   59717
(406) 994-4041

University Center Courses
University of Montana
Missoula, MT   59812
(406) 243-4383

Learner's Exchange
Education Clearinghouse
323 W. Alder St.
Missoula, MT   59801
(406) 543-3371

New Hampshire

Another Place
Rt. 123
Greenville, NH   03048
(603) 878-1510

Carroll County Learning Center
Box 801
Conway, NH   03818
(603) 447-6650

Headrest
P.O. Box 221
Lebanon, NH   03766
(603) 448-4872

New Jersey

Free University
Community House
Seton Hall University
400 South Orange
South Orange, NJ   07079
(201) 762-9000 x570

Deaf Advocates
194 Oak Ave.
River Edge, NJ   07661
(201) 343-8139

New Mexico

Freedom University
P.O. Box 40122
Albuquerque, NM   87196
(505) 266-6719

New York

Freespace Alternate U
339 Lafayette St.
New York, NY   10012
(212) 228-0322

Open Space
Loeb Student Center 109
566 LaGuardia Place
New York, NY   10012
(212) 598-2001

Brooklyn Skills Exchange
2242 E. 28th St.
Brooklyn, NY   11229
(212) 646-6800

Suffolk Cooperative Library System
P.O. Box 187
Bellport, NY   11713
(516) 286-1600

Free University
609 Clarendon St.
Syracuse, NY   13210
(315) 472-4157

Community Learning Exchange
P.O. Box 6263
Syracuse, NY   13217
(315) 422-4062

Clinton Free School
Hamilton College
Box 73
Clinton, NY   13323
(315) 859-4011

Binghamton Learning Exchange
P.O. Box 862
Binghamton, NY   13902
(607) 724-1973

Concepts & Creations
123 Seymour College Union
SUC Brockport
Brockport, NY   14420
(716) 395-2631

The Learning Exchange
8 Elm St.
Albany, NY   12208
(518) 434-8421

The Learning Network
Westchester Library System
280 N. Central Ave.
Hartsdale, NY   10530
(914) 761-0771

Communiversity
Vocations for Social Change
Genesee Street Corporation
713 Monroe Ave.
Rochester, NY   14607
(716) 461-2230

New York Network for Learning
56 E. 11th St.
New York, NY   10003
(212) 260-6670

International Skills Exchange
330 W. 58th St.
New York, NY   10019
(212) 757-0322

Free University
c/o Human Development
NTID, 1 Lomb Memorial Dr.
Rochester Institute of Technology
Rochester, NY   14623
(716) 475-6200

Community Self Reliance Center
140 W. State St.
Ithaca, NY   14850
(607) 272-3040

The Learning Web
318 Anabel Taylor Hall
Cornell University
Ithaca, NY   14853
(607) 256-5026

Genesee Valley Learning Exchange,
   Inc.
P.O. Box 159
North Greece, NY   14515

Padua Learning Community
Lake Ave.
Watkins Glen, NY   14891

Each One–Teach One
Langston Hughes Community
   Library Cultural Center
102–109 Northern Blvd.
Corona, NY   11368
(212) 651-1100

The Learning Connection
Nassau Library System
900 Jerusalem Ave.
Uniondale, NY   11553
(516) 538-9100

North Carolina

Share (Skills, Hobbies, Arts,
   Resources, Education)
554 E. Hargett St.
Raleigh, NC   27601
(919) 834-9534

University of North Carolina–
   Greensboro
Elliot University Center
Greensboro, NC   27412
(919) 379-5510

Alfonso Elder Student Union
P.O. Box 19495
North Carolina Central University
Durham, NC   27707
(919) 683-6486

Ohio

Free University
Student Union
John Carroll University
Washington Blvd.
University Heights, OH   44118
(216) 932-7252

The Learning Connection
65 Jefferson Ave.
Columbus, OH   43215
(614) 228-7441

The Defiance College
Defiance, OH   43512
(419) 784-4010

J. C. Williams College Center
Franciscan Way
Steubenville, OH   43952
(614) 283-3771 x235

Case Western Reserve University
1111 Euclid Ave.
Cleveland, OH   44106
(216) 368–2660

Wittenberg University
Springfield, OH   45501
(513) 327–6231

Interest Link
1161 Sherman
Akron, OH   44301

Division of Continuing Education
#146 University of Cincinnati
Cincinnati, OH   45221
(513) 475–6932

Oklahoma

Community Extra-Curriculum
731 Elm St., Room 316
Norman, OK   73019
(405) 325–6873

Praxis Project
Canterbury Center
2839 E. Fifth St.
Tulsa, OK   74104
(918) 592–6233

Supplemental Education
c/o Student Activities
Oral Roberts University
7777 S. Lewis
Tulsa, OK   74105
(918) 492–6161 x2442

Choctaw Community Education
14625 N.E. 23rd
Choctaw, OK   73020
(405) 390–8418

Oregon

Free University
Lewis and Clark College
Box 10
Portland, OR   97219
(503) 244–6161 x576

ASOSU Experimental College
Memorial Union East
Oregon State University
Corvallis, OR   97331
(503) 754–4683

SEARCH
EMU 11, Suite 1
University of Oregon
Eugene, OR   97401
(503) 686–4377

Community Skills Bank
340 S. Pioneer
Ashland, OR   97520
(503) 773–3818

Everyone's U
Room 334
Stevenson Union SOSC
Ashland, OR   97520
(503) 482–7986

Linn-Benton Community College
6500 S.W. Pacific Blvd.
Albany, OR   97321
(503) 928–2361

Associated Students of Oregon
    Institute of Technology
Oregon Tech Branch
Klamath Falls, OR   97601
(503) 882–6321 x193

Pennsylvania

Neighborhood Talent & Resource
    Registry
612 S. Dallas Ave.
Pittsburgh, PA   15217
(412) 521–3416

Venango Center for Creative
    Development
P.O. Box 382
Franklin, PA   16323
(814) 437–5822

Villanova Free University
Office of the Dean of Men
Box 207, Tolentine Hall
Villanova University
Villanova, PA   19087
(215) 527-2100 x739

Free University
223 Hetzel Union Building
University Park, PA   16802
(814) 863-0038

Trade-Off
Box 1446
Bethlehem, PA   18018
(215) 867-1972

The Drop-In Centre
1810 North Park Mall
Temple University
Philadelphia, PA   19122
(215) 787-7435

Communiversity
LaSalle College
5501 Wister
Philadelphia, PA   19144
(215) 951-1577

Juniata College
Huntington, PA   16652
(814) 643-4310

College Union Activities Council
University of Pittsburgh–Bradford
Bradford, PA   16701
(814) 362-3801

Penn State/York Business &
    Economics Club
1031 Edgecomb Ave.
York, PA   17403
(717) 771-4555

Rhode Island

Providence Free University
41 Radcliffe Ave.
Providence, RI   02908
(401) 272-9253

Brown Resource Center
Learning Exchange Network
Brown University
Box 1825
Providence, RI   02912
(401) 863-2419

Rhode Island College Programming
    Staff
Office of Student Activities
Providence, RI   02908
(401) 456-8034

South Carolina

Free University
Russell House University Union
Box 85141
University of South Carolina
Columbia, SC   29208
(803) 777-7130

Clemson University Union
Clemson University
Clemson, SC   29631
(803) 656-3311

South Dakota

Free University Committee
Union Board
Dakota State College
Madison, SD   57042
(605) 256-3551 x279

Tennessee

Free University
Student Government
341 University Center
University of Tennessee
Knoxville, TN   37916
(615) 239-8177

University for Many
Center for Health Services Sta #17
Vanderbilt Medical Center
Nashville, TN   37232
(615) 322-4773

Texas

The Good Tyme Classroom and
  Penneywise Adventure Company
3618 Cortez
Dallas, TX   75220

Dallas Public Library APL/CAT
1954 Commerce
Dallas, TX   75201
(214) 748–9071 x364

Free University
Student Center, Box 355
Southern Methodist University
Dallas, TX   75275
(214) 692–2378

SFASU University Center
Special Interest Classes Committee
Stephen F. Austin State University
Box 3056
Nacagdoches, TX   75962
(713) 569–3401 x26

Free University of Denton
Box 13615, NTSU Station
Denton, TX   76203
(817) 464–3155

Baylor Free University
Baylor University Student
  Government
Baylor University
Waco, TX   76703
(817) 755–2369

Sundry School
Campus Activities
University Center
University of Houston
Houston, TX   77004
(713) 749–1253

The Class Factory
Suite 229
5326 W. Bellfort
Houston, TX   77035
(713) 721–2230

The Community Education
  Cooperative
College of the Mainland
8001 Palmer Highway
Texas City, TX   77590
(713) 938–1211

Free University
Texas A&M University
Memorial Student Center
P.O. Box 5718
College Station, TX   77844
(713) 845–1515

Coates Center Courses
Trinity University
Coates University Center
715 Stadium Drive, Box 51
San Antonio, TX   78284
(512) 736–8525

The Learning Network
2510 Rio Grande
Austin, TX   78705
(512) 476–0427

Texas Union Classes
Texas Union, 4.312
University of Texas–Austin
Austin, TX   78712
(512) 471–3654

LEARN
University Center Programs
Texas Tech University
Lubbock, TX   79409
(806) 742–3621

Leisure Learning Unlimited
Box 35043
Houston, TX   77043
(713) 721–7299

Courses a la Carte
John H. Crooker University Center
University of Saint Thomas
3812 Montrose Blvd.
Houston, TX   77006
(713) 520–7000

Utah

Campus Capers
c/o Campus Recreation
University of Utah
HPER E–214
Salt Lake City, UT 84112
(801) 581–8516

Utah State University Center
Leisure Courses Program
Box 1189 USU PO
Logan, UT 84322
(801) 752–4100 x7642

Virginia

Short Courses
Squires Student Center
Virginia Tech Union, Program Office
Virginia Polytechnic Institute and
  State University
Blacksburg, VA 24060
(703) 951–5661

YMCA Free University
c/o Cooper House
305 Washington St.
Blacksburg, VA 24060
(703) 951–4432

Free Learning Exchange
Chi Psi Lodge
Rugby Road Extended
Charlottesville, VA 22903

Washington

ASUW Experimental College
Student Union Building, FK 10
University of Washington
Seattle, WA 98195
(206) 543–4375

Health and Life University
4½ W. Main
Walla Walla, WA 99362
(509) 529–7000

Common Skills Exchange
1015 E. Fourth
Olympia, WA 98501
(206) 352–9910

Northwest Free University
Vibing Union
Western Washington University
Bellingham, WA 98225
(206) 676–3460

Wisconsin

B'nai B'rith Hillel Foundation
611 Langdon St.
Madison, WI 53703
(608) 256–8361

Free University
McMillan Hall
University of Wisconsin–River Falls
River Falls, WI 54022
(715) 425–3551

Free University
Cartwright Center
University of Wisconsin
LaCrosse, WI 54601
(608) 785–8547

Wisconsin Union Mini-Courses
509 Memorial Union
University of Wisconsin–Madison
800 Langdon St.
Madison, WI 53706
(608) 262–3156

Milwaukee Public Library System
North Milwaukee Library System
3310 W. Villard Ave.
Milwaukee, WI 53209
(414) 278–3079

People's Interest Exchange
Campus Assistance Center
420 N. Lake St.
Madison, WI 53706
(608) 263–2400

Wyoming

Wyoming Free University
1127 E. B Street
Casper, WY   82601
(307) 237–5460

Multiversity
University Station
Box 3625
Laramie, WY   82071
(307) 766–6340

Canada

The Skills Exchange
482 Brunswick Ave.
Toronto, ONT   M5R 2Z5
Canada
(416) 921–3357

Index

313